BIG BEND NATIONAL PARK

AMERICA'S NATIONAL PARKS SERIES

Char Miller, Pomona College, *Series Editor*

America's National Parks promotes the close investigation of the complex and often-contentious history of the nation's many national parks, sites, and monuments. Their creation and management raises a number of critical questions from such fields as archaeology, geology and history, biology, political science, and sociology, as well as geography, literature, and aesthetics. Books in this series aim to spark public conversation about these landscapes' enduring value by probing such diverse topics as ecological restoration, environmental justice, tourism and recreation, tribal relations, the production and consumption of nature, and the implications of wildland fire and wilderness protection. Even as these engaging texts cross interdisciplinary boundaries, they will also dig deeply into the local meanings embedded in individual parks, monuments, or landmarks and locate these special places within the larger context of American environmental culture.

Death Valley National Park: A History
by Hal K. Rothman and Char Miller

Grand Canyon: A History of a Natural Wonder and National Park
by Don Lago

*Lake Mead National Recreation Area:
A History of America's First National Playground*
by Jonathan Foster

*Coronado National Memorial: A History of Montezuma Canyon
and the Southern Huachucas* by Joseph P. Sanchez

Glacier National Park: A Culmination of Giants
by George Bristol

*Big Bend National Park: Mexico, the United States, and a Borderland
Ecosystem* by Michael Welsh

Big Bend National Park

Mexico, the United States, and a Borderland Ecosystem

Michael Welsh

UNIVERSITY OF NEVADA PRESS *Reno & Las Vegas*

America's National Parks Series
Series Editor, Char Miller, Pomona College

University of Nevada Press, Reno, Nevada 89557 USA
Copyright © 2021 by University of Nevada Press

LIBRARY OF CONGRESS CATALOGING-IN-PUBLICATION DATA
Names: Welsh, Michael E., author.
Title: Big Bend National Park : Mexico, the United States,
    and a borderland ecosystem / Michael Welsh.
Other titles: America's national parks series.
Description: Reno : University of Nevada Press, [2021] |
    Series: America's national parks series | Includes
    bibliographical references and index. | Summary: "Big
    Bend National Park: Mexico, the United States, and a
    Borderland Ecosystem is the story of binational
    cooperation along the Rio Grande/Río Bravo corridor.
    Audiences in Mexico and the United States may find
    compelling the description of public and private efforts
    to create a unique memorial to friendship, even as it
    reveals how often cultural differences get in the way"—
    Provided by publisher.
Identifiers: LCCN 2020051249 (print) | LCCN
    2020051250 (ebook) | ISBN 9781948908825
    (paperback) | ISBN 9781948908832 (ebook)
Subjects: LCSH: Big Bend National Park (Tex.)—
    History. | Big Bend Region (Tex.)—History. |
    Mexican-American Border Region—History.
Classification: LCC F392.B53 W45 2021 (print) |
    LCC F392.B53 (ebook) | DDC 976.4/932—dc23
LC record available at https://lccn.loc.gov/2020051249
LC ebook record available at https://lccn.loc.gov/2020051250

The paper used in this book is a recycled stock made from
30 percent post-consumer waste materials, certified by FSC,
and meets the requirements of American National Standard
for Information Sciences—Permanence of Paper for Printed
Library Materials, ANSI/NISO Z39.48–1992 (R2002).
Binding materials were selected for strength and durability.

First Printing

Manufactured in the United States of America

25   24   23   22   21   5   4   3   2   1

CONTENTS

ILLUSTRATIONS

Following page 62

FIGURES

MAPS

The year 2019 marked the diamond jubilee of the establishment of Big Bend National Park. Much has been written for the past seventy-five years and more about the region of Far West Texas and northern Mexico that includes the landscape known as the Big Bend. Given this name for the turn in the river called the Rio Grande (Great river) on the American side and El Rio Bravo (The wild river) to the south, the Big Bend country has drawn the attention of the scholar, the novelist, the artist, and the photographer for over a century. So it was intriguing to have a colleague from my graduate school days at the University of New Mexico, Art Gomez of the National Park Service (NPS), propose in 1994 that I write an administrative history of this vast stretch of 801,000 acres.

While on the staff of the Santa Fe office of the park service, Art had published his own institutional analysis of the region for the years before establishment of the park, entitled *A Most Singular Country: A History of Occupation in the Big Bend* (1990). What the NPS needed, said Art, was a thorough assessment of its operations and management of the natural and cultural resources that the agency had guarded since 1944. A recent study of the park, published in 1996 by John Jameson, had appeared on the fiftieth anniversary of Big Bend's creation. The book examined key individuals and moments of change in park history, offering a welcome addition to the shelf of literature about Big Bend's flora, fauna, and colorful historical characters.[1]

With these studies in print, the value of an organizational analysis of Texas's first national park seemed appropriate. As surely as the flow of the Rio Grande carved the landscape of the Big Bend, so too did Art's statement affect my research and writing: "In the long term, the Park Service made the most longstanding contributions to the region's final settlement." Given the environmental distinctiveness of the area, and its profound social context, it seemed wise to connect these important themes with the broader story of the area that became known in the nineteenth century as a "borderland." This initial effort appeared as an NPS publication entitled *Landscape of Ghosts, River of Dreams: An Administrative History of Big Bend National Park* (2002).[2]

In the years after its appearance on the NPS website, this latter study drew interest from scholars and the general public, as did the Big Bend country itself. New scholarship emerged on its themes, emphasizing breakthroughs in the areas of environmental, transnational, and imperial history. Academic innovations stressed admixtures of social and ecological change along the geographic corridors above and below Big Bend. It seemed appropriate in the second decade of the twenty-first century, with its political and media attention on the broader arc of the boundary between the two nations, that the story of Big Bend be introduced to a new generation.

ACKNOWLEDGMENTS

This book owes much to many people who, for the past six years, have offered advice and guidance on its content, images, organization, and importance to our understanding of a world that others made along the Rio Grande / Rio Bravo corridor.

To Char Miller, editor of the series on National Parks for the University of Nevada Press, go many thanks for seeing a story that had been embedded in a larger administrative history about Big Bend National Park, written nearly two decades ago. In like manner, the directors of the University of Nevada Press, Matt Becker and Clark Whitehorn, provided encouragement about the process of publication to coincide with the National Park Service's centennial commemoration.

The book would not be as complete without the excellent counsel offered by Kenneth Orona, a student of the environment and the cultural landscape of the Southwest, whose ideas about binational policy filled in many gaps that the previous institutional history contained. Ken and his wife, Luana Vigil, read chapters for accuracy, in the process demonstrating the importance of reaching a wide audience with this story. Others who gave of their time to review the text and offer their thoughts include Derek LeFebre, whose appreciation for new stories of the border is much appreciated.

Current and former staff at Big Bend National Park, among them Tom Alex, Mary Anne Neubert, and Superintendent Robert Frumenaker, made available their photo archives, many of which appear for the first time in this volume. June Gallegos of the National Park Service's Technical Information Center at the Denver Service Center assisted with her identification of maps and drawings of the park from the 1930s. These contributions reminded the author of the highly professional support and vision of the park administration in the 1990s, among them Superintendents José Cisneros and Frank Deckert, and regional historian Art Gómez.

The author also must note the valuable assistance of his family in the editing and review of this work. Edward Welsh read the manuscript several times, helping to redesign its format for a university press. So too did his sister, Jacqueline Welsh, bring to the task her skills as a research librarian and her knowledge of the cultural complexities of Mexico and Texas. My wife, Cindy, whose family roots run deep in West Texas, reminded this author often that many people in both countries will benefit from knowing that their history is as much about what they share as about where they differ.

Finally, this story would not be possible without the efforts made for a century and more by residents of the Big Bend country, both Mexican and American, to represent what is best about binational cooperation. Whether private citizens or public officials, whether local or international, they inhabit a world that is at once a mystery and one that is easy to admire. To them this book is dedicated, as they live in a land bisected not by a border but only a river.

BIG BEND NATIONAL PARK

Introduction

Whether the focus is on the various peoples who occupied the Big Bend or the array of plant and animal life of the desert, Big Bend always has piqued the curiosity of settler and student alike. The environmental backdrop linking the interior of Mexico with the American Southwest proved to be hospitable to cattle raising. Lands to the east of Big Bend along the densely covered grasslands of the Texas Hill Country, in particular the Guadalupe and Brazos valleys, lured ranchers for their grazing stock. "Here Andalusia cattle," notes historian Dirk Raat, "a hybridized offshoot of semi-wild, black Iberian bulls and all-purpose, lighter colored European cows, ran wild and multiplied prodigiously." In the world of animals, the imperial reach was remarkable. According to environmental historian Dan Flores, by the 1900s more than thirty thousand head of cattle grazed in the Big Bend area. Thirty years later, an assortment of horses, goats, and sheep had joined the larger-hoofed animals to overgraze much of the groundcover of the Big Bend.[1]

Along with Flores, there were other scholars attentive to similar data points, seeking to recast the story of the Big Bend as prime territory for their assessment of the Spanish frontier. Its villages, presidios, and missions radiating north from central Mexico formed what Herbert Bolton called the "rim of Christendom"—a zone that reached deep into Texas along the Brazos and Nueces Rivers to San Antonio.[2] A competing arc of French influence from the Mississippi River valley as far north as the Missouri River pushed to the west and south, fanning across Texas in the eighteenth century. In history writ large and providing a grand view that centered European rivalries on the southern plains, Jeremy Aldeman and Stephen Aron track motives, material forces, and grand imperatives as they describe imperial rivalries infiltrating the Rio Grande valley and its Big Bend.[3] The greater US-Mexican border region, write Alderman and Aron, offers the reader "a timeless legacy of cultural continuity [that] shrouds the rise and fall of empires, the struggles between emerging independent nation-states, and the fate of increasingly dependent indigenous and metis/mestizo peoples." No matter the century, say Adelman and Aron, the Big Bend projects itself onto the world stage with its meaning and its lessons. The possibilities for exploring new alignments and agency thus are thought-provoking. Most appealing is the fact that these scholars assigned to Native American societies a critical role at the center of power. Such authors view indigenous tribes as masters of their own fates, propelled by their own self-interests, and contributors (for better or for worse) in the grand sweep of global change.[4]

These works also offer a new dynamic in which to cast the narrative of history in the Big Bend. "By the [nineteenth] century's end," write Aldeman and Aron, "treaties [had affected] international diplomacy." Competition for trade, and "not for territorial dominion," say the authors, had become "the guiding framework of power politics." Whether stated explicitly or inferred, Adelman and Aron leave their readers with the tantalizing prospect of exploration. They start from an outer casing and narrow one's point of view, with Big Bend serving as their core. If the linchpin for change was the new set of relationships and arrangements that constituted the transition from empires to nation-states, the conflict between the United States and Mexico played a pivotal role. Viewed as a series of castings that establish overarching contexts and coordinates, the early part of this story of Big Bend thus becomes a prism through which to view many layers of human and natural history.[5]

What continues to haunt the area's history, if not the scholarly mind that tries to understand this part of the planet, is the process of reconciling an area fraught with polar oppositions. The fact that we start with water as the unifying feature of Big Bend and the larger Rio Grande basin speaks volumes about the accommodations that had to be reached and the spirit of cooperation to be achieved, linking the destinies of both the United States and Mexico. As early as 1824, when the Republic of Texas was in its infancy, the young, upstart nation communicated with authorities from as far south as Tamaulipas and as far north as Chihuahua "to secure from them common agreement for concessions on the Rio Grande as it passed through their domains," writes historian Pat Kelly.[6]

The prospect of utilizing a navigable waterway fired the imaginations of both countries. Twenty-four years later, under the Treaty of Guadalupe Hidalgo, the US-Mexico border became a line that ran directly through the middle portion of the river at its deepest points. This further emphasized the importance of the shared resource. Yet as much as the river provided constancy and continuity, it represented also a break between the two nations. Part of that break involved a remapping of spatial identities and social arrangements. The early part of the book addresses the place between extremities.

Once the reader engages the middle portion of this book, he or she will see Big Bend as an outgrowth of world depression and conflict in the 1930s and 1940s, followed by the prosperity of the postwar years. Both Mexico and the United States encountered opportunities seldom seen in either nation's past. The citizens of the United States, writes one scholar, had become a "people of plenty," while the nation to its south experienced what some called the "Mexican Miracle."[7] As much as Big Bend remained ensconced in its cultural and ecological mold, its stature grew to assume international dimensions.

Conceived as one unit in a nation of parks, as an international peace park reflecting Franklin Delano Roosevelt's wishes for a good-neighbor policy, and as the fulfillment of a mutual need to reinforce trade agreements, Big Bend thus emerged as projecting its influence outward, even as it continued to reflect inward. Historians may continue to debate degrees of open and closed frontiers. Whether those markers reside within our borders or outside our national boundaries, Big Bend remains a fascinating place from which to ponder such questions.

At the dawn of the twenty-first century, on the eve of the park's diamond jubilee, few could have imagined that on September 11, 2001, the United States would experience the most horrific attack in the nation's history. Fewer still could have envisioned that, two decades later, the United States would retreat from its place on the world stage, entertaining a mixture of isolationist and nationalist impulses. Nor could many have realized that a nation of immigrants would construct a fence spanning 650 miles of the border between Mexico and the United States, entertaining calls by political leaders for more.[8]

Big Bend is best understood as the sum of its parts rather than taken whole by any one scholar of any given time. The park's history, particularly in light of the new scholarly trends, encourages the reader to reimagine Big Bend as constructed of a diverse ensemble of personalities. The totality of these narratives helps provide a necessary vocabulary and set of coordinates to make the park's history more comprehensible, if not yet complete.

Every writer, like every visitor, has come to Big Bend with the freedom to draw on their imagination to describe things both great and small. In the best of America's pragmatic tradition, the mix of general reason, independence of mind, and freedom of expression is all that is needed to extract meaning from a place shaped by the vagaries of time. Many a writer has reconsidered a fixed position after visiting Big Bend. They have been afforded the opportunity to clarify as much as obscure its meaning. To grapple with Big Bend is to exercise a flexibility of mind as well as body. As a part of things great and small, bringing forth clarity and ambiguity, examples abound in this book.

While Big Bend can be understood in vernacular terms, its idioms also connect to a larger and more vibrant tapestry of place. Big Bend inhabits an awe-inspiring landscape yet yields to a simple, almost idyllic representation as an immutable space, one that has inspired generations to explore and ponder its changing message. Acknowledgment of the unique physical origins, and appreciation of its limits and prospects for change, allows us to recognize the greatness of the human condition as can be found within the larger patchwork of National Park history. Big Bend and its vast environs of canyon and desert frame not only the setting for which natural and human history unfold. Like the river that has flowed for millennia through the Big Bend, they also shape the contours of an impressive portfolio of national and international story lines of the past, present, and future.

CHAPTER I

Once There Was Only a River— The Cultural Landscape of Big Bend

The famed environmental writer Edward Abbey found special satisfaction in visiting the wonders of Big Bend National Park. A former seasonal ranger at Arches National Park in southeastern Utah, the controversial and opinionated author of such works as *Desert Solitaire* (1968) and *The Monkey Wrench Gang* (1975) recalled in the late 1970s that "half the pleasure of a visit to Big Bend National Park . . . lies in the advance upon the object of desire." Calling the Chisos Mountains "a castled fortification of Wagnerian gods," Abbey also likened them to "an emerald isle in a red sea." He appreciated the cultural heritage of this rugged land, remarking that "we have good reason to think of frontier history as we drive steadily toward the looming mass of the Chisos Mountains." Then in a statement that echoed his love of undeveloped landscapes, Abbey declared, "I'd rather be broke down and lost in the wilds of Big Bend, any day, than wake up some morning in a penthouse suite high above the megalomania of Dallas or Houston." The author promised readers of *One Life at a Time, Please* (1988), "We will return, someday, and when we do the gritty splendor and the complicated grandeur of Big Bend will still be here."[1]

For those who have tried to control it, the country known as Big Bend is a landscape that demands much and offers little. More than one chronicler has acknowledged that the place, all 801,163 acres, must be accepted on its own ecological terms of aridity and isolation. Before the arrival of the Spanish speakers in the seventeenth century, no evidence exists of any particular cultural group being able to exercise dominion over the land and its scattered peoples. Whether Apache, Comanche, Spanish, or the Texas Rangers, even the fiercest and most cunning most often traveled through El Despoblado (The unpopulated land) en route to more lucrative settlements deep in Mexico or along the rivers of eastern Texas.

The English speakers, the last to enter the Big Bend country in the decades after 1850, had moments when one enterprise or another (cattle grazing, mining, cotton cultivation, railroads, tourism, or the narcotics trade) promised to make the land accommodate the American will. Only when conservationists on both sides of the Rio Grande / Rio Bravo embraced the intractability of Big Bend did human use patterns begin to return to the state of nature once known to the settled tribes (whom the Spanish called Jumanos), or whoever else carved their images on the ancient rocks to let posterity know that they had passed by.[2]

Now that the park service has managed the vastness of Big Bend for three-quarters of a century and more, a clearer picture emerges of the interplay of natural and human forces that defined the region. The landscapes reflect the value of linking folklore with scholarship to define the essence of a land ranging from 7,825 feet in the Chisos Mountains (Emory Peak) to a mere 1,800 feet along the banks of the Rio Grande. "No other national park," writes Frank Deckert, a chief naturalist and later superintendent at Big Bend National Park, "has this combination of size and remoteness coupled with the romance and mystery of the Mexican border."[3]

Deckert notes that millions of years ago Big Bend lay below a huge ocean: "The skulls and skeletons of sea creatures piled one upon another until they formed layers of limestone thousands of feet thick." The fossilized relics, now exposed as reefs, stretch in a triangular fashion from the Guadalupe Mountains to the lower Pecos River and the southern portion of Big Bend, each telling reminders of Big Bend's deep geologic past. Modern visitors to the park, similar to the Native and Spanish inhabitants of long ago, often marvel at the spectacle of warm-water creatures fossilized in the stones, where less than seventeen inches of precipitation fall in the mountains each year, and but ten inches at lower elevations.[4]

Acute aridity and isolation, the sweep of geologic time, and a dramatic geographic dimension shaped Big Bend National Park and became a theme of substantial historical research in the late twentieth century. Scholars recognized that the environment has realigned itself many times through phenomena like fire, wind, rain, erosion, and volcanic and tectonic upheaval. Sometimes the change is incremental; sometimes it is violent. Yet these physical forces were but the precursor to human land-use patterns of the Big Bend landscape that follow a similar trajectory of change. Over time, erosion carried boulders and rocks down such streams as Tornillo and Terlingua Creeks, which respectively constitute the eastern and western drainage basins of present-day Big Bend National Park. Volcanic forces shaped the Chisos Mountains north of the Rio Grande during the Tertiary period from twenty-eight to forty-five million years ago.

Then the cutting action of the Rio Grande (named the Rio Bravo, or "wild river," by the Spanish) and the sharp turn of the river from which the park and the region get their name etched the limestone layers that form the signature canyons of Santa Eleña, Mariscal, and Boquillas.[5]

Whoever first set foot in the future Big Bend National Park noticed these conditions and thought of strategies to adapt the land to their wishes. Nature's will ensured that only the hardiest of plants, animals, and humans would grace the landscape. Ninety-eight percent of the park is Chihuahuan desert, yet most visitors prefer the coolness of the Chisos Mountains or the greenery of the Rio Grande and its canyons. In the desert, where ground temperatures in summer can reach 180 degrees Fahrenheit, a keen eye can detect over sixty species of cactus (eleven alone of prickly pear), fifty-six species of reptiles, and over one hundred variations of grasshoppers. The richness and beauty of the area's flora and fauna continue to attract visitors from around the world.

One plant that served well the Native, Hispano, and Anglo dwellers was *candelilla* (wax), whose properties when boiled yield a substance used in perfumes, lubricants, and the like. Another plant that lured humans was agave, or mescal, which the Indé people (whom the Spanish also called Mescaleros, or "the people of the mescal plant") ate to gain sustained energy for their journeys through the desert.

Park archaeologist Tom Alex noted in a 1997 interview that early human interaction with the land was not sporadic but, in Alex's terms, "heavy and constant." At least eight thousand years ago, desert tribes traveled down the drainage corridors of the Big Bend, leaving behind fire rings and campsites in large numbers. "Over 200 kinds of foods were available to these people," writes Frank Deckert, "who used parts of a variety of plants and animals." Distinguishing characteristics of these ancestral peoples emerged with the establishment of permanent communities some sixty miles up the Rio Grande from the western park boundary, the place that the Spanish called La Junta de los Ríos (The joining of the rivers). There the Rio Conchos flowed north and east to meet the Rio Grande, itself coming south from its headwaters high in the Rocky Mountains. Even today, the most substantial population base between the park and El Paso (a distance of over three hundred miles) is the border area of Presidio, Texas, and Ojinaga, Chihuahua, located at the confluence of the Rio Conchos and Rio Grande.[6]

Scholars still refer to these people by the term the Spanish gave them: Jumanos. No translations for this term are offered in historical texts of the Big Bend, even as archaeological evidence links these people to the communities of farmers far to the north and west in New Mexico whom the Spanish identified as Los Pueblos (translated as "villagers"). This may indeed be the case, as the word in Spanish for "human being" is *humano* (written in sixteenth-century Castilian with a *j*). All tribes in the Southwest, and for that matter throughout North America, referred to themselves as "people" or "human beings." Hence the possibility that the Jumanos typified one behavioral trait in the Big Bend region as settled agriculturists who had solved the mystery of survival through ingenuity and cultivation of the soil.

The disappearance of most of these communities, and their persistence in one area around La Junta, may stem from the presence in the Big Bend of another type of Native society—the migratory hunters and warriors whom the Spanish would encounter. Collectively, the Spanish referred to the peoples throughout the southern Great Plains and the high deserts of the Southwest as Los Indios Bravos. These "wild" tribes would not submit to the demands of the Spanish for labor, tribute, concubinage, or conversion, preferring their own survival strategies in a harsh desert expanse. In later years these tribes included such generic names as Apache (the Zuni Pueblo word for "enemy"), Comanche (from the Ute Indian word Koma'antsi, for "the people who fight us all the time"), and the mysterious Chisos people, from whence comes the name of the most prominent mountains of Big Bend National Park.

Interaction between Spanish speakers and the Jumano and Bravo peoples they met formed the early narrative of the Big Bend for the better part of three centuries. Scholars have uncovered in the study of Spanish-Native history evidence of cultural interaction as well as conflict. Such is the case for the Big Bend and the people who dwelt there from the mid-sixteenth century to the arrival of the Americans three hundred years later. Students and aficionados of Texas history attempted to link the Big Bend country to the first Spanish explorers and the party of Alvar Núñez Cabeza de Vaca. His historic journey from the Gulf Coast of Mexico has been well chronicled, often as an important adventure story that hinted of treasures that lay to the north. Recent maps and close readings show Vaca entering from the southern rim of Big Bend and skirting the Rio Grande until the Spaniard made his unequivocal appearance at Rio de los Juntos. Perhaps most significantly, Vaca's trek through the wilds of West Texas and northern Mexico in the 1530s produced stories so fabulous that in 1540, Spanish royal officials commissioned the famed *Entrada* of Francisco Vasquez de Coronado to see whether Vaca's captivating accounts were true.[7]

One way to consider Big Bend's role in the history of the Southwest is to think about two geographic zones moving toward each other. The Apache inhabited the first area, comprising communities in and above Big Bend. The second was a concentration of Spanish settlements moving in a northeasterly direction. This unit, commonly referred to as Nueva Vizcaya, was a politically advancing, economically developing, and continuously changing jurisdiction as Spain claimed authority over new lands and peoples. Spanish institutions of Mission and Presidio forged a slow but inexorable pathway, often following mining strikes beginning in the 1540s, from the interior of Mexico until ultimately reaching the Big Bend area in the 1770s.

The hardiness of the Spanish brought them to the lands along the Rio Grande and laid the foundation for later exploration. One well-documented sojourn began in 1581 with the exploration of the Rodriguez-Chamuscado party (the customary military escort that accompanied missionaries traveling to distant outposts). The latter's journey down the Rio Conchos included a mix of soldiers and missionaries, who encountered Jumanos. The Native villagers told the Spanish of contact with Vaca over forty years earlier. Chamuscado and Rodriguez then ventured northwest along the Rio Grande in search of slave labor.

When word reached Mexico of the failure of this latest effort to capture slaves, or to protect the delegation of friars, a relief party retraced their footsteps the following year under the command of Antonio de Espejo. He claimed to have seen ten thousand Native people residing in five substantial villages around the juncture of the Conchos and Rio Grande. It also was Espejo who spoke of the wild tribes of the Big Bend at Los Chizos, who perhaps fled to the area to escape Spaniards seeking workers for their silver mines. This group may have been Apache, but the historical record is silent because for nearly a century after the Espejo journey, the Spanish did not return to the Big Bend area.[8]

By the late 1600s, the Apache had dispersed along mountain ranges and valleys throughout the American Southwest. They expanded their range of influence north to the Arkansas River valley, east to the Texas Panhandle, and south toward San Antonio and the lower Rio Grande. In and above Big Bend, the Apache established settlements from the Guadalupe to the Davis and Chisos Mountains. In seasonal migrations, the Apache occupied a constellation of farming plots near sources of water, hunting buffalo on the plains before settling down for winter. By the time they had acquired the horse, Apache regularly participated in trade fairs as distant as Pecos and Taos in New Mexico.

Historian Thomas A. Britten notes that eastern bands of Apache (often called the Lipanes in Spanish) spent their summers near agricultural villages along the Pecos River and upper Rio Grande, where they traded with Spaniards and Pueblos. In autumn, they returned eastward to hunt along the San Saba, Llano, and Pedernales Rivers. During the winter months, some bands ventured farther north into the Colorado and Brazos River regions of modern-day Texas to continue their hunting activities, while others occupied the foothills and plains just east of the Pueblos. As spring approached, the Apache diverted back south to exist on a variety of wild plants, nuts, and berries.[9]

While the seventeenth century produced in northern New Mexico a permanent Spanish *provincia*, and later the Pueblo Revolt of 1680, Spain's inability or lack of desire to establish control of the Big Bend country left the latter on the margins of Spanish imperial dominion. The flight of the Nuevomexicanos and their Native allies southward to El Paso in 1680 did not eliminate Europeans from the region. Instead, the Spanish in 1683 entertained a delegation of Jumanos who sought protection from bands of Apache who had raided deep into West Texas. La Gran Apacheria, as the Spanish called the huge area from modern-day Kansas to southeastern Arizona, witnessed a higher concentration of "the Enemy." This in turn threatened the lives of the more sedentary Jumanos. The leader of the delegation to El Paso, a man whom the Spanish called Juan Sabeata, included in his quest for safety a plea for conversion to the Catholic faith. The Spanish interpreted this as an admission that the Apache posed more of a threat than the very same Spaniards whom the New Mexican Pueblos had expelled just three years earlier.[10]

Still stinging from their retreat from Santa Fe, and a decade removed from a successful Reconquista, Spanish officials in El Paso agreed in 1698 to send three priests down the Rio Grande to La Junta: Nicolas López, Juan de Zavaleta, and Antonio de Acevado. Soon thereafter, New Mexico's governor-in-exile, Domingo Jironza Petríz de Cruzate, dispatched a military unit under the command of Captain Juan Domingues de Mendoza to survey a new mission. The latter's journey took him downriver as far as the Rio Conchos, and then by a circular route northeastward to what would become known as the Davis Mountains. These Mendoza called Los Reyes (The kings), for their regal presence over the plains of West Texas.

Before returning to El Paso, Mendoza met with Juan Sabeata at Horsehead Crossing on the Rio Pecos, near present-day Fort Stockton. There the Jumano leader gave Mendoza a French flag, evidence to the Spanish that a new European power had traveled far into the Southwest. This gesture reinforced in the minds of Spanish officials the importance of laying claim to the area of the Big Bend, and the magnitude of winning the allegiance of Native peoples.[11]

Spain's fears of foreign competition from West Texas to the Gulf Coast compounded the obstacles of distance, isolation, aridity, and resistant Native people who had hindered Nueva España since the days of Francisco Coronado. In Texas, the French presence along the Mississippi River (the province of Louisiana) forced the Spanish to defend their claims with presidios and missions in San Antonio and Nacogdoches (the latter known as La Misión de Los Adaes).

Meanwhile, both the Apache and Comanche responded to the squeeze of Spanish and French Empires, "relying on the bequests of imperialism: the horse from Spain and the gun from France. . . . The Texan and New Mexican equipoise, with presidio and mission as the outer-edge bulwarks of the Spanish presence," ultimately did not outlast the force of ongoing Apache and Comanche raids. History texts of the Southwest speak of the efforts of eighteenth-century Spanish rulers (the Bourbon family of France) to modernize the colonial empire through strengthened defenses and expanded trading zones. In 1747, the *audiencia* of Mexico reported, in the words of historian Art Gomez, "that not a single presidio existed" between San Juan Bautista, near present-day Piedras Negras / Eagle Pass, and El Paso, a distance of over 360 leagues (approximately 540 miles).[12]

To meet these challenges, Carlos III ordered a thorough examination of all Spanish frontier garrisons. The appearance in the Southwest of the Royal Corps of Engineers, Spain's version of the French military academy of Saint Cyr (and later the United States' Military Academy at West Point), precipitated a review of Spanish military readiness. Spain's final commitment to improvement of imperial defense came in 1768 under the command of the famed Marqués de Rubí. Inspired by the French model of science and engineering, the Royal Corps sent Rubí to suggest a radical departure in its strategies for protection of the Rio Grande. What prompted Rubí's historic inspection was Spain's embarrassing defeat by England in the Seven Years' War (1762), a humiliating loss of Spanish colonies in Havana, Cuba, and in the far-off Philippines.[13]

If the losses of territory were only brief (Spain returned to both areas as part of the Treaty of Paris the following year), the military setback exposed Spanish weakness and vulnerability abroad. Such unpreparedness caused authorities to evaluate and reassess their defenses. Accompanied by his assistant, Nicolás de Lafora, Rubí journeyed from the Native towns near Tucson (the people who called themselves the Tohono O'Otham), to the Sabine River in central Texas. Over the course of two years, traversing more than six thousand miles and encountering much of northern New Spain's most desolate and rugged terrain, Rubí inspected twenty of Spain's twenty-one northern garrisons. He described the Indian villages, sources of water, mineral deposits, and flora and fauna and made suggestions for roads and trails. In his report, Rubí warned his superiors that it would be impossible for Spain to provide military garrisons for every settlement located south of the Rio Grande.[14]

Rubí also criticized the decentralized process of presidio alignment, as these had appeared whenever a community desired one, rather than following a coherent plan of defense. His conclusion marked a significant shift in official thinking about the Big Bend area. Spain thus abandoned its military posts in East Texas, except for San Antonio and San Sabá. Instead the Spanish emphasized protection of the coastline of Texas, with its accessible ports and waterways, and along the Rio Grande to the far northern reaches of Taos and Santa Fe. In what came to be known as the Provincias Internas (Internal provinces), authorities in New Spain refashioned their military hinterlands.

Spain's insular turn signaled things to come as the world power became more circumscribed and protectionist in its thinking. The Spanish government adopted

Rubí's recommendation for three new presidio sites in the Big Bend region: a village at San Vicente Pass, south of the Chisos Mountains (the future location of the villages of San Vicente on both sides of the Rio Grande); another at San Carlos, a dozen miles or so south of modern-day Lajitas; and a third at the thriving communities around La Junta de los Ríos.[15]

Despite the merits of Rubí's judgment, the reality of Spain's imperial decline (and eventual ouster from Mexico in 1821) meant little funding in the years after 1750 for such an elaborate scheme. This coincided with the arrival of the Comanche bands onto the southern Great Plains, forcing the once-mighty Apache farther into Mexico and exposing villages there to constant fear of raiding and retaliation.

The first commandant of Las Provincias Internas arrived in 1767, when the Spanish sent to the new presidio at San Vicente an officer of Irish descent, General Hugo Oconor (called El Gran Colorado for his flaming-red hair and beard). Knowing that the Apache sought refuge in the Chisos Mountains, Oconor and his troops marched down the Rio Grande to La Junta, then eastward to the Big Bend area. Before reaching the Apache stronghold, Oconor visited the presidio at San Carlos, where he placed Captain Don Manuel de Villaverde in command of fifty soldiers and their families. He then stopped at San Vicente to install Captain Francisco Martinez as commander, in hopes that a unified defensive line along the Rio Grande would drive the Apache northward. The only problem with this presidial strategy was that it pushed the Apache back into the path of an emerging force on the southern plains: the Comanche.[16]

The Apache had maintained independent communities in Arizona, northern Mexico, and southeast New Mexico, finding proximity to Spanish villages for spring trade, sustaining themselves on the bounty of mountain ranges and passes, and engaging in kinship networks that cemented trade relations. Much of their migration had occurred on foot, characterized by the dispersion of a common linguistic stock. Once the Apache acquired the horse, their territorial domain grew exponentially. Access to buffalo on the plains fostered trade relations with Spaniards. Kinship ties reinforced commercial networks with neighboring Apache *rancherías* throughout the southwest.

In contrast, the Comanche established a greater degree of political homogeneity and centralized authority beyond the scope of what the Apache had attained. The rise of the Comanche dates back to the early 1600s, as these desert people related to the Shoshone and Paiute peoples evolved into the preeminent empire on the southern plains. The Comanche partnered with their relatives, the bands known as the Nuuche ("People of the Sun," or the Ute). They soon drove Apache bands southward into the interior of Mexico. Where the once self-sufficient Apache had migrated freely between winter camps, hunting grounds, and agricultural plots, they now found themselves forced to prey on northward-moving

Spanish settlements. The Comanche seized on established trade networks fueled by Spanish gifts in exchange for peace. The Comanche also engaged in a lucrative slave trade with Spaniards, both in the north and for suppliers of labor for mining camps in Mexico.

After waging sustained warfare throughout much of the eighteenth century, the Comanche bartered for trade goods from neighboring allies, such as the Pawnee, Wichita, or traders from France, England, and later the Republic of Texas. A trade nexus that radiated outward across the central plains to the Mississippi River augmented Comanche settlement on the southern plains, where rolling hills teeming with abundant grass and fortified with watering holes supported animal foraging unequaled in the area's history. Don Bernardo de Miera y Pacheco, writing in 1778, said of the Comanche, "They acquired horses and weapons of iron, and they have acquired so much skill in handling both that they surpass all nations in agility and courage. They have made themselves the lords of all the buffalo country, seizing it from the Apache nation, which formerly was the most widespread of all known in America." After detailing the rise of Comanche hegemony, Miera y Pacheco ended by alerting Spanish officials that the once-distant Apache, rather than vanishing from the plains, now "have pushed to the frontiers of the King's provinces."[17]

Whatever his credentials and accomplishments, Oconor's decision to constrain the Apache in the Big Bend did not please Teodoro de Croix, the commandant-general of Spain's internal provinces. Taking his directive from King Carlos III, the French-born Croix preferred to approach Indians by "the gentle and effective means that the Laws of the Indies provide; cajolery, good treatment, persuasion by missionaries, gifts, and secure offers of sovereign protection." Croix thus pursued a complicated alliance with the Comanche to defeat the Apache. Croix also believed that the presidios at San Vicente, San Carlos, and La Junta were unnecessary and called for their removal.[18]

Croix ventured into the Big Bend area in early 1778 from northern Chihuahua, only to be attacked by a party of five hundred Apache. Based on this incident and his personal review of the Big Bend presidios, Croix concluded that the garrisons barely supported themselves and lacked adequate grazing land for the soldiers' mounts. A decade later, the Spanish decided to engage in an elaborate scheme of treaties and coercion to succeed where presidios and frontal assaults on the Apache had failed.

The following year (1789), Juan de Ugarte, governor of Coahuila, moved to pursue the Apache north of the Rio Grande. Several years of effort resulted in the Spanish victory at the battle of El Aguaje de Dolores (The watering hole of sorrows) in the Chisos Mountains. Two years later, three Apache band chiefs sought peace, which entailed settling on land around Presidio.[19]

The same could not be said for the Comanche, as they surged through the Big Bend country. They continued raiding throughout the remainder of the Spanish era, reaching Spanish villages as far as Zacatecas, over five hundred miles south of the Rio Grande. Few residents of the Big Bend, whether Spanish or Native, noticed in 1821 when the Mexican Revolution ended and the new government of Mexico City declared a republic to replace imperial Spain. Even more so than the urban centers of New Mexico and central Texas, the Big Bend reverted in the Mexican interlude (1821–1846) to a state that one visitor in 1828 to San Carlos called "a half-wild Indian and Mexican settlement on the Rio Grande."[20]

Just as the Mexican independence movement meant little to the villages and presidios along the bend of the Rio Grande, the advance of America's Army of the West through New Mexico and California during the Mexican-American War (1846–1848) brought few changes to daily life. General Stephen Watts Kearny and his six-thousand-member force sent no one southeastward from El Paso to survey the new territory. Nor did American forces under General Zachary Taylor show much interest in the Big Bend country as they moved south that year from modern-day Brownsville, Texas, to capture the Mexican state of Coahuila. The corridor from San Antonio to Monterrey that Mexican president Antonio López de Santa Anna had taken in 1836 to recapture the Alamo had no spur lines westward to Big Bend. The United States claimed an area about which it knew little, and which required much in the way of defense, scientific study, and economic support.[21]

More substantial for the future of the Big Bend under American domination would be negotiations for the peace treaty held near Mexico City, and the boundary survey ordered by the treaty commissioners. The Treaty of Guadalupe Hidalgo, signed in the Mexican community of the same name on February 2, 1848, contained clauses about citizenship, land-grant rights, and protection against Indian raiding that appealed to Mexicanos throughout the Southwest. Article XI promised that the United States would perform the task of preventing Indian attacks along the US-Mexico border (Mexican negotiators had referred to them as *tribus selvajes*, or "savage tribes"). Article V specified that each nation appoint agencies to collaborate on the establishment of an international boundary line. These two mandates brought the same US Army to West Texas and the Big Bend that had defeated Santa Anna and the Mexican forces months earlier. They also launched the first of several scientific and diplomatic studies of the region.[22]

While the treaty negotiators hailed their accomplishment, another event occurred that linked the Big Bend more closely to the orbit of American power and influence. In January 1848, a supervisor of sawmill workers in California's Sierra Nevada found traces of gold in the millrace. The discovery unleashed the most dramatic surge of people across the continent that America had ever seen.

While the preferred route involved sailing around South America, some hardy souls trekked across the desert Southwest to avoid the Rocky Mountains. The forty-niners also found relatively flat land between the Texas coast and San Diego, making a southern route to California a priority for the federal government. The potential for Indian resistance only heightened as thousands of gold-seekers poured across the central and southern Great Plains in 1849 and 1850, with West Texas especially vulnerable because of the intractable Comanche and Apache.[23]

The US Army and its Corps of Topographical Engineers accepted the dual challenge of surveying the Mexico-US border and opening travel corridors across the interior West. In March 1849, Major Robert S. Neighbors led a unit of army troops westward from the state capital of Austin toward the desert outpost of El Paso. Their plan was to identify a wagon road for military and civilian traffic that would link central Texas with the far Southwest. That year, Lieutenant William Whiting led a force from San Antonio with the assistance of Brevet Second Lieutenant William F. Smith. The Whiting-Smith party became the first Americans to survey the Davis Mountains. They camped on Limpia Creek, near the future site of Fort Davis (constructed six years later to guard travelers along the San Antonio–El Paso wagon road). From there the party headed southwestward to Fort Leaton, established in 1848 near the town of Presidio (the Spanish La Junta), and on to El Paso. Turning downriver, they attempted to float from El Paso to Presidio, eventually deciding to survey the river by land. It was Whiting who christened the area "the Big Bend." His report, in the words of Art Gomez, "recommended that the neighboring region be thoroughly reconnoitered as it represented the last expanse of frontier in Texas known only to its native residents."[24]

That survey came in 1849 as part of the work of the United States–Mexico Boundary Commission. Departing from their base in San Diego, the group encountered a host of obstacles (the Gold Rush–induced inflation in California, civilian-military competition, and sectional politics in California, in the nation's capital, and between North and South). The commission nonetheless took the field, with Mexican and American officials collaborating on the enterprise. One of its prominent members was Corps of Topographical Engineers lieutenant William H. Emory, who as chief astronomer conducted many of the measurements for the team. When the commission reached Presidio in August 1852, it detached a crew under the direction of Marine T. Chandler, a civilian meteorologist, to study the canyons of the Rio Grande by boat. They had few scientific documents to consult, with the exception of a map drawn by the Mexican exploration party of Colonel Emilio Langberg.

In 1851, Langberg had undertaken the first general inspection of the northern Mexican states since the war. He reported that while frequently the target of

Indian raids, San Carlos was also a major trade center for surrounding tribes friendly to both the Spanish and the Mexicans. The colonel had crossed the Rio Grande into US territory along the Comanche Trail into the Chisos Mountains. These Langberg described as being "like a chain of hills running uninterrupted as far as San Vicente, presenting a vision of distinct figures resembling wondrous castles and towers." The Langberg party followed an old Indian path eastward to a place he called La Boquilla (The little mouth) and then turned upstream toward the old presidio of San Vicente. Even though the adobe walls lay in ruins, Langberg saw its potential once more as a defensive site against Indian raiding. He also noted the inscriptions on the adobe walls, bearing the names of a generation of soldiers who had passed before him in search of Indians.[25]

In retracing the steps of the Langberg party, the Chandler crew had managed to travel by boat from Presidio to Santa Eleña Canyon. Once there, Chandler had to climb the walls of the Mesa de Anguila to plot his course. This reconnaissance convinced him to avoid the narrow cliffs and rushing waters within the canyon by riding around it. From there the party spotted a mountain that they named Emory Peak, in honor of their chief astronomer (who did not accompany them through the Big Bend). This became their azimuth for triangulating distance and altitude in the area.

Chandler and his fellow surveyors then plunged into Mariscal Canyon, passing mountains that they referred to as Sierra San Vicente. After a two-day journey, they emerged from Mariscal Canyon and followed the river to the San Vicente presidio ruins. Finally reaching an opening that they named Cañon de Sierra Carmel (modern-day Boquillas Canyon), Chandler and his peers agreed that they had neither the endurance nor the will to continue downstream. A number of corps members suffered from malnutrition, while others lacked suitable clothing and footwear to attempt the journey any longer. The boundary commission thus gained little knowledge of the river valley at least one hundred miles upstream from its intersection with the Rio Pecos.[26]

Neither the United States nor Mexico chastised the Chandler party for its failure to survey the canyons of the Rio Grande. Evidence of the limits that nature had placed on the boundary commission appeared in 1859, when the Camel Corps of the US Army sent a detachment through West Texas to determine the feasibility of these desert animals as beasts of burden. Second Lieutenant Edward Hartz, along with Brevet Second Lieutenant William Echols, journeyed south with their North African mounts to the area later known as Willow Spring (south of present-day Marathon). The Camel Corps ventured through Dog Canyon (near the northern entrance to the future Big Bend National Park), then south along the east flank of the Chisos Mountains and across the Rio Grande at Presidio San Vicente.

Hartz and Echols explored and mapped the area between Boquillas and Mariscal Canyons for about a week. They then returned north along Tornillo Creek to Fort Stockton, unable to identify a site in the Big Bend for a military post. The army sent Echols back into the area in 1860 with a camel unit from Fort Davis to survey the area from Presidio to Santa Elena. Echols recommended a site several miles downstream from the mouth of Santa Elena Canyon for an army post, but the onset of the Civil War drew attention away from the region.[27]

Between the boundary survey and Camel Corps expeditions, the United States addressed the challenge of border defense against Indian raiding required by the Treaty of Guadalupe Hidalgo. The US Army placed outposts far to the east of the Big Bend at Fort Duncan (modern-day Eagle Pass) and 120 miles northwest of the river at Fort Davis. The military had targeted San Antonio and Austin for maximum protection, with the road to El Paso included in their strategy. Gomez notes that "Mexican newspapers were quick to editorialize their outrage towards the United States for failing to comply with its obligation under the Treaty of Guadalupe Hidalgo." Conditions along the border had deteriorated such that by 1852, "Chihuahuan authorities sought permission in Washington for Mexican forces to cross the Rio Grande in an all-out offensive against the Indians."[28]

The challenge of containing Indian raiding along the US-Mexico border coincided with protecting new territory that the neighbor to the north had acquired in the Gadsden Purchase. The United States in 1853 had paid Mexico $15 million for land west of El Paso and south of the Gila River (including the *villa* of Tucson). More important for the Big Bend region, the agreement contained language abrogating Article XI of the Treaty of Guadalupe Hidalgo. Says Gomez, "No longer committed to the protection of the Mexican frontier, the War Department devoted its full attention to Texas, and the remaining southwestern territories." This meant more troops and supplies for Fort Davis, which in the mid-1850s housed over four hundred uniformed personnel, and the establishment of Fort Stockton in 1859 to ensure delivery of the US mail along the San Antonio–El Paso road.[29]

The Gadsden agreement resulted also from conscious efforts by the Mexican government to establish communities along the Rio Grande. After 1848, Mexico created some eighteen *colonias* in areas traversed by nomadic tribes, among them the old presidios of San Carlos and San Vicente. In 1850, Mexican officials invited two hundred members of the Seminole and Kickapoo tribes to reside along the border. These Indians, displaced from their ancestral homes east of the Mississippi River in the 1830s by war and removal policies, had disliked their new homelands in eastern Oklahoma. A third group accepting the Mexican offer of settlement were the Black Seminole, descendants of runaway southern slaves who had intermarried with Seminole in Florida, and who were targeted in the Indian Territory by slave raiders.

These mixed bands, led by such luminaries as the Seminole chief Coacoochee (Wild Cat), served as mercenaries against the enemies of the Mexican communities of the Big Bend area. Their bravery and willingness to run the enemy tribes to the ground led Mexico to offer them farmlands deeper into Coahuila and Chihuahua. One such site was the community of Nacimiento de los Negros (Birthplace of the Black people), and another near the town of Muzquiz, about sixty miles directly south of the future Big Bend National Park. With the Civil War ended and slavery abolished, most Indians and Blacks returned north. A small number of Black Seminole remained along the border with the Indian-fighting US Army (the famed Seminole Negro Scouts).[30]

Such joint efforts of the United States and Mexico to terminate raiding by a common enemy affected the Big Bend region after the Civil War in several ways. The presence of soldiers at posts like Fort Davis, Fort Stockton, and Fort Concho (near San Angelo) attracted ranchers and farmers to supply the army with food, fiber, and horses. A combination of military defense and procurement stabilized the economy of the region, making it attractive to families seeking new opportunities in the postwar era. Francis Rooney and John Beckwith established ranches in the Big Bend after 1870 to feed soldiers at Camp Peña Colorado (south of Marathon), and at Camp Neville Springs in the 1880s (within the confines of the future Big Bend National Park). Daniel O. Murphy came to the Fort Davis area in the early 1880s in anticipation of the arrival of track belonging to the Galveston, Harrisburg, and San Antonio Railroad. The railroad connected his cattle town of Murphysville to East Texas, a community that he would rename Alpine to appeal to potential eastern investors and tourists.[31]

Once the route passed through the Big Bend in 1882, more ranchers and community builders arrived. Within five years, they had succeeded in carving out Brewster County from the much larger Presidio County. That process of homesteading, so important to the state of Texas and the federal government, began in the late 1870s in the Big Bend with the appearance of John T. Gano. The son of a former Confederate army general, Gano arrived in 1879 in Presidio County as a surveyor for private land claimants. Within a decade, Gano and his family had acquired some fifty-five thousand acres of land, much of it in trade with other ranchers for their surveying work.

By 1890, the Ganos ran over thirty thousand head of cattle between Terlingua Creek and the Chisos Mountains, with line camps at sites within the future boundaries of Big Bend National Park (Santa Eleña Canyon and Oak Creek Spring). On the southeast side of the future national park, E. L. Gage herded cattle near McKinney Springs, northeast of the Chisos Mountains in the shadow of the Sierra del Carmen. He later moved his operations northward to the railroad town of Marathon. There in the 1920s, he built the Gage Hotel to house his guests and white-collar employees, as these had become too numerous for the private accommodations on the Gage ranch.

The intersection of government, the railroad, consumers of beef, and eastern investors seeking new opportunities made West Texas ranchers prosperous in an area that had challenged many who had come before. A survey of statistical data for Brewster County from its inception in 1887 until the economic collapse of the 1930s indicates how small the population was, yet how much opportunity did surface, especially after the opening in the 1890s of the quicksilver mines in Terlingua and the fluorspar mines in Boquillas. It also reveals the lag between economic development of the Big Bend and that of the state of Texas (itself undergoing change in an urbanizing America).

As the nineteenth century drew to a close, the Big Bend area reflected many national trends, and in some cases surpassed them. When residents of Alpine asked the state of Texas in 1887 to separate them from the far-distant county seat of Presidio County, the new county of Brewster had only 307 people scattered over some five thousand square miles. The first official enumeration of Brewster County occurred three years later, with US Census officials noting the presence of 710 people. Of Brewster County's total population, 666 that year lived in Precinct 1 (the term for the town site of Alpine). An additional 44 lived in Precinct 2, the remainder of the vast county.

To place Brewster County in regional perspective, Texas in 1890 ranked seventh in the nation in population, with over 2.2 million people. Of that number, only 11 percent lived in towns of 2,500 or more (the US Census Bureau's definition of an "urban" area); this at a time when the national average of "urbanites" stood at nearly 40 percent. Among Brewster County's 710 individuals, 695 were classified by race as "white," an intriguing reference in that this included Hispanics (who often were not considered white by local Anglos). The county that year also claimed a dozen residents identified as "colored" (the term used for Blacks, or African Americans), and three people of "all other" races.[32]

More revealing of change in Brewster County was the data uncovered by the Census Bureau in its 1900 enumerations. The state of Texas had grown by 36.1 percent, 15 points higher than the national average. Brewster County maintained its isolated character vis-à-vis Texas and the nation. Whereas the United States in 1900 was 48 percent urban, Brewster County had fewer than two people per square mile (the Census Bureau's calculation since 1890 of a "frontier" area). Yet the presence of mining communities in the southern portion of the county (and the farms to support them) shifted the balance of population substantially. Precinct 1 (Alpine), with 778 people, now fell behind Precinct 3 (the town and ranching area of Marathon), which claimed 799 people. Two new precincts, both near the Rio Grande, had formed by 1900: Terlingua (Precinct 2), with 197 people, and Boquillas (Precinct 4), with 218 people.

The 1900 census also offered more compelling data in its manuscript records. These revealed that the county was not a haven for young, single, male outlaws (men outnumbered women by only 1,345 to 1,011). In addition, the census now listed Mexicans in the foreign-born count, with Brewster County registering 733 Mexican natives. By comparison, Germans formed the next-largest ethnic group (a mere eleven people in the county's population). The vast majority of Mexican nationals resided in Terlingua, where they represented nearly all of its citizens, taking jobs listed as "miner," "laborer," or "freighter."[33]

While the historical record is mostly silent on the explicit motivation for famed geologist Robert T. Hill's journey down the Rio Grande at the century's end, there are two potential reasons. First, Hill was an admirer of the legendary Major John Wesley Powell, who in 1869 had ventured into the "great unknown" of the Colorado River. Powell first wrote about his journey in a series of articles for *Scribner's* magazine, expanding on his findings in a book-length manuscript. Three decades later, Hill published for *Century* magazine his own account of traversing the area popularly known as Big Bend. His byline read that he served in an official capacity on the United States Geological Survey, that being the person "in charge of the expedition."

As a geologist, Hill took on the romantic and poetic cast of what historian William H. Goetzmann describes as the "Second Age of Discovery," during which explorer-adventurers wrote as lyrically as they did scientifically about the continent. When Hill journeyed down the Rio Grande and around Big Bend, he joined the elite company of Stephen Long, Powell, John C. Frémont, and others who had surveyed and documented the western American landscape.[34]

A second reason Hill took to the canyon lands of the Rio Grande was his deep and abiding curiosity about nature. One year before his departure down the 123 miles of the Big Bend, Hill delivered a keynote address to the Department of Geology at the University of Texas. There he extolled the virtues of forging connections with physical landscapes. Explained Hill, "In fact, no man can come in contact with natural history without becoming to some extent refined." One's "sympathies will increase," Hill argued, with "his power for observation extended; his love for the beautiful developed, and his whole intellectual and religious horizon expanded from narrow egos to broad field of toleration for all human motives and activities, and if this be true of the individual, it is also true of the age." A return to nature embodied society's vision, as citizens immersed themselves in urban landscapes and acquainted themselves with civilizing institutions.[35]

Born in Nashville, Tennessee, in 1858, Hill had spent his childhood years under the shadow of the Civil War. After 1865, Hill's older brother, Joe, invited Robert to stay with him in Texas working as a typesetter for a local press in Comanche County, between Abilene and Fort Worth. The young Hill was struck by the stark environmental contrasts between what he had known as the American South and what he encountered in the American West. The differences presented themselves not only in contrasting landscapes and topography but also in his imagination. Texas was alive in its distinctive and cultural allure, and little understood in its geological formations. As Hill remembered, "I looked at the big-hatted and moustached men, most of them with a six-shooter on and wearing jingling belled cartwheel spurs." He continued, "All around me were sights and sounds new and uncouth to me. I stood amazed at this gateway into the old-time Indian fighting, desperado, swashbuckling, buffalo-killing, cowboy-yelping, ranger-ruling Texas frontier of 1873–74, as wild frontier days as this country has ever known." The images of the US Cavalry escorting the last of the great Kiowa and Comanche leaders to reservations in Oklahoma still lingered in Hill's memory decades later.[36]

The Texas geologist took to the Rio Grande in the fall of 1899 to describe in detail and for the first time the sights and sounds, rhythms and tempos of the river for a popular reading audience. His specially designed boats stretched thirteen feet long and three feet wide. They came equipped with cleated bows to withstand abrasive contact with the sometimes shallow and rocky river bottoms. As Hill and his crew descended the Rio Grande at Presidio, he apprised his readers of the significance of the undertaking: "Few Americans realize the impregnability and isolation of this frontier, or that it represents a portion of our national boundaries which heretofore has never been completely traversed or explored."[37]

The narrative that Hill produced captured in vivid and dramatic terms the characteristics of both the river and its wider surroundings. After following its slow, meandering course during the first portion of his journey, Hill exclaimed, "Almost in the twinkling of an eye we passed out of the desert glare into dark and silent depths of its gigantic walls, which rise vertically from the water's edge to a narrow ribbon of sky above." The river, enclosed between towering fissures, settled to a murmur as the group glided through a deep waterway of narrow canyons. The escarpments were wedged so tightly together that any member of the group could nearly touch the walls on either side by simply extending his oar at arm's length.[38]

The most interesting part of the trip was their encounter with a rockslide of debris blocking human navigation. Here the water simply had worked its way through the crevices during heavy runoff. Hill noted that "the boulders were mostly quadrangular masses of limestone, fifty feet . . . or more in height, dumped in a heterogeneous pile, like a load of bricks from a tip-cart."[39] For three days Hill and his crew portaged the rocky slope, using an assortment of techniques including lassoes and rope pulleys to lift and advance vessels and supplies. They named this section of the river Camp Misery for the toil they experienced.

After having traversed more than 350 miles of the vastness of the Big Bend country, Hill's river journey reached the railroad town of Langtry. In less than one month's time, and with long stretches of wading in water, days spent portaging stretches of the rocky river bottom, and enduring isolation, the mission's end came as a relief. Taking on nature's challenges, Hill confessed, "Beautiful as were these canyons, and prolific as they were in game and caves of wild honey the hardships we had endured were telling upon the temper of the party, and we no longer appreciated the noble surroundings. We longed only to escape from the walls, upon which we now began to look as a prison."[40]

Hill carefully recorded distances between canyons, accounting for both the volume and temper of the river at distinct points. In more pragmatic terms, the document led the reader down the primary stretches of the Rio Grande, establishing distance, proportion, and scale. Some parts of the river valley opened and extended for miles in each direction to distant buttes, mesas, and plateaus. Helpful in his account was his description of the river as it slowed and swirled in a quiet and seemingly motionless pool, only to move again in torrents of whipping and slapping rapids beating against riverbanks and collecting in foaming pools. From salvaged color plates, the famed landscape artist Thomas Moran, who had accompanied John Wesley Powell on his 1867 journey down the Colorado River, illustrated Hill's journey.

By the turn of the twentieth century, the Big Bend of the Rio Grande had changed much, and not at all. Nomadic peoples had come and gone, some with temporary success as conquerors, some as victims of their fierceness. Settled villagers, whether Native, Spanish, or a combination of each, survived by cultivating the river's bottomlands, hunting its feral game, and watching as explorers from Spain, Mexico, and the United States marched or rowed along the river's shores. While the Big Bend country may not have been completely "unpopulated," as the Spanish believed when they called it El Despoblado, it remained for the Americans to enter the new century and believe that they had found the "last frontier."

CHAPTER 2

Saving the Last Frontier—
The Big Bend Park Initiative

Large-scale extraction of the country's natural resources began in the nineteenth century, evolving in the twentieth with a call to protect the republic's scenic wonders. In what is commonly known as the conservation movement, federal and state authorities joined a chorus of preservationists like John Muir to heighten awareness of America's diverse landscape and natural resources. Since the establishment of Yellowstone National Park in 1872, the federal government, sanctioned by President Ulysses S. Grant, had endorsed the idea of a centralized administration to manage the growing number of wildlife preserves, scenic wonders, and historic monuments.

Following the momentum established by Theodore Roosevelt, President William Howard Taft wrote in 1912 to Congress, "Every consideration of patriotism and love of nature and beauty and art requires us to expend money enough to bring all these natural wonders within easy reach of our people." He continued, "The first step in that direction is the establishment of a responsible bureau, which shall take upon itself the burden of supervising the parks and of making recommendations as to the best method of improving their accessibility and usefulness."[1]

Not until the presidency of Woodrow Wilson, however, and at the behest of his secretary of the interior, Franklin Lane, did the idea come to fruition of a public agency to administer America's national parks. Established in 1916, the National Park Service's first director, Stephen Mather, used advertising and promotion of designated scenic areas to showcase the nation's beloved spots to influential politicians and journalists. Mather, a westerner and self-made millionaire, invited important political officials to camp in a park. He then introduced them to its transcendent beauty or pointed out its dilapidated condition and need of protection. Either method worked for him as long as he garnered interest. In addition to working with newspaper and magazine editors, the newly formed government office aligned with transportation officials to connect rail lines and later roads for automobile transit to the nation's parks.[2]

As many of the nation's larger currents filtered into the Big Bend, it is not surprising that a growing and expanding populace opened its mind to local and state histories west of the Mississippi River. The state of Texas, proud of its distinctive pioneering roots, rugged individualism, and fierce independence, expressed an identity that embraced the Lone Star ethos but still championed the values of a state that once flew six flags. Enthusiasm for local history matched the nation's interest in learning more about itself. In Texas's Randell County, located in the northwestern Panhandle, boosters in 1913 endorsed a resolution promoting Palo Duro Canyon as a national park. Located twenty-seven miles south of Amarillo, the 150-mile natural wonder diagonally straddled both Randell and adjacent Armstrong Counties. The physical geography was a striking example of wind erosion exposing colorful geological strata. A chasm cut sharply into the desert, descending as far as eight hundred feet below a sea of grassy tabletop lands.

The area also exhibited a long and dynamic paleontological and archeological history. Just beyond Palo Duro to the west was the famed Llano Estacado, home to bison, vibrant Native cultures (Kiowa, Apache, and Comanche people), and a place of celebrated Spanish exploration. The measure showed the degree to which communities in the Texas Panhandle recognized the locale's strong historical past, and their passion to make their vision come alive. Two years after the Panhandle booster organization passed its resolution, a bill appeared in the Texas House of Representatives entitled "Palo Duro Canyon National Forest Reserve and Park." While the measure died in committee, the overture offered a strong indication of the earnestness that citizens in northwest Texas displayed for establishment of a national park.[3]

Equally as important as the boosterism of the Texas Panhandle was promotional literature, like that issued in 1916, that shed a bright light on one area while diminishing the prospects of another. In the popular brochure *Texas the Marvellous*, Nevin O. Winter claimed that Palo Duro Canyon "is the most picturesque feature of the Panhandle topography" and deserved recognition as a national park. The author continued, "One is lost in admiration of the strange and fanciful figures made by the washing of the waters in the rainy season in Palo Duro. Even Niagara [Falls] sinks into insignificance when compared with the wild grandeur of this great chasm with its deep abysmal solitude." In contrast, all he said of the Big Bend area was that "in descending the Rio Grande from El Paso there is really no important port until Eagle Pass." Winter employed a firm tone that shaped and informed public awareness about the merits of Palo Duro vis-à-vis the lesser-known Big Bend. It would not be long, however, before an alluring narrative of the border would draw attention to the ancient corridor of the Rio Grande.[4]

Before Carlysle Graham Raht sat down to write *The Romance of Davis Mountains and Big Bend Country* (1919), the native Texan already had traveled the American Southwest as a journalist, court reporter, miner, and cowpuncher. A graduate in history from the University of Texas at Austin, Raht was poised to write about an area that had matured with him. The author took special care to "eliminate the personal viewpoint," both his own voice and those of the historical contemporaries he studied. His compelling work lamented a bygone era (his own formative years) and offered a distinctive rendering of the past.

Using popular Spanish accounts, US military records, and settler recollections, Raht wrote an early history of Fort Davis and the Big Bend area to emphasize military campaigns that achieved the "winning" of the West. Nearly two decades into the twentieth century, he professed, "Like the buffalo and the red man, they are gone forever, but to us who linger along the trail we cherish them fresh and green in our memories as the richest experiences of life." In lucid and vivid prose, Raht described the Comanche attraction to natural springs and expounded on the journey of Alvar Núñez Cabeza de Vaca through the region. Raht's chronicle of the drama of the Big Bend echoed in advertising and tourism promotion for decades.[5]

Given the deep enthusiasm shown for the Texas Panhandle's illustrious past, an equally powerful and magnetic pull drew interest to the Big Bend area. The thoughts and attention of a handful of local enthusiasts, politicians, and scholars attracted to the rugged beauty, panoramic backdrop, and rich archeology of Big Bend propelled the region into the spotlight. Whereas the Texas Panhandle drew the attention of boosters and potential tourists traversing the new network of highways, Raht helped reorient public attention to the mysterious Big Bend by championing its regional distinctiveness and local color, encased in a majestic setting.

South of the Rio Grande, Mexico's evolving economic development and the dynamic interplay of cultures fused the two nations' histories. During the late nineteenth and early twentieth centuries, mineral-rich states like Sonora, Chihuahua, and Coahuila attracted US capital investment for Mexican railroads, mining operations, machinery, and labor. Big Bend thus functioned as a way station for commerce moving from San Antonio to the west. Several stretches of the Chihuahuan desert backed up against the most impassable part of the Rio Grande, hindering the flow of traffic and commerce. As historian Mark Wasserman notes, "With its vast mineral resources, cheap land, and close proximity to the United States, Chihuahua received more nonrailroad foreign investments than any other region in Mexico before 1910." Chihuahua's unique geographical setting created a distinctive reliance on goods transported by overland trade.[6]

Change had already arrived to transform the region on both sides of the border. For Mexico, and for Chihuahua in particular, rail facilitated the new social and economic order, exacerbating the divide between wealthy and poor citizens. From 1902 to 1907, Chihuahua experienced an unprecedented boom, and with greater material growth came rising expectations for economic prosperity. One factor was completion of the rail line that linked the interior of Mexico with El Paso, Texas. When a market downturn swept away capital, so went the aspirations for a better life. Scholar Manuel Gamio, working in the 1920s for the US Social Science Research Council, surmised that rail lines not only facilitated the flow of goods and movement of people between the two nations. The experience also provided Spanish speakers with hopes for the future. Gamio wrote, "When there were no railroads, and only desert lay between Mexico and the United States, revolution was a purely domestic product, for the echoes of great social movements elsewhere were faint in Mexico and scarcely reached people. When the railroads joined these two countries, however, Mexican immigrants came to the United States and returned with ideas and memories of a better way of living."[7]

The Mexican dictator Porfirio Díaz (1884–1911) had overseen political and economic change in Mexico, but his totalitarian command also stifled democracy and opportunity for most of the nation's landless poor. Díaz, who had once welcomed foreign investment from the United States, now targeted Yankee capitalists when integrated markets yielded to fluctuations. By 1913, political conditions had deteriorated to the point that Díaz's once-mighty federal army had succumbed to revolutionary factions.

In December of that year, nearly three thousand Mexican soldiers took refuge in the far northeastern town of Ojinaga, Chihuahua, across the Rio Grande from Presidio, Texas. Anticipating a fight with Francisco "Pancho" Villa's revolutionary army, soldiers spilled into the small rural community. Huddled in its assortment of adobe structures, they retreated to Ojinaga fearing a thrust from Villa's forces, as the latter had attacked Chihuahua City from the south en route to capturing El Paso, the largest city along the US-Mexico border. Not only soldiers fled to one of the last northern strongholds for the federal army. "Hundreds of refugees poured across the river," explained the radical journalist John Reed, "some on horseback driving cattle before them, some in wagons, and others on foot." Awaiting them after their eight-day journey across Chihuahua's harsh desert were US military officials and customs agents, patrolling for contraband.[8]

After Reed proceeded to Mexico's interior for more material and angles for his stories, Villa and his "Villistas" soon converged on the north. Villa's demeanor turned violent when the United States withdrew its support for him, instead acknowledging the leadership of a more tractable revolutionary, Venustiano Carranza. In March 1916, Pancho Villa crossed the border into southern

New Mexico and raided the small town of Columbus. On May 6, an armed Mexican party struck the Big Bend community of Boquillas, seeking money and supplies, and leading local residents to fear wholesale violence.[9]

While Colonel John J. Pershing led his Punitive Expedition of army troops in search of Villa through the state of Chihuahua west of the Big Bend, other American officers contemplated similar actions in and around Boquillas. Negotiations in April 1916 in El Paso between Mexican and US representatives had resulted in promises by the former to stop the raiding by bandits into the United States. With the collapse of the agreement a month later, General Frederick Funston decided to divide the Big Bend Military District into ten separate outposts in the face of Mexican attacks. One of these military installations, called Camp Saint Heleña, was an army post built at Castolon on land leased in October 1916 from Clyde Buttrill. This facility would offer protection for the quicksilver mines of Terlingua.

When the US Census Bureau returned in 1920 to the Big Bend area and Brewster County, it found a landscape altered by the fortunes of war and civil unrest. The nation that year had finally become "urban," as 51.4 percent of the population lived in towns of 2,500 or more. This had many implications for political and economic power in America, as rural constituencies feared the domination of cities and the corruption of their attendant lifestyles. Texas followed the national pattern of urbanization, with the state now fifth in population at 4.7 million (up 19.7 percent in a decade). More telling was the Lone Star State's urbanization (32.4 percent), which included rapid growth in such cities as Dallas, Houston, and San Antonio.

For Brewster County, however, the story was the reverse. Its population had fallen by 8 percent, to 4,822 people. Alpine had lost over 10 percent (to 1,989), even as Marathon grew to 1,928 (an increase since 1910 of 41 percent). The Terlingua and Boquillas census districts had merged in 1910, and their total declined from 1,567 that year to 905 people in 1920, a shrinkage along the border of nearly 60 percent.[10]

Interest in some sort of national park facility in West Texas began as early as 1921, when a group of civic officials petitioned the Texas state legislature to identify lands within the Davis Mountains for a state park. The rise of tourism generated by the popularization of automobile travel, and the passage in 1916 of the Federal Highway Act, opened the region to visitors seeking the exotica and wonders of the Far West. In a state with a population of nearly six million and a 500 percent increase in motor vehicles in the 1920s, Texas's leaders sought recreational destinations and roads and interstates that linked their vast landscape.[11]

In 1924, an Alpine doctor and state senator, Benjamin F. Berkeley, asked William C. Boyd of the Texas Fish, Game, and Oyster Commission about establishment of a twenty-five-thousand-acre park in the Chisos Mountains. The following year, US representative Claude Hudspeth introduced in Congress a resolution to appropriate $100,000 to purchase lands in the Davis Mountains. This idea died in committee, but it stimulated interest among local and state leaders to plan for road construction in and around the storied military post of Fort Davis. Nothing came of the initiatives for parks in the Davis and Chisos ranges, and Texas promoters of tourism and travel looked elsewhere in the late 1920s to invest their time and resources.[12]

When Pat Morris Neff entered the Texas Governor's Mansion in 1923, he proclaimed that given the state's landmass, ownership of public lands, and colorful history, "Texas should have led all the other states in the Union in the ownership and maintenance of State parks." Neff lamented, however, that the Lone Star State "did not reserve one beauty spot, nor set aside anywhere one acre of land to be used and enjoyed by the public in the name of the State." What struck Neff was that other states had made significant investments to identify, purchase, and publicize important historical sites and convert those spaces into state parks. At the time Neff made his remarks, twenty-five states had seen fit to designate sites for public parks. Michigan, Connecticut, and New York topped the list, with thirty, twenty-five, and twenty-two sanctioned state parks, respectively.[13]

In 1923, Neff authorized creation of the State Parks Board, a panel of six appointed members charged with the task of considering areas praiseworthy for designation. Neff's call received a rousing response of forty-three nominations of potential sites. After a careful screening process, that number shrank by 1927 to twenty-three state parks. When the Texas State Parks Board announced its first official park list, those areas amounted to 1,996 acres. They ranged in size from 200 acres to as small as 10 acres, an average of 86.7 acres per unit.[14]

Capitalizing on the momentum established by the National Highway Act of 1921, Neff reconfigured state laws enabling Texas to be eligible to receive matching federal funds. The proposed amendment, approved in January 1923, granted to "the state the power to designate, construct, operate, control, and provide for the maintenance of a state system of public highways." The governor also established the Texas Highway Association, a three-person board appointed to six-year terms. To fund the new department, Neff implemented a gasoline tax and levied fees on motor vehicle licenses. He contended that highways were the "arteries and veins" that stimulated commerce for the overall economic health of the Lone Star State. Coincidentally, roads also opened avenues for a reconnection with nature.[15]

Having grown up in the dense woodlands of East Texas where he spent most of his career east of the Brazos River as a lawyer, legislator, and businessman, Neff governed in an age of domestic calm, as reflected in his book entitled *The Battles of Peace*. He was attentive to civic behavior, experiences, and knowledge that shaped an informed citizenry and fostered local pride. Wrote Neff in 1925,

"The citizenship of Northeast Texas is unfamiliar with the beauties of the Rio Grande Valley. People who live in the Rio Grande Valley are strangers to almost every other section of the State." Neff wanted to bridge these distances by linking the east and west through highways and state parks.[16]

Like Neff, Walter Prescott Webb would begin to follow his life's passions in a time after war. When the future "dean" of Texas history arrived on the University of Chicago campus in 1919, the global conflict had just ended. Lessons to be drawn from the "war to end all wars" remained in the distant future. Yet the ideas of violence, the difference between winning and losing, and the importance of law and order (domestically and internationally) occupied the young scholar's mind. On a visit to Big Bend in 1924, Webb followed a route similar to that of Robert T. Hill, only he drove a Model T Ford down US Highway 287, cutting through ninety miles of the wildest and most picturesque portion of Texas—the Big Bend.

Perhaps the spirit of freedom enveloped the young historian, as Webb stopped often to observe the landscape. He sought the color and temper of a land that had shaped the world of the Texas Rangers (one of his favorite historical subjects). Webb could not help but note the material reminders of another past that decorated the countryside: broken windmills here and there, traces of barbed-wire fencing dangling on the ground, cattle and horses foraging on hillsides. With a flair for language and the gift of telling good stories, Webb wrote about the Texas Rangers in terms to match the landscape: expansive and grandiose.

Webb also echoed the sentiments of Governor Neff in thinking about the alignment of history and economic growth. Webb's *Great Plains* (1931) did not employ the same confrontational style as did his first article, published four years earlier in the nationally circulated *Scribner's* magazine. He delayed release of his Texas Rangers manuscript for nearly a decade, trimming back references to the direct confrontation between Texas cowboys and rangers and the Comanche. Something happened to him at Big Bend that changed his thinking in favor of cultural determinism, and of adaptation that gave way to modernity. It was then that Webb shelved the idea for a deep institutional history of the Texas Rangers. He began working instead on an equally valuable, if less bold, study of ranching, in particular its institutional and technological adaptation to aridity that made possible the occupation of the Great Plains.[17]

Webb also missed in his interviews with Texas Rangers the most important officer patrolling the Big Bend: Everett Townsend. The latter had changed with the times, becoming a sheriff and later politician. Born in 1871 in Colorado County, Texas, Townsend moved with his family to the border town of Del Rio, where he spent his formative years. Two decades later, Townsend volunteered for service as a Texas Ranger after altering his age so that he would be considered for the unit. Within two years, he had risen to the rank of deputy marshal.

Townsend came to the Big Bend in 1894 as a customs inspector, working out of Presidio. Nearly fifty years later, he would reminisce about his first exposure to the Rio Grande. "With Deputy U.S. Marshal Bufe Cline," wrote Townsend to a friend, "I was on the trail of some mules that had been stolen in Mexico and smuggled to this side of the Rio Bravo." When Townsend and Cline reached the top of Bandera Mesa, they saw "a vision of such magnitude as to stir the sluggish soul of a hardened human bloodhound trained in the relentless service of the Texas Rangers and now serving Uncle Sam as a River Guard, a business equally as grim."[18]

Townsend admitted in his 1943 correspondence, "I was too busy chasing men to visit it at the time." A few months later, he crossed the river again to marvel at Mexico's "deepest canyons and strange forests." The former Texas Ranger recalled, "The expansive desert basin, checker-boarded by intermingling colors as if daubed by the playful hands of careless children, extended for miles to the north and south." Years later, said Townsend, "it reached in so deeply that it made [me] see God as [I] had never seen Him before." The journey into the heart of the Coahuila frontier "so overpoweringly impressed" Townsend that he "made a note of its awesomeness in his scout book." He managed the E. L. Gage Ranch from 1900 to 1918, when he became sheriff and later state representative. What is remarkable about Townsend is that he interacted in two worlds that did not fit the mold of "ranger." From his lifelong experience with the people and the landscape of the Big Bend, Townsend came to advocate for establishment of a state park.[19]

Historians of Big Bend National Park, as did park service officials in the 1930s, often credit the park's origins to Townsend, who on March 3, 1933, coauthored House Bill No. 771 to create "Texas Canyons State Park." The impetus for that legislation also included Robert Wagstaff's inquiry two years earlier to J. H. Walker, who "became very much interested in the matter and made a careful check of the area." Wagstaff, another young state representative, recalled that Walker (then the Texas state land commissioner) "decided that it would be better to delay action a couple of years on account of the fact that some of the most desirable lands for a park, adjoining the main [Rio Grande] canyons, had been forfeited for non-payment of interest, but were still subject to reinstatement." The Texas lawmakers did, however, agree that year to adopt Senate Concurrent Resolution 9. It called on the federal government to conduct an immediate survey of lands in the Lone Star State for inclusion in the national park system.[20]

J. Frank Dobie, the noted author of Texas frontier novels, echoed these sentiments with his call in 1930 for a park in the "wild Big Bend." The Herbert Hoover administration had whetted the appetite of local interests further by declaring in the waning days of his presidency a series of "national monuments" in nine western states. One of these was the 250,000-acre gypsum field of New Mexico's

Tularosa basin that became White Sands National Monument. Momentum for creation of parks like Big Bend had accelerated, believed Wagstaff, strengthening his resolve to pursue the dream of a park for West Texas.[21]

During the transition between NPS directors Stephen Mather and Horace Albright, a shift in historical thinking took place that oriented Americans toward the patriotic lessons of the Civil War, the American Revolution, and veneration of important national figures. Before a place like Texas (itself a former Confederate state) could obtain national funds for public parks, it needed to establish state park units. When state senator Morris Sheppard requested that the Department of the Interior consider "as soon as possible a survey of lands that qualified for national Park status," Albright's retort was terse. The NPS director noted acerbically that six other projects in the Lone Star State were being considered, and that Big Bend would have to take its place in line.[22]

Under Albright's tenure (1927–1933), the NPS also had consolidated other natural and cultural resource missions of agencies such as the War Department, the US Forest Service, and the Department of Agriculture. Another challenge for Big Bend was the growing sense of nationalism about national park history and the place of parks in American culture. "One might suspect, in other words," writes Albright's biographer, "that the nativism and nationalism of the 1920s contributed to the rise of the National Park Service and helped account for Albright's success in starting a program of historic preservation." In an age when groups like the second Ku Klux Klan surged nationally, Albright saw no harm in accepting help from advocates of Anglo-Saxon superiority.[23]

Mexican immigrants, sometimes viewed as indispensable to agribusiness, were often dubbed radical subversives and potential threats to American social institutions. While conducting field research in the late 1920s and mid-1930s, the Berkeley economist Paul S. Taylor chronicled the complex economic and social arrangements prevalent throughout much of the Southwest. Among the myriad of social situations, Taylor wrote, "a variety of social distinctions which penetrate even the realm of business make publicly manifest the desire of Americans to avoid social contacts with Mexicans." A new American leader would soon address the economic plight of the nation and localities like Texas, helping to defuse racial animus toward Mexican immigrants by offering a new approach to US-Mexico relations.[24]

The arrival in Washington, DC, in March 1933 of the presidential administration of Franklin D. Roosevelt signaled a new era to the champions of Big Bend National Park. FDR wrote, "I have heard so much of the wilderness and the beauty of this still inaccessible corner of the United States and also, of its important archeological remains that I very much hope that some day I shall be able to travel through it myself." In a letter to a Texas congressman, the president stated,

"I feel sure that [Big Bend] will do much to strengthen the friendship and good neighborliness of the people of Mexico and the people of the United States."[25]

This latter point would be crucial to the success of any effort to bring Big Bend National Park into the NPS system. Until the 1930s, the park service only had endorsed areas of great scenic beauty; "crown jewels," in the words of many park admirers. Not long after FDR settled into his new position as president, Robert Wagstaff and Everett Townsend called for protection of the Rio Grande canyons of Santa Elena, Mariscal, and Boquillas. Wagstaff's colleagues approved the measure in short order, but problems that would plague the formation of the park for the next decade required another version for a special legislative session that September.

One such challenge was Section 2 of the new park bill, which held that "the legislature of the State of Texas hereby withdraws from sale all unsold Public Free School lands situated in Brewster County, Texas, South of North Latitude 29 degrees, 25 minutes; and said lands, estimated to consist of about 150,000 acres." These school lands would be valued at one cent per acre for payment to the Public School Fund (or the sum of $1,500). Wagstaff and Townsend agreed in the amended bill that "all minerals in and under the above described sections of land are hereby reserved to the Public School Fund, to be developed under present or future laws as minerals under other unsold school land." The name of the park also would be changed from Texas Canyons State Park to the Big Bend State Park.[26]

Section 5 of the new bill indicated the hopes of its sponsors for federal inclusion of Big Bend in the NPS network of parks: "The State of Texas owns additional lands located near the Canyons of the Rio Grande and in the Chisos Mountains of Texas, which are suitable for park purposes, and . . . Federal aid will probably be secured to improve said lands if they are taken over for park purposes." Townsend and Wagstaff cautioned their legislative peers, however, that "steps should be taken immediately to set aside said lands before they are acquired by private parties," a condition that "creates an emergency and an imperative public necessity."[27]

Between the signing on May 27, 1933, of the original park bill by Texas governor Miriam "Ma" Ferguson and her endorsement five months later of the vastly expanded Big Bend State Park, the Alpine Chamber of Commerce assumed the lead in gaining regional support for the proposed park site. Local sponsors, preeminent among them James Casner, a recent arrival in town who had bought the local Chevrolet auto dealership, knew that Congress that spring had passed legislation to create the Civilian Conservation Corps (CCC). This program, part of the "First Hundred Days" of legislation signed by FDR between March and June 1933, had as one of its goals, says NPS historian Richard Sellars, "protection of the nation's forests from fires, insects, and disease damage—goals that matched perfectly those of most national park managers."[28]

The CCC included a state parks assistance program that the Alpine Chamber of Commerce brought to the attention of park service officials in Denver, Colorado. If Brewster County could receive one of the CCC's six hundred units, two hundred young men would soon arrive, earning thirty dollars per month. Their presence also would stimulate the West Texas economy through purchases of construction materials, food, clothing, and shelter.[29]

CCC camps were not easy to acquire in the program's early days, and the Big Bend sponsors had to wait until May 1934 to welcome the first workers to their area. Conrad Wirth, assistant director of the NPS, wrote in July 1933 to Herbert T. Maier, director of the NPS's Denver office of state park conservation, to express his concerns about the efforts of promoters of parks in the Big Bend and Davis Mountains. Maier had offered to travel to West Texas to examine the sites, but Wirth preferred to wait until Roger Toll, the NPS's premier authority on potential park locations, could leave his post as superintendent of Yellowstone National Park and visit Big Bend. Wirth cautioned Maier that "the meager reports we have on these areas . . . would not indicate that they measure up to National Park caliber." The assistant NPS director did offer hope that "these reports do indicate that [Big Bend and the Davis Mountains] are excellent State Park material so perhaps they should be retained and developed as State parks." Since Wirth's office could not guarantee support for the Texas units, he also did not see how they could be included in the Emergency Conservation Work (ECW) program, an alternative to the CCC.[30]

Aware that politics affected park creation as much as their economics and aesthetics, the Alpine Chamber of Commerce undertook its own campaign for Big Bend. Chamber director Forest Robinson called on local business leaders to speak on behalf of the merits of the CCC, and to promise financial support if necessary. Casner and his colleagues convinced Maier that they needed not one but two CCC camps in the Chisos Mountains (a total of four hundred employees). F. A. Dale, Texas district inspector for the CCC program, wrote in September 1933 to Major John D. Guthrie, commander of the Eight Corps Area of the US Army (which oversaw the operations of the camps), suggesting that both camps be located at Government Springs, as the "camp site and water" had been "placed under lease by the Chisos Mountains park committee and the Brewster County Chamber of Commerce." The sites had access to the railroad town of Marathon, which consisted of employees transferred from other CCC districts. Dale then offered the logic that would prevail for the remainder of the planning process for Big Bend: "The National Park Service is particularly interested in this park on account of its outstanding qualities as a wilderness and recreational area."[31]

The reality of CCC funding, and the need for the NPS to understand the merits of Big Bend, affected the negotiation process attempted by the Alpine chamber and other champions of a national park for Texas. Maier, now the ECW district officer for Texas, warned Wirth in early October 1933, "I have told the Chisos [Mountain] people that the camps as first recommended for their area could not be awarded because two camps had to be withdrawn from the Texas list for Arizona." Budget constraints (the bane of many New Deal programs throughout the 1930s) required Maier to judge the Big Bend proposal carefully, and his decision revolved around the obstacles of distance and isolation. "The Chisos [Mountain] Camps," said Maier, "were decided upon for this switch because of their high altitude and very long dirt road."[32]

As Maier struggled to balance the Big Bend request with the onslaught of applications for CCC work, his district inspector continued to echo the sentiments of local promoters from Alpine. On October 6, 1933, Dale again reminded Maier that, "considering scenery, climate, flora fauna, and Indian relics, there is nothing approaching [Big Bend] closer than Colorado." ECW personnel who had visited the area judged it far superior to Palo Duro Canyon, the area south of Amarillo being promoted for NPS inclusion for its connection to the sixteenth-century Coronado expedition. "The Big Bend district," said Dale, "may not have much influence, but it certainly has the best park possibility now offered in Texas." He encouraged Maier to move quickly, as "the next six months have practically no rainfall—hence no objection from the Army on account of unbridged creeks, etc."[33]

Dale also noted that the army had rejected calls for a CCC camp along the Rio Grande at Santa Heleña in June because of "excessive heat." Should Maier adopt the Chisos basin site, Dale believed that "the area would be used extensively by vacationists from all over Texas and possibly adjoining states." He rationalized that the Chisos "and the Davis and Guadalupe Mountains are the only cool spots in Texas in the summer." The state of Texas could be counted on to improve the road from Marathon to the park, said Dale, "which would put the area within one and one-half days drive of Houston, San Antonio, Dallas, and Austin." Dale then closed his plea to Maier with the suggestion that "here is an opportunity to raise the standards of the E.C.W. parks in Texas." The state's natural attractions suffered in comparison to the more striking physical beauty of the Rocky Mountains and the desert Southwest.[34]

Maier would define this contrast more clearly when he wrote on October 12, 1933, to Townsend, apologizing for rejection of the Chisos camps after his favorable recommendation. Texas had to reduce the number of CCC sites from 178 to 14, and the army's judgment about the Saint Heleña camp influenced its thinking about the entire Big Bend area. The park service remained committed to promotion of the site, given the imperatives of the New Deal to improve the economic life of the nation, and the political realities of including Texas in the net of services and programs emanating from Congress. George L. Nason, director of the NPS's state parks division in Oklahoma City, asked Professor B. C. Tharp of the Department of Biology and Bacteriology at the University of Texas for his opinion of Big Bend. Tharp in turn supplied Nason with a research paper written by C. H. Mueller, one of his graduate students who in the summers of 1931 and 1932 had conducted fieldwork in the Chisos Mountains.[35]

While Tharp encouraged Nason to engage in much more thorough analysis of the area, he agreed with Mueller that "this region is of outstanding scientific value by virtue of the fact that it is the meeting place within the United States of representatives from Mexico and from the Rocky Mountain systems lying to the north." In addition, the Big Bend area housed "a rather surprising number of eastern species and of species from the arid west." Big Bend's scientific value from the standpoint of vegetation, Tharp claimed, was "further enhanced by virtue of the fact that the Chisos Mountains are not a range but rather a 'heap' whose diameter is essentially equal in whatever direction it is measured." The height of the mountains "above the surrounding plain is relatively greater than that of other mountains in the state," said Tharp, even though "the altitude above sea level is somewhat less than the maximum."[36]

None of these testimonials to the beauty and power of the Big Bend landscape mattered as much as the report filed by Roger Toll. The Yellowstone superintendent ventured through the future park site from January 8 to 11, 1934, accompanied by J. Evetts Haley of the History Department at the University of Texas; Townsend; John W. Gillette, president of the Alpine Chamber of Commerce; local rancher Homer Wilson (who also served as the outfitter for the surveying party); and other NPS officials. In a letter to Arno Cammerer, director of the Interior Department's Office of National Parks, Buildings and Reservations, Toll spoke to the concerns of the army and the park service regarding Big Bend's inclusion in the NPS system. "The Chisos Mountains . . . have attractive vegetation with some trees and plants not found elsewhere in the United States," Toll reported, and "the view from the South Rim is highly spectacular." The Rio Grande canyons of Santa Elena, Mariscal, and Boquillas had "spectacular gorges, from 1,000 to 1,500 feet deep," which the Yellowstone superintendent considered (along with the Chisos Mountains) to be "the chief scenic features of the area."[37]

Toll judged the Big Bend to be "a wilderness area," marked by its aridity and its "very sparse population." Most of the economic activity revolved around the raising of cattle, sheep, and goats, as well as "mercury ores and some other mineral deposits." Toll thus agreed with F. A. Dale that "the Big Bend Country seems to be decidedly the outstanding scenic area of Texas." Should the NPS construct a road to the three canyons and the Chisos, "the area would offer a scenic trip that would be of national interest." He further warned Cammerer, "The area will not have many visitors until the facilities of access and accommodation are provided."[38]

No sooner had Toll left the Big Bend area (and before he could file his report to his superiors in Denver and Washington), than did local supporters of the park resume their lobbying efforts with state park and NPS officials. D. E. Colp, chairman of the Texas State Parks Board, wrote to Maier in early February 1934 to ask that he "discuss this with Mr. Roger W. Toll as he inspected his property and I am sure the NPS would place a good deal of confidence in whatever he had to say about it." Colp informed Maier, "It is our plan to acquire something like one million acres in this area by getting small amounts at each session of the Legislature."[39]

Based on the appeals of the Alpine chamber, and the impending report of Toll, Maier moved quickly to submit the Big Bend State Park application to his superiors in Washington. Maier told Wirth in February 1934 that "the name, Big Bend, is being used because it is the ambition of the [Texas] Park Board to finally acquire the whole Big Bend area of a million acres for a National Park." The NPS wanted three CCC units, "all to become located at one point in the Green Gulch in the Chisos Mountains."[40] The park service's initial reviews of potential work included twenty miles of truck trails, seventy-two miles of fencing, an undetermined number of horse and foot trails, and overnight cabins, a concession building, and a telephone line.

Maier, operating on Toll's endorsement of the merits of Big Bend, asked whether the NPS realized "that the work would be outlined down there in such a way as to tie in with the final master plan for a national park," a task that Maier conceded "is not an easy thing to do." Toll further worried about "what effect our activity will have on the values placed on land still to be purchased by the state." In a telephone conversation between Colp, Toll, and Maier, Colp reported that "the people down in that part of the country have promised various parcels of land with the idea that either a state or national park will become an actuality." Maier worried that "since they [local landowners] have been turned down on [CCC] camps both in the first and second periods [of 1933–1934], they will lose all confidence in the project if it is turned down."[41]

To expedite the Big Bend project, Maier and Toll offered suggestions for the location of roads, trails, and buildings that revealed the distinctiveness (and the cost) of CCC work. Toll argued that "three roads will eventually run up the walls of the Rio Grande Canyon onto the Chisos Mountains." Toll and Maier called for CCC work at Santa Eleña, as "the state now owns two or three sections of land suitable for a camp." The NPS, however, would need at least two camps there, as a "road leading up the walls of the Rio Grande Canyon would have to be practically their sole project."[42]

Another site of interest to Maier called for a camp there with the primary tasks of "building foot and horse trails, the developing of water, some overnight cabins, and above everything else a survey of the road from here on." The NPS required special permission to "devote 90% of the [CCC] activity to the building of this road," as the CCC preferred spending the bulk of its funds on preservation projects. Maier considered Toll's opinion highly influential with the CCC, and "we might justify this as 100% conservation in that everything done in the area, whether road or otherwise, is being carried toward the permanent conservation of the area."[43]

This pattern of political maneuvering also concerned the NPS in matters of land ownership, as Toll did not believe that Texas had unrestricted access to the 105,000 acres projected for Big Bend State Park. In addition, Colp had succeeded in acquiring passage in the Texas state legislature of a measure allocating $50,000 for the Big Bend CCC program, and the state senate and the governor seemed equally inclined to support Colp. "You have certainly got to hand it to him," Maier told Wirth, and concluded about the camps, "Although we may not go into this thing, taking it all in I think it deserves to be classed as an 'A' project."[44]

Once Colp had convinced Maier to advance the Texas proposals, the latter official turned to Toll on February 19, 1934, for more specific details. Toll compared the process for the creation of Big Bend National Park to that recently used with Tennessee's Great Smokies, Virginia's Shenandoah, Kentucky's Mammoth Cave, and Minnesota's Isle Royale National Parks. "The danger of doing any development before the park has been established and the land secured," said Toll, "is that the valuation of the land will be increased by having the State and the Federal Government committed to the project, and by the expenditure for roads and other development on nearby land."[45]

The Yellowstone superintendent realized "the urge to start development with relief funds that are now available, but which may not be available in later years." He asked Maier to secure from Colp maps of the proposed park site, including notation of the state lands. Toll closed his recommendations by encouraging a first camp at Santa Eleña, because of its access to water from the Rio Grande, as opposed to the Chisos basin, where "the water supply is doubtful and the [CCC] men could not begin immediately on road work."[46]

While Brewster County park advocates reveled in their good fortune, in the spring and summer of 1934 the NPS accelerated the process of park surveys. By the end of that year, the park service had a much clearer idea of the opportunities and challenges awaiting Big Bend National Park. Yet the NPS also faced similar demands for reviews and planning throughout the country as its share of responsibility grew for economic recovery and resource preservation. The experimental nature of the CCC and related work programs, the lack of any experience with long-range planning for government employment programs, and the costs of operations in the isolated conditions of Big Bend rendered the exercise problematic for the NPS. Maier saw more potential for CCC work at Big Bend than at existing campsites at Stephenville and Lampasas. He made plans to move them once the army approved the Chisos Mountains proposal.

W. G. Carnes, chief engineer of the NPS's Western Division, noted that Big Bend's isolation and distance from a transportation hub "is not dissimilar to that of Grand Canyon, Zion, or Bryce [Canyon]" National Parks on the Colorado Plateau. He decided to send the assistant landscape architect at the Grand Canyon, Harry Langley, to join with a Phoenix-based engineer from the US Bureau of Public Roads to inspect the Big Bend. "It is so seldom," Carnes told L. I. Hewes, deputy chief engineer of the Bureau of Public Roads in San Francisco, that "we have a chance to influence the development of areas before they become National Parks." The reconnaissance would help the NPS avoid mistakes of the past, where poorly coordinated transportation planning hindered park service operations.[47]

For the boosters of Big Bend, the key figures in the area that spring were George Nason of the ECW program and Robert D. Morgan, superintendent of CCC camp SP-33-T. They came to the Chisos on May 21, 1934, with the first installment of the two-hundred-member work crew (80 percent of whom were Hispanic). The CCC bought the original camp acreage from ranchers Ira Hector and Waddy Burnham, using money provided by the Alpine Chamber of Commerce. That organization then had to recapture its investment through a bond election. The Texas State Parks Board "owned" the property occupied by the first and second CCC camps (the latter designated as SP-34-T). The board had informed the army that "the United States is authorized to use this property for camp sites for one year or as much longer as camps are retained on the Big Bend State Park, said occupancy to be without cost to the Federal Government." Colp then told the commanding general of the CCC, stationed at Fort Bliss, Texas, that "any and all buildings, structures or installations erected on these camp sites by the Government shall be and remain the property of the Government in any manner it may deem to be [in] its best interest."[48]

CHAPTER 3

Science Comes to a Wild Land

As the National Park Service examined Big Bend as a potential park unit, it also brought to Far West Texas its new mission of scientific research to preserve nature for the enjoyment of visitors. The park service had established a "Wildlife Division" in 1933, writes Richard Sellars in *Preserving Nature in the National Parks*, as an outcome of a private survey of natural conditions in NPS sites. The division was funded by George Meléndez Wright, an assistant park naturalist at Yellowstone National Park, who with this group of young scientists, says Sellars, "promoted an ecological awareness in the Service and questioned the utilitarian and recreational focus that dominated the bureau." The Wildlife Division, housed originally on the campus of the University of California at Berkeley (Wright's alma mater), brought to their studies of places like Big Bend a belief, according to Sellars, that "the greatest value of the reserves lay in providing scientists with the opportunity to learn what certain portions of the parks were like in their original, unmodified condition." Wright hoped to accomplish with his cadre of scientists an immediate isolation of park lands from further intrusions by humans, followed by careful "biological modifications" to restore their primeval conditions.[1]

Protection of the NPS's interests in the Big Bend, and acquisition of knowledge about its resources, led the park service to send technicians into the field and to promote their findings. In April 1936, NPS naturalist George F. Baggley received an invitation to speak about Big Bend at the annual meeting of the Society of Mammologists. Baggley asked Maynard Johnson to craft an argument that would appeal to his audience, and the NPS regional wildlife technician responded by linking the American and Mexican portions of the Big

Bend. This would give scientists, said Johnson, "an approximately complete biological unit," making Big Bend "the only national park that does so." Johnson also praised the future park's inclusion of the Chisos Mountains, as they were "separated from any other mountains by wide stretches of desert flats." This meant that "the fauna will be better protected in certain respects than is possible in any other national park."[2]

Johnson remarked that another distinctive feature of Big Bend was "several Mexican species that enter the United States only at this point," most notably the "weeping Juniper (*Juniperus flaccida*)." The wildlife technician noted that the "most characteristic plant" of the plains surrounding the Chisos Mountains was the creosote bush, with mesquite, ocotillo, lechuguilla, and prickly pear the other representatives of lower Sonoran Desert cacti. The higher that one climbed into the Chisos, said Johnson, the more one encountered Upper Sonoran species like the Mexican buckeye, desert willow, Apache plume, oak, piñon, juniper, Arizona cypress, Douglas fir, and yellow pine.[3]

Johnson hoped to impress upon Baggley that "the study of the flora of this region is in its infancy." While scientists already had identified some 450 to 500 species, much remained to be accomplished. As an example, Johnson cited disparities in naming oak trees in the future national park. "There are probably nine or ten species and varieties of oaks in the Chisos Mountains," wrote Johnson, "some of which may be new to science and some of which are probably hybrids." Since Baggley's audience would focus primarily on mammals, Johnson mentioned that "tree squirrels, and porcupines, are among the mammal groups absent from the area—perhaps because an extensive area surrounding the Chisos Mountains is treeless semi-desert." In the proposed park area as a whole, the mammals most frequently seen were Texas jackrabbits. The "most abundant" of mammals "are various species of Peromyscus—especially in the mountains, and perognathus—especially on sandy lowlands."[4]

With the close of the summer research season, NPS officials in 1936 had a wealth of data from which to plan future development of Big Bend National Park. Erik Reed, assistant archaeologist for Region III, completed what would be the most thorough assessment of cultural resources in the park area for the next five decades. As had his peers in biology and geology, Reed outlined the distinctive features of human habitation of the Big Bend area. "The Big Bend proper," reported Reed, "is less rich in specimens than other sections" of the United States, "especially the lower Pecos [River]." Yet the NPS archaeologist found that "many good collections have been made there; of sandals, matting, wooden implements, basketry, etc."[5]

Reed told his superiors that "the historic occupants of the Trans-Pecos (Jumanos, Lipanes, etc.) are not very thoroughly known, and the affinities of the prehistoric cave-dwellers are a matter of controversy." This was "in contrast to the northern Arizona-southern Utah area," where "the culture of the Basketmakers of the northern part of the arid southwest is fairly well known." Archaeological evidence there had identified "the irruption of a new people into the Pueblo civilization, and connection somehow with the historic Shoshoneans of the Great Basin." Unfortunately, reported Reed, "none of these statements apply to the west Texas cave-dwellers."[6]

Despite the lack of scholarly interest in the cultures of the Rio Grande basin, Reed found of value their survival skills in the desert. "The group under discussion," wrote the NPS archaeologist, "lived in caves and probably also crude brush shelters, had very little agriculture (none on the Pecos; some maize grown in the Big Bend; apparently none in the Hueco-El Paso area)." While these ancient peoples made no pottery, a feature that enamored archaeologists of the Pueblo cultures of northern New Mexico and Arizona, Reed learned that "they wove quite good baskets—twined and coiled, especially split-stitch coiled—and twilled matting." Their sandals were "roughly woven of yucca leaves, in several techniques," while "little else is known of their clothing." For weapons, the Big Bend cultures "used the atl-atl or dart-thrower," and evidence abounded of the use of the bow and arrow (which Reed noted was "not known to the southwestern Basketmakers until the beginning of Pueblo immigration"). They also used the "carved rabbit stick" that archaeologists associated with the Basketmakers and the historic Shoshonean of the Great Basin.[7]

It was the comparison with the more prominent ancestors of New Mexico's Pueblo peoples, whom the NPS had begun to study in depth in the 1930s at sites like Chaco Canyon, Bandelier, and Mesa Verde, that drew much of Reed's analysis. He did report that "one cannot safely link them [the Big Bend peoples] at all strongly with . . . the Lipan Apache, the Patarabueyes or Jumanos, and the Basketmakers of the Southwest." The Big Bend cultures, the New Mexican Native communities, and ancient villages whose residents were known to park service archaeologists as "Ozark bluff-dwellers," "all have many points of similarity, but are nevertheless separate entities." Reed placed these groups "all on about the same level of cultural development, at a stage that many cultures pass through." He then stated that "there is no need to suppose that these three peoples spoke the same language, were more closely related than any other widely separated groups of aboriginal Americans or were even contemporary—although all this is perfectly possible." Reed believed that "the Patarabueyes who were settled at the mouth of the Conchos (where now is Presidio, Texas) in the sixteenth century are to be connected with the west Texas cave-dwellers."[8]

More likely for Reed was evidence from "two additional groups of archaeological finds in the west Texas area." These he labeled "the discovery of extremely ancient sites in Guadalupe Mountains in Texas and in New Mexico and farther north around Clovis and Roswell, New Mexico," as well as "the 14th century occurrence of Pueblo culture around El Paso." Reed claimed that "it is perfectly possible that the Big Bend cave-dwellers were descendants of the very early inhabitants of the Guadalupes." He also suggested that "the folk who lived in the El Paso pueblos and manufactured crude polychrome pottery were a branch of the cave people become sedentary and relatively civilized under Puebloan influence from the Mimbres-Chihuahua basin."[9]

It was easier for Reed to distance the Big Bend cultures from the Lipan Apache, "who are the most important people of west Texas in historic times." He argued that, "despite great superficial similarity," one would have to accept "very unlikely hypotheses." One such theory held "that the whole cave-culture dates from after the 13th century (or else that the Apache came into the southwest much earlier than is at present believed)." Reed added to this scenario the idea that "agriculture was abandoned, that certain arrowpoint types disappeared and quite different ones replaced them (instead of one type gradually evolving into another)." The NPS archaeologist, however, did find "definite connections southward of the west Texas cave-dwellers—with a very similar but little-known cave culture in the mountains of Coahuila." Yet Reed declared it "impossible to specifically link them with any historic or prehistoric group in the United States." At best, the scientific evidence revealed that the Big Bend culture "is very like that of the Basketmakers and that the two groups may well be cognate representatives of the same fundamental stock."[10]

Given this dilemma of identity, Reed could speak with more certainty about "their place in time." He reported that "the west Texas cave-dwellers may have been in existence as such two thousand years ago and they may have still been there when Cabeza de Vaca traveled through Texas [in 1541]." The archaeologist noted that "an antiquity comparable to that of the Basketmakers (i.e., going back a few centuries before the time of Christ) has been postulated and is supported by the finding of cave-dweller materials in association with an extinct species of antelope (Tetrameryx)." A "competent and trustworthy archaeologist" had found shards of fourteenth-century Pueblo pottery ("El Paso polychrome notably").[11]

This led Reed to theorize "that the west Texas cave-dwellers inhabited the region from fairly early times on down to about the fourteenth century." At this point, they were overrun by the Lipan Apache and either vanished into the mountains of Coahuila or became the Patarabueyes at the confluence of the Conchos and the Rio Grande. Reed concluded about the identity of the cave-dwellers, "They present an interesting problem, in whose solution the discipline or technique to be most utilized is that of the shovel and trowel."[12]

As did other NPS scientists who came to Big Bend in the summer of 1936, Reed and his archaeological crew examined cultural resources on the Mexican side of the Rio Grande. Reed's journey south into Coahuila and Chihuahua revealed that "very little archaeological work has been done in northern Mexico in general, and almost none in this region." He learned that "the more westerly part of Chihuahua has been studied extensively, with very little reference to the mountains of eastern Chihuahua." In the area of Coahuila to become part of a future international park, Reed noted that a survey team from Harvard College had spent time there in 1885. "This has never been completely published," reported the archaeologist, "but the cultural material recovered is still at the Peabody Museum in Cambridge, Mass."[13]

Reed then spoke of his conversations with local rancher Elmo Johnson about cultural resource sites in Mexico. "A good part of [the Johnsons'] collection comes from south of the river," wrote Reed, with one particular site "a largish cave in which were a great number of burials, the skeletal material being in quite good condition apparently." Reed lamented that "this site is totally lost to science, due to Johnson's digging therein," but he hoped that "there may be others like it" in the area. Reed himself only had time to visit one site in Mexico that summer: Cañon de los Altares in Chihuahua, which he reached from Santa Elena. There he reported "an unusually extensive set of petroglyphs." Reed also recognized "camp-sites along the Mexican side of the Rio Grande as on the Texas side," while "back into the hills there are shelter sites and camps." In addition, said Reed, "there are interesting early Spanish sites at a few places on the river, notably presidio San Vicente."[14]

The most dramatic environmental survey conducted in the Big Bend region in the summer of 1936 was that of Ernest G. Marsh Jr., a graduate student in botany at the University of Texas. On October 11, Marsh filed with Region III officials "A Preliminary Report on a Biological Survey of the Santa Rosa and Del Carmen Mountains of Northern Coahuila, Mexico." His findings, while not complete, were such that the regional NPS office sent press releases to all newspapers in the Southwest heralding his achievement. Marsh had accepted an appointment "to spend three months in the Muzquiz-Boquillas region of northern Coahuila."[15]

The trip began eighteen days late, with the University of Texas researcher "awaiting permission from the Mexican government to enter the country as a government employee." Then "a delayed rainy season broke heavily two days before [his] arrival in Muzquiz." Marsh faced "continual rains, the loss of seventeen bird specimens, and a shortage of time" that prompted "abandoning the avifaunal and reptile collections for the Muzquiz area." He then made "successive trips of one week's duration to the Sabinas River, the Zacate-Encantada, and the Mariposa-Gacha," turning his attention to the more northern regions of Coahuila.[16]

Marsh's descriptions of his journey, and of the places that he surveyed, read more like an adventure novel than a scientific report. It took him nearly one week to drive from Muzquiz to the Big Bend area, where he encountered the two-thousand-foot Carmen escarpment (which could be crossed only on a wagon road). Once in Piedra Blanca, some 175 miles north of Muzquiz, Marsh had to abandon his vehicle and transfer his equipment to "a more favorable mode, the burros." On July 30, he made camp at Cañon de las Vivoras, south of the Haciendo del Jardin, or 35 miles west of Piedra Blanca.[17]

From this base Marsh observed that "the northern Del Carmens are represented by two chains of mountains running parallel in a general northeastern direction." He then wrote that "the more western chain ends abruptly in probably the highest peak of northern Coahuila, La Sierra del Jardin." Marsh noted that "the complexity of the rough country and the slow method of travel force me to concentrate my efforts to a portion of the area rather than the whole." Claiming that "for no reason other than that it was a bit farther removed from inhabitants," Marsh "chose the western side of the western chain, a fifteen mile stretch of deep canyons and towering peaks."[18]

For the next six weeks he studied the Sierra del Carmen, coming to appreciate "the immensity of problems arising within such a small area of unexplored mountains." His hikes took him to the "great bare slope that leads up to approximately 6,000 feet to terminate in an abrupt Escarpmento de las Fronterizas." After making two excursions into the mountains, Marsh found himself riding out onto "the wide stretch of flats along the Chihuahua line." From there he "retraced the road to Muzquiz to spend seven days working in the Muzquiz Swamp and the canyons of La Mariposa." When it came time to leave, said Marsh, "it was almost with regrets that on September 23 I saw the last horizon of old Mexico pass behind me, and I was back again to the point of beginning."[19]

Marsh's survey marked the most detailed explanation to date of the Mexican side of the Rio Grande available to the park service. His collections included four species of amphibians from the Sierra del Carmen, one of which (the leopard frog) Marsh described as "the largest specimen I have ever seen." He also gathered samples of thirty-nine species of birds, out of some eighty-three species that he recorded in the Coahuila range. He recorded (but did not collect) thirty-one species of mammals on his tour. The University of Texas graduate technician also collected some 850 specimens of plants, 400 of which came from the Sierra del Carmen. In addition, Marsh carried out "some thirty five or forty species of cacti, which, as yet, have not been determined." Of reptiles, Marsh could report preserving nineteen species. Completing Marsh's work were one hundred photographs of animal and plant life, as well as scenic shots of the Sierra del Carmen, the Santa Rosa Mountains, and the town of Muzquiz.[20]

It was Marsh's description of the communities and landforms that he encountered, however, that gave the NPS for the first time a detailed picture of life in what one day would become Mexico's protected areas along and near Big Bend National Park. Muzquiz was "a picturesque Mexican village of 6,000 population," wrote Marsh, "lying off the south escarpment of the Santa Rosa Mountains." He had learned that "for many years this town was the most important mining center of northern Coahuila," a distinction that had faded with time. "Coal, copper and silver are still mined," reported Marsh, and "ranching has grown much in importance over the last twenty years." Thus "the little town of Muzquiz now devotes the major part of its business toward the several large ranches extending to the east and north."[21]

Two of these ranches (El Zacate and La Encantada) were owned by Americans, reached "by journeying east from Muzquiz, and north through the Santa Anna Canyon." Beyond the Encantada ranch, "there is no road for vehicles," said Marsh, "and to reach the great FRESNOS MESA country one must travel by horse." In Santa Anna Canyon, Marsh found "a forty-mile expanse of walled valleys, offering the one gateway to the west." From there "a seldom used trail strikes west from the Zacate to cross the arid west plains of Coahuila and into the State of Chihuahua."[22]

To the east of Muzquiz, and "swinging north around the southern tip of the Carmen escarpment," said Marsh, were "three other ranches, LA MARIPOSA, LA GACHA, and LA ROSITA." Marsh found there "deep canyons and grass-filled valleys radiating down from the mountains [that] furnish them with abundant pasture lands." To the north of La Rosita he encountered "the famous LA BAVIA ranch, once owned by Spanish royalty, but now by an American capitalist." Marsh described the ranch as "a great valley floor 40 miles from east to west, and 100 miles long, watered by mountain springs." This he called "the most perfect ranching country in all of northern Coahuila."[23]

Beyond La Bavia to the north, Marsh found Santo Domingo, "a German owned ranch," and Conejo, "a government inspection post inhabited by two customs officials." The small village of Piedra Blanca was "ranching territory owned by an American living in Del Rio, Texas," wrote Marsh. He marveled at the grandeur of El Jardin, "a local term applied to the highest and most northern peak of the Del Carmen mountains."[24]

This term also applied "to the extensive land holdings of a Mexican diplomat," and constituted "the Jardin Ranch which includes almost the whole of the northern Carmens, west to the Chihuahua line and north to Boquillas." Within the ranch, Marsh found the "American Club," which the botanist described as "probably the most beautiful part of the lovely Carmen Mountains, owned by a party of American sportsmen who visit there during the hunting seasons." The eastern terminus of Marsh's journey was Boquillas, which he described in his 1936 report as "a small Mexican border town of 200 inhabitants, located near the southern tip of the Big Bend area, originally settled as a gate for the transportation of mineral ore from the Carmens into Texas." With the decline of the mining industry, said Marsh, Boquillas was "now dependent upon the small cattle and goat farms along the Rio Grande River and the Fronteriza Escarpment."[25]

In the spring of 1937, the park service received the final report of Marsh on his survey the preceding summer of the Sierra del Carmen and the Santa Rosa Mountains of Coahuila. In this more detailed account, Marsh told his superiors of his difficulties in gaining access to Mexico, as he had been told by the office of the Mexican consul in San Antonio "that other than my having to have the necessary collecting permits from the Mexican department of Caza, Pesca y Forestal for which negotiations were already underway," he should have no problems. Then the University of Texas botanist discovered that "the Mexican immigration officials in Piedras Negras insisted on making a very technical interpretation of my entrance, to cause me a prolonged delay." For eighteen days, Marsh "worked with the Mexican officials to have one question after another arise as we progressed." The student technician's every answer would be transmitted to Mexico City for an official ruling "before my permits were in order and my equipment bonded under the rules and regulations of Mexican law pertaining to the 'Transuente' passport issued to me."[26]

Heavy rains some fifty miles south of Piedras Negras slowed Marsh's travel substantially, requiring seventeen hours to reach the interior town of Muzquiz. From there he joined with local guides Victoriano and Fidel Villarreal to head north into the Sierra del Carmen. At the small village of Piedra Blanca, the party left their automobile, loading their equipment onto pack mules for the remainder of the journey. "During the next month," Marsh would recall, "I experienced alternating sieges of good luck and misfortune." At times "I was truly fascinated with the wilderness of virgin nature that lay on every side," only "later to find myself damning my incompetence and fate." Marsh managed to spend "long hours in the field," covering "quite thoroughly the canyons along the western sides of the northern Del Carmens."[27]

After a month in the field, "certain losses from the plant and bird collections made me think it better to return to Muzquiz and thence to Eagle Pass rather than to follow the original plans of passing at Boquillas." It took ten days to retrace his steps "over La Gacha, La Mariposa and the Canyons along the Santa Rosa Escarpment." From there Marsh had an uneventful drive to Piedras Negras, returning home to Austin in late September.[28]

Marsh's final report to the NPS included the most thorough set of color slides of northern Coahuila yet available to park service planners. The student technician took extensive notes of the flora and fauna in each picture, often remarking on their beauty and uniqueness. He also caught on film community life in Muzquiz and other villages that few Americans had ever seen. Marsh saved his most effusive comments for the fauna of the Sierra del Carmen, noting the abundance of the band-tailed pigeon, "appearing in great numbers with as many as one hundred birds flying together as they feed on the acorns and wild cherries growing in the arroy[o]s of the upper foot-hills."[29]

The Texas graduate student told his superiors that "this beautiful bird has evidently found its perfect habitat here in the northern Carmens." With an "abundant food supply" and "the absence of its most destructive enemy, man," the band-tailed pigeon flourished in the north, a condition that changed the farther south Marsh observed the bird. He also saw at least four species of doves and five species of hawks, and had several sightings of the golden eagle. "The question often has been raised," wrote Marsh, "as to whether the Golden Eagle actually does kill young stock animals." The technician examined a report of seven young calves killed by eagles on La Mariposa Ranch. Marsh could not link the mutilations to the golden eagle, but he did report that "in the Del Carmen Mountains, I saw an eagle kill a large jackrabbit and fly several miles with it dangling from its claws." He surmised that "the occasions are few when [the eagle] finds it necessary to attack animals so large as calves, but when there comes the time, his great strength and courage can serve him well."[30]

Mammals of all types abounded in the Sierra del Carmen as Marsh and his guides hiked the canyons and mesas. One of the most commonly sighted creatures was the opossum, which local residents referred to as the "chicken hunter." The student technician also marveled at the number and variety of bats in the Sierra del Carmen. "The little Canyon Bat," he reported, "is very abundant throughout the Western Hills," and Marsh considered it "a rare sight to see with the aid of a long-range light after nightfall the thousands that feed over the Western Hills tank." Black bears proliferated in northern Coahuila, but they also faced the hazard of hunters. Until 1932, wrote Marsh, American hunters killed several bears annually on the Jardin Ranch. That year "the owner of the north Carmen country, an official in the Mexican Diplomatic Corps, began to refuse permission to hunting parties." As a result, "only three bears are reported as having been taken since by residents who have stock on parts of the range."[31]

Marsh contended that "the heaviest drain on the bear in the northern Del Carmens over a fifteen-year period" came from "hunting activities of members of the American Club, located across the mountains from the Jardin Ranch." In recent years, however, "impassable roads" had rendered the club "inactive." Marsh could report in 1937 that, "in general, the present status of the bear in the Del Carmen and Santa Rosa Mountains is excellent." Mexico had placed "no rigid rules of enforced preservation" on hunting bears, but Marsh believed that the animal faced "little danger of depletion." Instead, "under such ideals of habitat as are furnished by the inaccessible rocky canyon country and a bountiful food supply of acorns, madrona berries, wild cherries, and persimmons as well as small mammals," wrote Marsh, "there is every evidence of significant increases."[32]

The NPS technician could not say the same about smaller animals such as the raccoon. "I saw no sign of this intelligent little fur bearer north of the Rosita Ranch," reported Marsh, as "the last raccoon taken from the northern Del Carmens was caught by a trap in 1930." Farther south toward Muzquiz, Marsh learned of sightings of raccoons, but "the status of the raccoon could be improved." The technician believed that "in those regions where he is adapted to live," the raccoon "is persecuted continuously by an abundance of dogs and men." The striped animal "is forced to take refuge in the mountains and live in discord to his preference." Marsh believed that "after seeing the region that raccoons were once quite common around Muzquiz and in the lowland valleys as far north as Piedra Blanca." He told the NPS that "with some enforced protection," the raccoon could be restored to the Sierra del Carmen.[33]

More surprising to Marsh was the presence of small fur-bearing animals like the mink and spotted skunk. The NPS technician caught some thirty specimens of the long-tailed Texas skunk, which he "found abundant throughout the Del Carmens and Santa Rosa Mountains." Marsh also had trapped a Mexican badger, but could not locate the Arizona gray fox. Coyotes were quite common in the Sierra del Carmen, said Marsh, and "hardly a night goes by without the 'music' of this desert hunter." He most often spotted coyotes that were "small and buffy-white shading to black." Yet Marsh also recognized a larger coyote with longer and lighter hair. The student technician found

"astonishing the number of coyotes which can be brought together by drag-
ging the viscera of a butchered cow over several miles of cattle trails."[34]

Marsh recalled, "Among my pleasantest experiences have been the times
that I lay hidden on the leeward side of frequented trails and watched the coyote bands pass in the moonlight." He counted as many as twenty animals traveling together, and also remarked that "even though the coyote lives in such
abundance to the region, it is seldom condemned as a predator." Marsh learned
that "occasionally it is accused of killing goats or sheep," and in such cases "a
few animals are trapped each year," in one case by "two dogs trained as killers
that had the reputation of having betrayed many a coyote into his death."[35]

Marsh spoke at length also about the Mexican gray wolf, known as the
lobo. Santo Domingo, to the east of the mountains, wrote Marsh, "reports
200 cattle killed in 1934 and 1935 by ravaging bands of lobo." The NPS technician learned from local ranchers that "over the last fifteen years, the number of
domestic stock pastured in northern Coahuila has more than doubled." Yet
"reports of a wolf caught by trap are rare, principally because the wolf is a
wary creature and the average Mexican trapper has not learned to match his
wits." Another species of predator that Marsh noted was the Mexican cougar
(sometimes called a mountain lion). "The accounts of the lion are many," wrote
Marsh, "though he is seldom seen alive." He also observed that "a number of
hides are found used as rugs in every hacienda." Local hunters attributed to
the cougar the "killing of young horses and deer." A "Mr. Pauly of the Encantada [Ranch]" told Marsh that "a lion [had] killed three colts in his remuda on
four consecutive nights in 1935," with one of the horses "found dead forty
miles from the site of the killing the night previous." Marsh reported "no
wholesale persecution of the lion over the region," yet "once a killer lion makes
his appearance, he is pursued at once."[36]

Based on his extensive fieldwork, Marsh surmised in the spring of 1937 that
"wildlife research in the Sierra del Carmen be made continuous from this
study as a cooperative program between the Department of Parks in Mexico
and the National Park Service." His travels through the frontier of Coahuila
indicated that "such a program would be welcomed and beneficial to the Mexican department." In addition, joint studies "would stimulate a very desirous
spirit of cooperation between the corresponding departments in the two
nations." Finally, wrote Marsh, this collaboration "would facilitate in time,
money, and results the rehabilitation of the Big Bend Park area."[37]

He noted that NPS officials like William McDougall, Maynard Johnson,
and James O. Stevenson had called for "the making of certain ecological studies in order to determine the original status of plants and animals over the
land area." Marsh also thought it wise to "observe the relation of one species

with another toward the end of rehabilitation of the depleted wildlife." This latter initiative would "accomplish an understanding of the physical environment most conducive to a favorable propagation and distribution of native plant and animal species."[38]

Marsh had evidence of this because of the stark contrasts between the ecology of the Big Bend area and northern Mexico. "Subjected for many years to the adverse influence of man and livestock," wrote Marsh, the future NPS site "has been sorely used." Even "such environmental conditions as could be generated on experimental plots for ecological study could not be of the most desirable character." Marsh believed that "once a maladjustment is stimulated, even though the cause is in time removed, the original set-up cannot be established except over long periods of years." The NPS could not afford the luxury of such lengthy studies, as "the need of results is for the immediate future in order that a directional influence can be placed upon phases of the Big Bend wildlife to accomplish a timely restoration."[39]

Given this scenario, the NPS technician viewed the Sierra del Carmen as, "structurally and biologically, a region essentially identical to that of the Texas Big Bend and the Chisos Mountains." He conceded that "the Del Carmen Mountains and the surrounding plains for a number of years have been subjected to the influence of man." Yet he considered this "to such a lesser degree, that excepting certain localities, words [such] as overgrazing and depletion are not needed in descriptive phrases." He noted that "certain large areas in the mountains and on the plains have been free of livestock for twenty years and longer, while more extensive tracts have seen little detrimental effect from the few live stock that they have held." This condition had occurred with "little enforcing of game laws by officials in northern Coahuila."[40]

One reason was that "upon those large ranches that hold the bits of concentrated population, the ranch owner takes great pride in the game upon his property, and under such conditions of abundance as exist, comparatively little hunting is encouraged." Marsh found this "reflected into the unrestricted areas free from molestation," where "the wildlife responds positively." Journeying out from Muzquiz, "the most impressive feature is the apparent abundance of wildlife and the congeniality it holds for its progeny." Marsh then concluded that "for a true understanding of an original, unmolested environment, and for a less expensive, more satisfactory program," Mexican and American park planners should select portions of the Sierra del Carmen to be "studied extensively, the results of which will be applicable immediately to the corresponding areas in the Texas Big Bend."[41]

Marsh's words went unheeded by NPS officials, as more pressing needs prevailed on the American side of the Rio Grande. Rollin H. Baker, a graduate student at Texas A&M College, worked in the summer of 1937 as a technician conducting an entomological survey of the future park location. Over the course of more than one hundred days, Baker went first to the Chisos Mountains and then fanned out across the lower elevations of southern Brewster County. The technician noted the presence of "a beautiful, tiger-striped, long-winged butterfly" in Juniper Canyon as one of the more unusual species. Nights spent on foot in Boot Canyon were punctuated by "the growls of bobcats and foxes," while during the day Baker and his crew observed "many deer, eagles, and other wild animals."[42]

He found most interesting the hike to Boquillas, where "the farmers irrigate their land along the river affording insects a wonderful playground amid the thick vegetation of the irrigated flood plain." Boquillas had a great variety of butterflies, among them the milkweed butterfly "clustering on all types of vegetation." Baker and his partners made note of a party from the Field Museum of Natural History in Chicago that "spent several weeks in camp with us in late July and early August." This group sought reptiles and mammals, and Baker "enjoyed several collecting trips with them learning much from them in the ways of collecting."[43]

Baker also traveled westward to Santa Eleña Canyon, where he found that its "insect fauna . . . closely resembled that of points further down the river." He concluded, "Though I have collected in the Big Bend Proposed Park Area some two thousand specimens of the insect fauna, I feel that three and one-half months in an area as large as this region is not fully adequate for more than a beginning on an entomological survey." He suggested to the park service that "the area can be worked a great deal more for insect abundance and types, and there are many interesting ecological studies to be dwelt upon before a final survey can be accomplished."[44]

From the spring of 1942 until the months before the opening of Big Bend National Park (June 1944), the park service conducted no formal scientific surveys of the future NPS unit. In September 1943, James O. Stevenson, a former park service official, sent to chief naturalist Victor Cahalane "a few comments—the personal opinions of the writer" on the NPS's plans for "the development of Big Bend International Park." Stevenson conceded that the plan for facilities and visitor services development in the Chisos basin "was o.k., but we must guard against overdevelopment and spread of structures, roads, etc., throughout the northern two-fifths of the Chisos Mountains." To do otherwise, said Stevenson, meant that "the whole wilderness flavor of the area will be dissipated." He argued that "the view from the South Rim should not be denied to anyone willing to make the trip the way it should be made—on foot or on horseback."[45]

Stevenson recalled the comment of the NPS's Hermon C. Bumpus that "one should earn his way from the bowl (the Basin) to the rim either by a hard ride on horseback or a harder hike through a virgin country." Bumpus, chairman of the advisory board of the NPS and a prominent biologist, had contended that "the achievement will consume a day, but a day never to be forgotten." Stevenson then described the rumor of a "cog railway" to the South Rim as "fantastic," quoting an unnamed scientist "who has a thorough knowledge and appreciation of the Chisos." Harvey Cornell, regional landscape artist with the NPS, would add to Stevenson's remarks the marginal note that "the cog railway was never a popular idea—and was made only as a substitute for a road, if [through] public demand it was found that a road or an equivalent would be unavailable." Stevenson then argued that "those who insist on viewing the Chisos wilderness from a car window will never find it." Instead, "those unwilling to walk or ride on horseback through the mountains will be better off elsewhere seeking other types of entertainment or recreation."[46]

Stevenson then offered to Cahalane his thoughts on the relationship of Big Bend to Mexico. "The Big Bend will not be a true International Park," he warned, "until Mexico acquires a sizeable tract of land south of the Rio Grande and provision is made for an interchange of travel by the people of both nations to both sections of the park." Stevenson agreed with the NPS's Minor Tillotson and Paul V. Brown that "developments should be so planned that each section complements the other rather than competes with it." Yet "until such time as the Mexican authorities give assurances that an adequate tract will be acquired in Chihuahua and Coahuila," said Stevenson, "park planning will necessarily be limited to the Texas portion of the area."[47]

The former NPS official nonetheless hoped that plans for a thorough biological survey would proceed. "No detailed investigation of the wildlife of the Mexican border area has been made," claimed Stevenson, citing a brief list of studies on the Sierra del Carmen, including the survey by Ernest Marsh. "The choicest area opposite the park in Texas," wrote Stevenson, "is the Fronteriza and Carmen Mountains regions." He admitted that "since the Carmen Mountain Hunting Club, owned by Americans, controls some 100,000 acres in the Carmens, acquisition of this important range may be delayed indefinitely." Then in a statement that presaged calls in the 1970s for creation of a "wild and scenic river" designation for Big Bend, he said that the park service should press for inclusion of "the entire river region opposite the park in Texas, including sizeable tracts bordering the three canyons." Stevenson believed that this would "reduce the possibilities of pollution and poaching, give increased protection to beavers and fish life, and provide necessary range (in Mexico) for any bighorns which may be re-established in the park."[48]

When Big Bend National Park opened in the summer of 1944, NPS officials called for a "faunal survey" of future interpretive and protection programs. Assigned as team leader was Walter P. Taylor, senior biologist with the US Fish and Wildlife Service. The aridity of the Big Bend would influence many conclusions at which Taylor and his ecological survey arrived. These included more-accurate records of weather and climate, previously collected intermittently at Johnson's ranch and Government Spring. Water supplies also concerned the surveyors, as they recommended that "location of the Park Service and concessionaire headquarters at the Graham or Daniels ranch sites should encourage greater attention to the resources of this interesting stream and heightened appreciation of its values." Taylor claimed that "already the general public (July 1944), due very largely to the fishing in the Rio Grande, regularly pass by the Chisos Mountains and go to the river, even in the hot weather of late spring and summer." Taylor also noted that "the hot springs at intervals along the river, especially between Hot Springs and Boquillas, form an added tourist attraction."[49]

One problem facing the NPS was reduced streamflow, "as the Mexicans take more and more water for irrigation above the Big Bend and as additional water is used for the same purpose by Americans in New Mexico and West Texas." The surveyors identified seventy permanent springs in the park area, "which may be depended upon to afford sufficient water for wildlife." Some of these springs suffered from cattle grazing, as "an abundance of manure and urine of domestic stock and rotten animals or scattered remains, either in or near the water, are all too characteristic." Taylor believed that the park service should clean out the springs damaged by stock raising, leaving the sites "the way Nature made them."[50]

The same policy would apply to the rock bowls, or *tinajas*, in the Dead Horse Mountains, Mariscal Mountain, and the Mesa de Anguila, and the "tanks" built by ranchers. "While these tanks are unnatural," said Taylor, "they may as well be left alone," as "they will disappear in short order if they are not sedulously maintained." As for dams and reservoirs, the surveyors conceded that these might "increase the amount of water available for mule deer and other animals." Yet "such developments," concluded Taylor, "would not be natural and cannot be recommended."[51]

In matters of species restoration, Taylor and his colleagues did not support "any overt action," as they observed "sufficient seedstock of all the plants and animals in the park (except the bighorn sheep and the pronghorn antelope) eventually to populate the area to an optimum degree after the livestock are taken off." With bighorn sheep, no one could explain why they disappeared, or why they had stayed in areas of "ultra dry Edwards limestone types with no springs or other water except in tinajas." Hunters decimated the population, said some local residents, while "possible infection with the diseases of domestic sheep and goats, may have had something to do with it."[52]

In 1941, J. Stokely Ligon had written a report for the US Fish and Wildlife Service noting that "the policy of the National Park Service, in protecting *all* native wildlife within park boundaries, is not such as to encourage the introduction of a vanishing species." Instead, Ligon suggested that "immediate efforts to save seed stock of the bighorn sheep might well be confined to the present range of the sheep in the Sierra Diablo Mountains, north of Van Horn, Texas." Taylor and his associates agreed, suggesting that "if proper protection can be given to the Park, and an international park developed on the Mexican side of the Rio Grande, there eventually may be some natural restocking of the Park with bighorns from across the river."[53]

This feature of the proposed international park merited substantial attention from the ecological survey. Taylor and his coauthors wrote that "it is a fact that the river affords no appreciable barrier, in a distributional sense, even to some small rodents." Should the park service identify "a plentiful stock of bighorn sheep, prong-horned antelope, black bear, gray wolves, and other species on the Mexican side, it would only be a matter of time until some individuals would appear on the American side." Taylor and his colleagues claimed that "Mexico is probably the center of abundance of some of the Big Bend mammals." This would include bighorn, antelope, "birds, many of the mammals, including predators and fur animals, as well as game species, insects, and indeed most forms of wildlife." Taylor and coauthors again suggested that "if the Mexican park can be set up and protection given to existing stocks on the Mexican side both inside and outside of the proposed park, there is no reason why, over a term of years, restoration cannot proceed across the Rio Grande."[54]

Yet another section of the park boundary of concern to Taylor and the survey team was the Rio Grande. "Without a fence along the river," warned Taylor and associates, "it will be impossible during times of low water (which are apparently increasingly more frequent) to keep livestock from trespassing into the Park from Mexico." This would be an issue of resource management for decades at Big Bend, and Taylor and his coauthors noted that "this consideration emphasizes the desirability of encouraging Mexico to set up a park upon her side of the Rio Grande and to eliminate the domestic livestock therefrom."[55]

Fencing, meanwhile, would hinder the "free ingress of such game animals as peccary, antelope, bighorn, mule deer, and white-tailed deer, as well as some of the predatory animals, including the mountain lion, the wolf, and the bear."

Taylor and his colleagues wanted these animals to be "encouraged to enter the Park area." For that reason, they hoped that "all existing fences within the boundaries of the Park should be removed as soon as practicable [because] these fences interfere with the free movements of native animals, and are contrary to Park Service policy."[56]

Visitor access and points of interest then received mention in Taylor's report, with a lengthy list prepared of natural and cultural resource sites. Among these, said Taylor and colleagues, were a "small cemetery at Chilicotal Spring," "Indian writings on the Chimneys," "old candelilla factories at La Noria and Glenn Spring," and "sites of old ranch headquarters in the Park (McKinney's, Boquillas, Hot Springs, San Vicente, Johnson Ranch, Glenn Spring, Dugout, [and] Grapevine Spring)." Taylor and his coauthors stated that "the whole Big Bend National Park, to a considerable extent, is an area of especial interest because of its unique combination of high and low plant-animal communities." They argued that special notice should be given to "the portion of Mexico in the Mexican states of Chihuahua and Coahuila," as "it is characterized by wild wastes of desert and mountain country with some possibilities for the increase in game and other wildlife."[57]

Taylor and colleagues remarked that "there are probably few locations in North America which are more primitive in character than these lands across the Rio Grande." This led the surveyors to the conclusion that "there is no question but that, as time goes on, more and more persons will cross the Rio Grande and enjoy themselves in this rugged mountainous and desert country."[58]

Fire suppression needed to be part of this strategy, wrote Taylor and his associates, as "no woodcutting whatever should be permitted within the National Park area." They wanted "fallen trees, shrubs, or parts thereof, and accumulating brush and litter . . . left in place, except as clearly needed for a limited number of camp fires in pack trips." The authors claimed that "such debris affords home and shelter to numerous small animals, such as fur animals, rodents, insects, birds, and game." From this came mulch that would "protect the soil from erosion," while "litter and brush are often of the utmost help in the rehabilitation of grasses and other plants, protecting them from grazing and browsing animals during their critical period."[59]

Taylor had heard that "cutting of timber has been carefully regulated on the Mexican side of the Rio Grande," with "a permit required from the local forest officer" to cut trees. "On the American side," wrote Taylor and his coauthors, "this has not been the case." As a result, "it is said that native Mexicans have crossed into the United States and removed timber from the American side of the line." In addition, "trees growing along the river have also been used freely by Americans who, up to this time, have occupied ranch and farm land along the river." Such woodcutting "must necessarily be eliminated so that the natural vegetation can restore itself." The surveyors had discovered that "much of the mesquite along the river is second growth," but Taylor and his coauthors hoped that "in 50 or 100 years Park visitors may be able to see what a well-developed mesquite forest (a beautiful woods by the way) looks like."[60]

At the conclusion of the Taylor report, the surveyors devoted several paragraphs to recommendations on the "international aspects" of Big Bend's future. "Every assistance and encouragement should be given the Government of the United States of Mexico to set up a great Mexican national park across from the Big Bend National Park," wrote Taylor and colleagues. They admitted that "our own Big Bend Park cannot be effective as an ideal wildlife area until this is done." The authors wanted protection for "the natural plant and animal life in a broad belt on the Mexican side of the line." They reminded NPS officials that "the Mexican area ultimately should function as a restoration area from which some of the most interesting animals in the Southwest would be fed into our own Big Bend National Park."[61]

Taylor and his coauthors then addressed the issue of "the removal of the small Mexican population from the American side of the land." In so doing, the NPS "will make a trip into old Mexico of greater interest than ever." Taylor and colleagues suggested that "accessible from the Rio Grande in this vicinity should be a number of settlements in Mexico, notably San Carlos, directly across from Lajitas." The surveyors believed that "the setting apart of the Mexican national park, along with the Big Bend National Park," would "greatly enhance the interest to all, both citizens of Mexico and the United States." Such "a truly international enterprise should go far to promote more friendly relations between the two countries." Beyond this diplomatic initiative, said Taylor and his associates, "the value and interest of our own park project would be at least doubled and perhaps tripled if there were an international setup in the region."[62]

Appended to the Taylor report was a document prepared by Thomas K. Chamberlain, an aquatic biologist with the US Fish and Wildlife Service station at Texas A&M College. Chamberlain detailed his findings on marine life in the park. "To call the Rio Grande fishing 'sport fishing' requires a broad interpretation of the term," said Chamberlain. "Yet people come daily," he reported, "every month of the year, some from great distances, expressly to fish these waters." Chamberlain remarked that "this fishing has a high recreational value," despite the fact that "there is little or no sport fishing as that term is usually understood." No regulations existed for Rio Grande use, and "there has been a tendency for a few individuals to monopolize the fishing."[63]

Chamberlain found the river to be "a rich catfish stream," with that species constituting 95 percent of the anglers' catches. Visitors and local fishermen alike reported that "the average size of these fish runs [was] large, probably exceeding six pounds." It was not uncommon for fishermen to bring in thirty-pound yellow catfish, and some had caught fish weighing one hundred pounds. "The general opinion," wrote Chamberlain, "is that when the catfish are in the mood to feed nearly anything will serve as bait." Fishermen used minnows, goldfish, and "at such times a piece of soap will serve as well as any meat." The proliferation of catfish also permitted most anglers to set lines in the river overnight, returning in the morning for their catch.[64]

Chamberlain found this latter practice most disturbing, as it contributed to "commercial exploitation and excessive fishing." With no rules, "undoubtedly many pounds of fish go to waste because fishermen make larger catches than they can utilize." Chamberlain recalled "a typical case" where "two men, their wives, and two older children put out 125 set lines, each with a number of hooks." In order to string bait for so many lines, the party shot several rabbits on park grounds. Another fishing party slaughtered a goat "to bait some long trot lines containing hundreds of hooks each." Chamberlain heard of a party "catching, the year before, an average of 500 pounds of catfish per night for 10 nights." The average weight of these fish was fourteen pounds, with several ranging from thirty to sixty pounds. Still another angler boasted of catching a catfish "over six feet long." Chamberlain reported that when the angler was asked what he did with it, he said that "it was too big for him to handle or to use, but as it had swallowed the hook, he killed the huge fish to get his hook back and then threw the fish away."[65]

To halt this abuse of the river, Chamberlain called on the NPS to devise regulations "aimed at rationing those fish by enforcing reasonable limitations on fishing." He predicted that "fishermen are sure to enter the Park in increasing numbers in the years to come." He also spoke out against allowing "one small party of fishermen to put out so large a number of set lines as to tie up one or more miles of fishing channel." Chamberlain had learned from Mr. and Mrs. A. R. Davis, of Marathon, that "the use by fishermen of any kind of boats, but particularly power boats, to set their trot lines, is the most serious threat to catfishing on the river." Chamberlain believed that "it is reported to be a violation of national law to use boats on the river." Yet "this is continually being done," and "the use of power boats permits anglers to run their trot lines through canyon waters that otherwise would be natural spawning refuges, such as the Boquillas Canyon, Mariscal Canyon, and the Grand Canyon of the Santa Elena."[66]

His research indicated that "the large species of catfish favor spawning in depressions and various sheltered places in riverbanks and cliffs which abound in these canyons." Chamberlain noted that "the precipitous canyon walls would preclude fishing in these waters were it not for the use of boats." The Fish and Wildlife consultant recommended limiting visitors to the use of poles and handlines. "No wild land animal occurring within the Park may be used for fish bait, even when found dead," said Chamberlain, who would make an exception for turtles caught in the river. Boats would be prohibited on the Rio Grande, bag limits would be twenty pounds, and "a record shall be turned in to the Park officials of all food fish taken in the Park area."[67]

The NPS's emphasis on scientific research in the Big Bend region had drawn the attention of the president of the local college in Alpine. Howard Morelock had convinced Arthur Kelley, chief of the park service's archaeological sites division, to visit his campus and judge for himself the potential for scientific research at Sul Ross State Teachers College. Kelley learned that Morelock "envisaged a collaborative arrangement with the National Park Service in which his institution with its laboratories, buildings, personnel, and other facilities for interpretation would serve as an orientation center for the millions of visitors to Big Bend National Park." The Sul Ross president defined Alpine as "the gateway to the park," with Big Bend serving as "a laboratory, a vast open-air reservoir for the original sources and natural models in place to illustrate the peculiar blend of scenic and natural phenomena." In addition, the new national park would offer "the folk atmosphere of Mexico, Spanish-America, and Anglo-America; the threshold of history in rancheria, squatter's cabin, Apache and Comanche camp sites, cave habitations of the Texas equivalent of the remotely prehistoric Basket-Makers, and beyond that the ancient hearths deeply exposed in arroyos which reflected the settlements of Early Man."[68]

Beyond Morelock's quest for a nationally prominent (and federally funded) resource program at his college, Kelley reported to the NPS director that "the dominating idea was not simply a collaboration by which there would be a division of functions between the orientation center and the natural laboratory." The NPS archaeologist stated that Sul Ross's "business is specialized in the field of producing primary school teachers." Kelley believed that "the most potent and all-pervasive educational influence which could operate to affect the largest number of highly impressionistic persons is the school teacher." He claimed that at Sul Ross, "in a Southwest setting, where many citizens are already bilingual, where four centuries of continuous cultural evolution have produced distinct but genetically related varieties of a common pattern of Spanish-American life, there is much promise for achieving an understanding between the peoples of North and Central America."[69]

As much as Kelley wanted to endorse Morelock's vision, he doubted Sul Ross's capacity to deliver on its promises. "These advantages are real," wrote Kelley, "but are not mutually exclusive." He noted that "the Universities of Texas, New Mexico, and Arizona possess these same attributes in varying degree." Kelley agreed with Morelock that "the advantage of geographic position, with particular reference to Big Bend National Park, of course lies with Sul Ross." Yet "the ultimate objective of making our southwestern areas function in the over-all pattern of Pan-American cultural relations," said the archaeologist, "has a strong advocate in the University of New Mexico and Chaco Canyon National Monument."[70]

Kelley reported that the "Chaco Conference has become a southwestern institution, and as the number of visiting historians, archaeologists, anthropologists, and museologists increases, with the studied effort of the University of New Mexico to embrace the Americanists in future scientific conferences, that area tends to bulk largest in the minds of many of our neighbors." Kelley further noted the University of New Mexico's effort "in salvaging the moribund Laboratory of Anthropology in Santa Fe" as "an event which needs to be evaluated by the National Park Service."[71]

Morelock's contention that proximity to Big Bend mattered more than programmatic capacity also failed to influence Kelley, who saw the Austin campus as the Lone Star State's only university with "the national and international prestige, the funds and endowments, the faculty and curriculum, and the established contacts with other institutions in Latin America." When examining the University of Texas's programs in Spanish or Latin American literature, Latin American history, political science, economics, and geography, said Kelley, "the same disproportion will be found." He also worried that "Indianization is a culturally conditioning fact in most of these [Latin American] countries which it is difficult for an Anglo-American to understand."[72]

For Kelley, "only the ethnologist, the archaeologist, or the student of sociology concerned with acculturation, can bring to these people that dignity and pride in origin and achievement which our genealogists, historians, and patriotic organizations concerned with the heroic performances of their ancestors provide." The NPS archaeologist noted that while "Teotihuacan, [and] Monte Alban are not prehistoric monuments . . . they are to the majority of Mexicans a living symbol of tribal greatness." Park service researchers needed to remember that Mexican history "is native American; ours is still unconsciously perceived to be derived European, and only secondarily by the accident of historical transplantation American."[73]

Morelock's plea to Kelley prompted the NPS archaeologist to correspond with Carl Russell, seeking the opinion of top-level park service officials. "I admire Mr. Morelock's initiative," Russell told his colleagues in Chicago, and like regional NPS officials in Santa Fe, he wanted the park service to "encourage [Morelock] in his program for promoting international understanding." The NPS "will find it advantageous to establish a relationship with the Sul Ross Museum," said the interpretation chief, but he also warned that "it is a mistake to adopt a policy of excluding museums and museum work from the Big Bend itself." Russell had long held that "each National Park is a museum and that our entire Service program in each park is a specialized type of museum program." Thus "to conclude that the Service will not engage in museum work at Big Bend is irrational."[74]

If the NPS agreed to house its scientific laboratory in Alpine, contended Russell, then "it would be reasonable to say that administrative work will center at Sul Ross State Teachers College." The interpretation chief noted that Ross Maxwell had initiated a promising program of research and specimen storage. "We should strive to replace the naturalist's workshop," Russell advised, "and employ a naturalist as a member of the minimum staff first appointed." The interpretation chief saw this as "museum work even though it makes no immediate contribution to public contact work—and it cannot be done advantageously at Sul Ross."[75]

Undaunted by the opinions of Russell and Kelley, President Morelock cast about in the winter of 1942–1943 for additional support for his Big Bend–Sul Ross partnership. Two avenues that opened for him were a program headed by Nelson Rockefeller, coordinator of inter-American affairs for the US State Department, and Emery Morriss of the Kellogg Foundation. Morelock wanted Rockefeller to establish on the Alpine campus a "Pan-American House," with its goal the promotion of "International Understanding and Good Will [a program of the Kellogg Foundation]." Newton B. Drury, director of the NPS, congratulated Morelock "on all that you have done to bring this program to the attention of important leaders in Inter-American affairs."[76]

Drury had reviewed Morelock's scheme for collaboration between the park service and Sul Ross, but believed that "you do not intend that the National Park Service should commit itself to the full extent of your statement that 'all scientific material in the park area will be placed in the museum on the college campus.'" The NPS director acknowledged that "we shall look to the talents and facilities at Sul Ross to assist with research and interpretation of the Big Bend country."[77]

As a federal agency, however, the park service could not "agree to any arrangement that would limit other scientific activities or direct the placing of all scientific materials at the College." The constraints of wartime funding prohibited any long-range planning, but Drury advised the Sul Ross president that "any postwar activities should be determined as carefully and exactly as possible." The NPS director informed Morelock of his conversations with Russell, telling him that Kelley would return to Alpine "to review with you the research and interpretative programs that have been conducted in other national park areas."[78]

Morelock's quixotic search for federal support and a national identity did not abate with the caution of NPS director Drury. Three days after learning of Drury's opinion, the Sul Ross president wrote back with plans for an "International Shrine" on the border of Texas and Mexico. He then asked Drury his thoughts on "a broadcasting station in Alpine for the purpose of promoting international goodwill through the Big Bend National Park set-up here." Morelock conceded that "the outlook is a little gloomy, but if some foundation could set up the money *now*, we could have everything ready for a big publicity program at the proper time."[79]

The Sul Ross president had plans to travel to Fort Worth for meetings with Amon Carter, where he hoped to convince the *Star-Telegram* publisher to apply "a part of the $25,000 'working fund' to subsidize a station here." Morelock then informed Drury of the response that he had received from Rockefeller, who "indicated that he had referred my request for scholarship students and for money to expand our Library on International Affairs to the 'Committee on Science and Education.'"[80]

Because the park service took seriously the challenge to understand the landscape of Big Bend, NPS scientists and technicians discovered much of value in the years before creation of Texas's first national park. The grandeur of its canyons, and the astonishing variety of its flora and fauna, would fascinate practical officials of the park service as much as the romance and drama had affected Walter Prescott Webb and J. Frank Dobie. Yet the callous disregard of local landowners for these features of nature and culture angered park service officials and saddened park advocates like Everett Townsend.

One ironic feature of the NPS's campaign for scientific research in Big Bend was the discovery that northern Mexico's isolation and poverty had preserved the contours of the land far better than had the ambitious *norteños* (a Spanish colloquialism for "people of the north," or US citizens). The dream of an international park may have faced severe opposition among politicians and ranchers on both sides of the Rio Grande. Yet the chance to restore an American park with flora and fauna from Mexico did not escape the notice of NPS surveyors and policy makers. Finally, the park service's power to save the land could not extend to the campus of Sul Ross State Teachers College, as federal regulations and park facility development denied President Morelock's wish for a better school, with a stronger identity, than local conditions or state funding could make possible. It would remain for the park service to enter the "last frontier" in the summer of 1944, and to redefine land-use patterns, economic strategies, and border relations as it sought to protect one of the most striking ecological zones in North America.

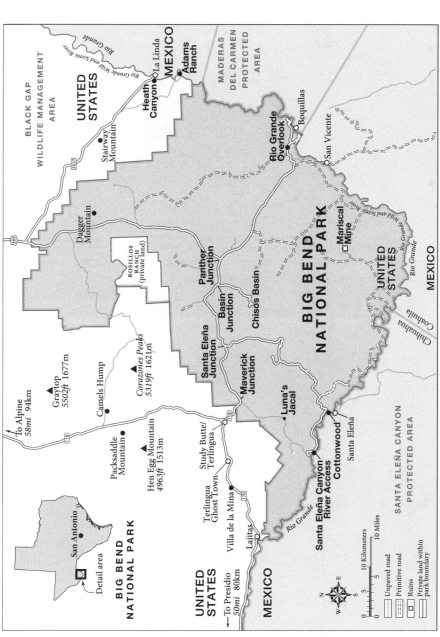

National Park Service map of Big Bend National Park (2020). Courtesy of Big Bend National Park.

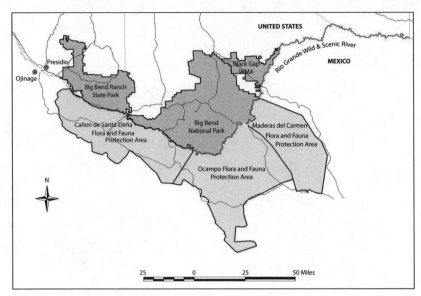

Map of protected areas in Mexico adjacent to Big Bend National Park (2020). Courtesy of Big Bend National Park.

Kickapoo Indians from Mexico at Rio Grande Hot Springs (ca. 1920). Courtesy of
Big Bend National Park.

US Geological Survey of Rio Grande Canyons (1899). Robert T. Hill, leader of expedition,
is second from left. Courtesy of Big Bend National Park.

North Peak of Chisos Mountains (1899). Photograph taken by Robert T. Hill. Courtesy of Big Bend National Park.

Santa Eleña Canyon (1899). Courtesy of Big Bend National Park.

US Geological Survey crew crossing boulders in Santa Eleña Canyon (1899). Courtesy of *Century* magazine.

Walter Prescott Webb
(1942). Courtesy of Big
Bend National Park.

Civilian Conservation Corps camp in Chisos Basin (1934). Courtesy of Big Bend
National Park.

ccc workers on the Window Trail (1934). Courtesy of Big Bend
National Park.

CCC roadwork (1934). Courtesy of Big Bend National Park.

Miguel Angel de Quevedo, director, Departemento Forestal, Caza y Pesca, Republic of Mexico (undated). Courtesy of Big Bend National Park.

Daniel F. Galicia, chief inspector, Departemento Forestal, Caza y Pesca, Republic of Mexico, preparing for overflight of proposed International Park (January 1936). Courtesy of Big Bend National Park.

George Meléndez Wright, chief, Wildlife Division, National Park Service, upon return from overflight of proposed International Park (January 1936). Courtesy of Big Bend National Park.

International Park Commission vehicle being towed across the Rio Grande in Big Bend (January 1936). Courtesy of Big Bend National Park.

International Park Commission staff and oldest residents of San Carlos, Chihuahua, Mexico (ca. 1936). *From left to right:* Balentin Chávez (age 76); Ingeniero Raul Ybarro, Departmentento Forestal, Caza y Pesca; Everett Ewing Townsend, former Texas state senator, US Customs agent, and advocate for Big Bend National Park; and Santiago Luján (age 76). Courtesy of Big Bend National Park.

International Park Commission in Boquillas, Mexico (January 1936). Members include Roger Toll (*fourth from left*), Daniel F. Galicia (*fifth from left*), and George Meléndez Wright (*far right*). Courtesy of Big Bend National Park.

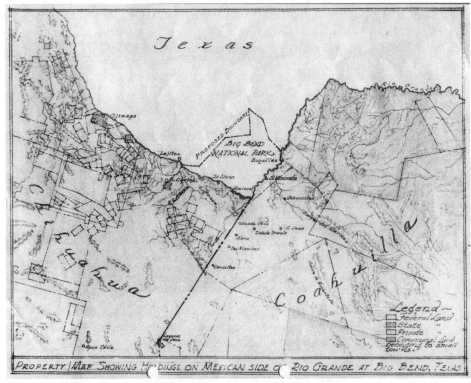

Property map of Mexican landownership in proposed international park (1936). Large shaded areas owned by Mexican and American cattle companies. Courtesy of Big Bend National Park.

Visitors at American overlook of Boquillas, Mexico (ca. 1950). Courtesy of Big Bend National Park.

Big Bend park visitor on outskirts of Boquillas, Mexico (1965). Courtesy of Big Bend National Park.

Lady Bird Johnson and Interior Secretary Stewart Udall entering canoe for river trip through Mariscal Canyon (April 1966). Courtesy of Big Bend National Park.

CHAPTER 4

Dreaming of a Park for Peace

Of all the initiatives pursued by the park service in the 1930s, few had the drama or complexity of the international peace park. Stimulated by policies in Mexico City and Washington, DC, the idea of a joint park along the Rio Grande at Big Bend received its most serious attention in the depths of the Great Depression. In the process, each nation learned a great deal about the conditions of the past that had separated them, while facing the obstacles of economic and ecological devastation that triggered Franklin D. Roosevelt's New Deal and Lázaro Cárdenas's reform movement. Optimism was in the air as officials at the highest levels explored the means of cooperation, while NPS personnel prepared for inclusion of the international park in the larger universe of Big Bend planning.

While much has been written about the conservation and Good Neighbor policies espoused by Roosevelt, less is known of the work on environmental protection of Mexican president Cárdenas and his advisers. Lane Simonian writes that, "indeed, the exploitation of natural resources has been the dominant theme in Mexican environmental history." He argues that "if the conventional wisdom is true that poor people cannot afford to protect natural resources, then there would be no basis for conservation in Mexico." Yet that is precisely what occurred in the 1930s, when Cárdenas asked Miguel Angel de Quevedo to lead the newly created Departemento Forestal, Caza y Pesca (Department of Forestry, Game and Fish). Quevedo, who would work closely with NPS officials in 1935 and 1936 on the joint-park proposal, had studied forest conservation in Paris at the Ecole Polytechnique, receiving in 1889 a degree in civil engineering.[1]

His exposure to American conservation programs began in 1909, when outgoing president Theodore Roosevelt invited Quevedo to Washington to attend the International North American Conference on the Conservation of Natural Resources. Consultations with the likes of Gifford Pinchot, Roosevelt's chief of the US Forest Service, helped Quevedo develop an interest, says Simonian, that "lay less with the establishment of a forest industry based upon the principles of sustained yield than it did with the protection of forests because they were biologically indispensable."[2]

Quevedo's journey from the halls of the White House to the Big Bend of the Rio Grande symbolized not only the history of Mexican conservation but also that of border relations and the twentieth-century Mexican political economy. Eager to promote his ideas of forests and parks, Quevedo sought to interest revolutionary leaders like President Venustiano Carranza, who agreed in 1917 to establish outside Mexico City the first Mexican national park: El Desierto de los Leones (The desert of the lions). Five years later, Quevedo had formed the private Mexican Forest Society and petitioned President Plutarco Elías Calles "to establish national parks in areas with high biological, scenic . . . and recreational values." Calles did not implement Quevedo's plan, and Simonian summarizes Mexico's conservation ethic by the 1930s as "weakened by the disinterest of powerful Mexican officials and by a lack of general public support."[3]

Quevedo's persistence, and his hopes for a true national park system in Mexico, would rise when President Cárdenas announced that, in the words of Simonian, "conservation was in the national interests and the irrational exploitation of the land must come to an end." Historians Michael C. Meyer and William L. Sherman describe Cárdenas as "intensely interested in social reform." The Mexican leader also "had that special charismatic quality of evoking passionate enthusiasm among many and strong dislike among some." He inherited a nation that was but 20 percent urban, and where rural "per capita income, infant mortality, and indeed life expectancy lagged behind that of cities." To address these inadequacies, says Simonian, Cárdenas's "administration undertook the largest land reform program in Mexican history, extended irrigation projects to small farmers, experimented with alternative 'crops,' such as silkworms and sunflowers (for the oil), created rural industries, and established fishing and forestry cooperatives."[4]

Cárdenas also approved of Quevedo's efforts to mitigate erosion caused by deforestation of Mexican lands. From 1934 to 1940, Quevedo oversaw the planting of some two million trees in the Valley of Mexico alone, and four million more throughout the republic. This commitment encouraged Quevedo to press for more work, in that "Mexico's forest problem was so complex and so difficult that only a permanent campaign that enlisted the support of the entire citizenry on behalf of forest conservation could succeed." Finally, Quevedo worked with Cárdenas to establish some forty national parks in Mexico, although, in the words of Simonian, "Twenty two were less than the size of Hot Springs National Park [in Arkansas], the smallest national park in the United States."[5]

The limitations that Cárdenas placed in the summer and fall of 1935 on Quevedo's plans for national parks would hinder negotiations with the United States. "Like their U.S. counterparts," writes Simonian, "Mexican officials rarely created national parks that incorporated whole ecosystems." Quevedo identified park lands based on their "scenic beauty, recreational potential, and ecological value." Much like their American counterparts, the parks in the Mexican system would be promoted for their "therapeutic value." Finally, Quevedo "believed that international tourism would further cooperation between Mexico and other countries," a key feature of FDR's Good Neighbor Policy and his New Deal ventures into natural and cultural resource preservation.[6]

This prompted an emphasis on park development in and near the population centers of Mexico, especially its capital city. "Quevedo created a national park system," says Simonian, "whose centerpiece was the high coniferous forests of the central plateau." How this concentration of resources and attention far to the south of the Rio Grande would affect negotiations for a joint international park became clearer as the two countries planned meetings along the border, talking at the highest diplomatic levels about a partnership never before attempted.[7]

Given the circuitous journey taken since 1935 to establish an international park in the Big Bend area, the speed with which American and Mexican officials moved that year engendered hope for the future of the partnership. Interior Secretary Harold Ickes had asked Secretary of State Cordell Hull to formulate the diplomatic protocol for planning such an endeavor. Ickes himself envisioned naming the new park (or at least the American side) the Jane Addams International Peace Park. John Jameson writes that the interior secretary saw this as "a fitting memorial to a fellow Chicagoan and the winner of the 1931 Nobel Peace Prize in recognition of her lifelong commitment to international peace and understanding."[8]

Addams had brought to the immigrant neighborhoods of late nineteenth-century Chicago the British concept of the "settlement house," where educated reformers (both male and female) would teach middle-class values and American citizenship. Popularized in her book *Twenty Years at Hull House*, Addams's outreach programs increasingly included Latinos recruited to the Midwest to replace the European ethnic groups she had first encountered in the 1880s and 1890s. Ickes, who had worked in Progressive Era reform programs in his hometown of Chicago, saw a strong connection between Addams's service to Latinos, the president's initiatives for better relations with Mexico, and the appeal of an international park dedicated to peace in an era of escalating tensions in Europe and the Far East.

Word of Mexico's commitment to the discussions came in late July, as US ambassador Josephus Daniels wrote to Hull, "It is my understanding that the

Bureau of Forestry of the Mexican Government has written to the Foreign Office expressing its interest in the project." Daniel Galicia, chief of the Mexican forestry bureau, informed Daniels that "he was sending an expedition into Coahuila and Chihuahua in about three weeks to study the possibility of establishing a corresponding reserve on the Mexican side of the Rio Grande." Galicia had asked the American diplomat "especially for a map showing exactly the areas involved in the American project and any other [particulars] which might be of assistance to him in making plans for a Mexican park." Galicia's superior, Quevedo, also asked Daniels to coordinate a meeting with US officials on the initiative. "I found Mr. Quevedo personally most enthusiastic at the idea," said Daniels, with "his chief interest [being] the possibility of making the park a great game reserve."[9]

Quevedo mentioned to the US ambassador that "the big game in the northwestern part of the State of Coahuila, some of the finest in the country, is in danger of extinction." Daniels believed that "the Government already owns much of the land in this section and that the President has approved the drafting of a bill for submission to the next Congress authorizing the Forestry Department to issue bonds for the purchase of any additional lands necessary for national parks." Quevedo and Daniels also discussed "the naming of the park," and the former stated that "this was a matter on which [the Mexican] Congress and the authorities of the States concerned would probably wish to be consulted."[10]

To expedite the request of Galicia and Quevedo, American and Mexican officials met in El Paso on October 5 to plan for a larger conference in that border city the following month. There Herbert Maier learned from Galicia and from Armando Santacruz Jr., Mexico's commissioner to the International Boundary Commission (IBC), of that nation's interest in water projects along the Rio Grande. Maier quickly corresponded after the meeting with L. R. Fiock, regional director of the US Bureau of Reclamation (USBR), about Santacruz's suggestion "that it is the plan [of the IBC] to erect three dams along the Rio Grande in the Big Bend area," one each at the mouths of Santa Elena, Mariscal, and Boquillas Canyons. "From what he said," reported Maier, "I gathered that the U.S. Federal Government tentatively favors the erection of these dams."[11]

Maier recalled that upon his most recent visit to the Big Bend, he had heard of "the possibility of such dam promotion." This he had dismissed because, "as you know, dams have been proposed for about every strategic point on about every river in the United States during the past decade." The NPS official told Fiock that "even if the Mexican government favors such a move, I am sure that it will be out of the line of normal policy to approve of our participation in these hydraulic ventures because . . . our national park areas are to be maintained in their wilderness state."[12]

Maier decided not to engage Santacruz in a discussion of NPS policy "because I did not wish to complicate the picture." He informed the USBR official that "it has been tentatively proposed that the area on the Mexican side be set aside as a large Forest and Game Preserve." He knew that the Rio Grande's international status meant that "such hydraulic ventures would have to be anticipated." Yet the United States, "on the basis of its future adoption of the area as a national park, can withhold participation in such ventures if that appears advisable."[13]

As Fiock had replaced the current US commissioner to the IBC, L. M. Lawson, Maier asked that Fiock supply him "with information as to what extent the U.S. Reclamation Service is seriously considering the erection of dams at these three canyons." He also asked that Fiock "hold the matter of my inquiry confidential," as Maier knew that the NPS's Washington office would handle all conversations with Mexican officials on this matter.[14]

Issues of water quality and quantity would affect management of Big Bend National Park from its inception. Fiock's response to Maier's confidential inquiry revealed how each nation would envision water resource planning in the Big Bend area. Fiock claimed that he possessed only "meager knowledge" of the "proposed construction of dams on the Rio Grande below El Paso." He had not worked on the surveys for water projects between that city and the Gulf of Mexico but had gained access to informal details within the USBR. "In 1919," Fiock recalled, "the Bureau of Reclamation through some cooperative arrangements with the Irrigation Districts of the Lower Rio Grande Valley (Brownsville section) made a preliminary investigation of possible storage reservoir sites." He also knew that "being an International proposition the International Boundary Commission . . . [had] interested themselves during the past several years in these matters." This led Fiock to believe that the IBC was "working cooperatively on plans, at least to the extent of collecting necessary essential data."[15]

The USBR official had visited the three canyons of the future park, considering them "exceedingly favorable for dam construction." He cautioned Maier that "it seems doubtful that there is a sufficient discharge of water in the Rio Grande at these points to fill the reservoir which could be created by either one of them." Fiock reminded Maier that "the flow of the Upper Rio Grande is entirely controlled by Elephant Butte Dam and Reservoir," north of Las Cruces, "and there are no large tributaries to the Rio Grande between Elephant Butte and the Pecos River," below the proposed national park. In Mexico the only stream flowing into the Rio Grande in the vicinity was the Rio Conchos, and "there is already constructed on the Conchos River a dam and reservoir almost identical in proportions with Elephant Butte [itself a storage basin of two million acre-feet of water]."[16]

Besides the lack of water in the Rio Grande through the Big Bend, Fiock also noted the use of irrigation far from the park. "Construction of dams in the canyons of the Big Bend," said the USBR official, "cannot provide major flood control to the lower Rio Grande Valley because of the tributaries which produce high runoff which causes the destructive floods entering the Rio Grande below the dam sites." Even if "international relations permit and funds [are] made available," said Fiock, "the first dams to be constructed will be as far down the Rio Grande as possible and still be above the Lower Rio Grande Valley." The USBR knew of two such sites: "the Salineño site for a dam and regulating reservoir and the El Jardine site for storage and flood control."[17]

Fiock then suggested that "there are no favorable sites between the El Jardine site and the canyons of the Big Bend." This meant that "possibly the Boquillas site or one even below that would be chosen if it is at all possible to find a satisfactory site on farther down the river." He hinted that "apparently the only reason there would be for consideration of the construction of more than one dam in the canyons of the Big Bend would be for the purpose of power development." Yet "the isolation of the territory from any large power market even if there was river discharge enough to generate any appreciable quantity of power," said Fiock, meant that "the chances of development of power possibilities are very remote indeed." Should that be the case, "dams could be constructed at each successive site which would back water to the dam next above and so on down the river through the entire canyon section of the Big Bend."[18]

The IBC's ambivalence about water projects in the Big Bend canyons led Maier to correspond with his superior in Washington, Conrad Wirth, about inclusion of this topic in the upcoming meetings with Mexican officials. Even though Maier had confidence that the Interior Department could block such projects, he told Wirth, "I want to have first-hand information as to just what the U.S. Reclamation Service and the International Boundary Commission down there really have had in mind." Maier had initiated his contact with the El Paso office of the USBR. "This had taken a little time," he told Wirth in explaining the lateness of his report on the October 5 meeting in El Paso with Mexican representatives. It also "has had to be handled carefully," Maier noted, "because we do not wish to 'scare' the Mexican officials away from the park idea."[19]

Soon thereafter, L. M. Lawson of the IBC contacted Maier to offer his thoughts on the Big Bend dam issue. Lawson's organization had "for some time been engaged in a study regarding the equitable uses of the waters of the Lower Rio Grande," said the US commissioner, and had "been active in the measurement of discharges of the main Rio Grande and tributaries." In recent years "extremely large flood flows and serious water shortages" throughout the length of the Rio Grande had raised "the question of flood control and conservation of water."[20]

In August 1935, President Roosevelt had signed legislation that gave the IBC authority to conduct technical and other investigations. These included ones concerning flood control, water resources, conservation, utilization of water, sanitation, prevention of pollution, channel rectification, stabilization, and other related matters on the international boundary. This had granted the IBC its access to the Big Bend area, though Lawson echoed the thoughts of the USBR when he told Maier, "The use of water, both in the United States and Mexico, above the Presidio Valley, which is the beginning of the Big Bend district, results in very little accumulation to the river from the upper Rio Grande." Records kept by the IBC "would indicate that about seventy percent of the Lower Rio Grande flow come from Mexican tributaries, with the remaining percentage from the Devils and Pecos Rivers of Texas."[21]

Lawson advised Maier that "while some flood control works are now being construction by the Commission on the Lower Rio Grande, others are planned in and below the Big Bend district." His agency had studied a number of dam sites with the view of developing storage and hydroelectric power. Mexico and the United States, Lawson conceded, "have not yet come to final agreement upon the equitable distribution of the international waters." The IBC commissioner also admitted, "Nor have final plans reached any definite form as to which storage site in the Big Bend district would be the most feasible and economical." Lawson assured Maier that "this decision . . . rests upon the joint determination of the undertaking." He then closed with the vague statement that "it can be assumed that at some future date plans will be carried out to some finality in taking advantage of the storage possibilities that exist between the canyon section of the Rio Grande in the Big Bend district."[22]

While planning for water projects worried Maier, he also had to oversee the details of the first major gathering in the twentieth century of Mexican and US officials on border issues. Less than two decades after the "raids" by Pancho Villa and the resultant Pershing expedition into Mexico, American and Mexican scientists, park officials, and diplomats agreed to assemble in El Paso. Even before this meeting on November 24, 1935, Maier coordinated a visit to Arizona by Daniel Galicia, Maynard Johnson, and Walter McDougall to accompany a US Biological Survey party in the King and Houserock Valley Refuge areas in Arizona. Their goal was consideration of the plans for the Ajo Mountain National Monument, later to become Organ Pipe Cactus National Monument. Galicia noted that this desert plant extended from southwestern Arizona to the Gulf of California. This shared ecosystem prompted calls for an international park on the Arizona-Mexico border similar to Big Bend.

Maier suggested to Wirth that this surge of interest by Mexican officials might be enhanced not only by the El Paso meeting. It also would be wise to extend invitations to Miguel Angel de Quevedo and other Mexican park officials to travel to Washington in January 1936 to attend the annual NPS superintendents' conference. "It occurs to me," wrote Maier, "that, after all, the final conference on the birth of the International Park should be considered rather an historic event."

In conjunction with the anticipated agreement between Mexico and the United States, Maier encouraged Wirth to extend the hand of friendship to the NPS's future partners at Big Bend. "This will not only impress them with the importance of what they are entering into," said Maier, "but should go a long ways towards assuring the success of the undertaking." In turn, the presence of Mexican park planners would "make a favorable impression on the National Park Superintendents and others attending this conference." Quevedo, Galicia, and their associates would thus represent the future of US-Mexico border relations in ways that no one could have anticipated even a decade earlier.[23]

Pursuant to this meeting, and the prior engagement in El Paso, Maier asked Johnson and McDougall for their thoughts on the boundaries for a Mexican park opposite Big Bend. The surveyors disappointed Maier, in that they had not traveled into the Mexican interior. In addition, said Johnson and McDougall, "we know of no one who has made a sufficient investigation of it to attempt a location of boundaries." CCC superintendent Robert D. Morgan did inform Maier that on July 4, he had entertained a Dr. Francisco Del Rio, who represented the governors of Coahuila and Chihuahua. Del Rio reported that the Mexican government was interested and would establish a park of such an area as would be in keeping with the one planned for the Big Bend. Morgan noted that Del Rio spent one day in the area, "but was not sufficiently familiar with it to make definite boundary recommendations."[24]

Johnson and McDougall did know that Galicia planned to go into the region for a preliminary survey and then to return later with a party of engineers and surveyors for a more thorough investigation. Galicia had indicated to them that he would make this trip after his survey of the international park at Ajo Mountain. For his part, the chief forester for the Republic of Mexico wrote to Maier on November 12 to indicate his support for collaboration with the United States. "I wish you'd know how glad I'm with it," said Galicia, "because we've found a probability to [e]stablish a[n] Inter-National Park in Punta Penasco, Sonora State, and game refuge along the border." He planned after the first of the year to visit the Boquillas area. "It would be very convenient for you and Mr. de Quevedo to [discuss] the matter over, on his [upcoming] visit to El Paso." Galicia then thanked Maier for sending him booklets on NPS units in the region, promising to devote time to discussing Big Bend and Punta Peñasco at the El Paso conference.[25]

As the international park meeting neared, NPS officials in Washington asked Mexican officials to visit other sites in the United States to observe how the park service operated. Arthur E. Demaray, acting NPS director, wrote to Juan Zinser, chief of the game division of the Departemento Forestal, Caza y Pesca, when he learned that Zinser had decided to travel to California after leaving the El Paso conference. "I hope very much," said Demaray, "that you will be able to visit some of our national parks on the way." This gesture emanated from "the recent resolutions of the Second General Assembly of the Pan American Institute of Geography and History urging park systems for other American countries."[26]

Demaray recommended the Grand Canyon "and some of the national monuments established to give protection to historic areas of great interest." In California, Zinser should see Sequoia and Yosemite National Parks. Then he should travel to San Francisco, where he would "find a group of [NPS] engineers and landscape architects who are fully conversant with park policy and operation." Finally, Demaray suggested contacting the California Fish and Game Commission, "the State organization with which Mexico has long cooperated in connection with fisheries off the coast of lower California." The acting director described "this outstanding conservation organization" as "typical of the machinery utilized by the states in enforcing regulations concerning fish and game in conserving natural resources." This effort by the NPS was well received by Zinser, whom Lane Simonian identifies as the member of Quevedo's staff who "established wildlife refuges, signed a migratory bird treaty with the United States, and fostered the establishment of hunting groups" in northern Mexico.[27]

When the historic day arrived, NPS and Mexican park officials demonstrated an eagerness for cooperation and partnership that overrode any concerns held by Maier about the details of an international park. Among the attendees from Mexico were Quevedo, Galicia, Zinser, Jose H. Serrano and Juan Thacker of Quevedo's staff, and Armando Santacruz Jr. of the IBC. Other Mexican representatives came from the states of Coahuila, Chihuahua, and Sonora (the last to discuss the Ajo Mountain park proposal). American officials included Maier; Frank Pinkley of the Southwestern National Monuments; Vincent Vandiver, regional geologist for the park service; Don A. Gilchrist, director of Region III of the US Biological Survey; and Charles E. Gillham, game management agent for the biological survey.

Maier reported to Wirth that "the primary purpose of the conference was to afford the Mexican representatives an opportunity for an official indication as to the extent of their participation in national park, monument, and wildlife undertakings immediately along the International Boundary." In so doing, "there was compiled a set of eight resolutions outlining preliminary policy covering the creation and administration of such areas along and extending over into both sides of the boundary."[28]

First on the agenda was the statement that "the Mexican Government accepts the suggestion of the United States Government for the creation of International Parks designed to include adjacent areas of outstanding scenic beauty on both sides of the International Boundary." From this would come "fostering of a closer understanding between the peoples of the two nations and inaugurating a joint effort for the conservation of natural resources." They saw as critical "the conservation of plants, animals and birds and of all such natural conditions." Each park unit "will be controlled by the proper Department of each Government, subject to joint Regulations to be agreed upon for the maintenance and conservation of the areas involved." Wildlife refuges would be an important feature of international park planning, with "regulations . . . to properly provide for the crossing of the Border by administrative forces as well as the wild life," while "peculiar and beautiful vegetation and outstanding geological phenomena" merited their own "National Reservations."[29]

Reflecting Quevedo's concerns for ecological zones shared by border towns, the conference resolved that "with a view to improving the esthetic and health conditions as well as for recreational value to the present communities along the Border[,] it is recommended that the two Governments cooperate in establishing forest plantations around these communities in both Countries." Finally, the attendees declared the need to make permanent the partnership forged in El Paso that day, with a joint commission created "to carry out at an early date the necessary investigations and surveys for the location of the areas to be included in the proposed International Parks, wild life Refuges, plant Reserves and forest plantations." They then called for another meeting in the Texas border city no later than January 15, 1936, with submission of their findings and recommendations to the leaders of their respective nations two months thereafter.[30]

Maier analyzed the tone and mood of this conference, finding much to commend. The NPS already had studied the American portion of suggested international park units at Big Bend, the Espuelos Mountains of Mexico and the Hatchet Mountains and Animas-Pelonicello areas of southwestern New Mexico and southeastern Arizona, and the proposed Organ Pipe Cactus National Monument (including the Rocky Point Area [Bahia Adair] of Mexico). The last site had garnered the support of Mexican park officials, who envisioned "a recreational area for fishing and bathing" that would be "accessible from the International-Pacific Highway leading from Mexico City and Guadalajara up the coast to Southern California."[31]

For Maier and his colleagues, the "only international park in which the National Park Service is, or is likely to be, interested in along the Boundary is the Big Bend." Maier liked Quevedo's suggestion of tree plantations at border communities, something that the forest, fish, and game chief had observed in his drive with NPS officials from Laredo to El Paso. Maier praised Quevedo for his "early outstanding record in the reforestation of land surrounding [Mexico City]" and agreed that "such undertakings will be highly worthy and could probably be carried out on our side under the extended CCC program." Southwestern National Monuments superintendent Frank Pinkley noted that each nation need not be bound by the designation given to an area, such as a wildlife refuge adjoining a national park, as "desirable ranges of scenery, fauna or flora, [should] be units rather than limited as at present to an arbitrary line."[32]

The NPS's Maier then offered his assessment of the mood of the attendees, describing that of the Mexican representatives as "earnest and enthusiastic." "Señor de Quevedo," said Maier, "although seventy, is a very energetic individual." Reiterating details of Quevedo's meeting in Washington in 1909 with Theodore Roosevelt and Gifford Pinchot, Maier noted that he also "is an honorary member of the Society of American Foresters." Quevedo informed Maier of "the legislation he now has in process of formation which will enable his Department to regulate and practically prohibit hunting along the entire Mexican-U.S. Boundary within a zone 150 kilometers [90 miles] south of the international line," a measure that Quevedo assured Maier "has already received the approval of Pres. Cardenas and the Cabinet."[33]

Maier then advised Quevedo on his itinerary of western US parks, hoping that he could see the Grand Canyon because of "a similar area in the State of Chihuahua which is also a mile in depth and which the Mexican government has under consideration as a national park [Copper Canyon in the Rio Conchos basin]." Quevedo did not have time to travel to Arizona, but "being primarily a forester," said Maier, "he desired above everything else to see the Sequoia."[34]

Most critical, however, were Quevedo's thoughts on Big Bend National Park. "The Mexican Government," Maier learned from Quevedo, "is prepared to prohibit all hunting on the Mexican side of the Big Bend at an early date." Quevedo also hoped that "the boundaries of the Mexican area shall be based upon biological as well as scenic considerations." While "the bulk of the land is in private ownership (large ranch holdings)," said Maier, "Quevedo stated definitely that he favors the undertaking of a program of land acquisition covering all lands within the boundaries to be proposed."[35]

Maier and Quevedo agreed that "this, of course, will be a long-term program." The American land-purchase program "will no doubt require several years for acquisition by the State of Texas," wrote Maier, "and just how rapid land acquisition by the Mexican Department will be, it is impossible now to [gauge]." Maier contended that "it is natural to assume that land acquisition may be more difficult for the Mexicans to effect than with us." Yet he saw hope in the suggestion by Daniel Galicia for "acquisition by exchange."[36]

With an eye toward accelerating the process of park planning, Maier suggested to his superiors in Washington that they select a small group to be assembled in Alpine on January 15 to spend some thirty days in the field. The Mexican government had named nine individuals to collaborate with the NPS, but Maier feared that "there is already danger of the party becoming unwieldy." He also noted that beyond Big Bend and Organ Pipe, "the remainder [of the suggested sites] are low in scenic and recreational values from a national park standpoint and should, perhaps, be set aside primarily for the conservation of their peculiar fauna and flora." The US Biological Survey could survey these areas in more detail, leaving the NPS-Mexico team to examine Big Bend and Organ Pipe.[37]

Policy makers in both the NPS and the Departemento Forestal, Caza y Pesca had much reason to celebrate in the first weeks of 1936, as the American secretary of state, Cordell Hull, announced on February 8 his appointments to the US Commission on International Parks. The list sounded like a who's who of natural resource agencies: Conrad Wirth, Roger Toll, Frank Pinkley, George Meléndez Wright, and Herbert Maier of the park service; L. M. Lawson of the IBC; and Ira H. Gabrielson of the forest service (replaced a week later by W. B. Bell). US representative Ewing Thomason anticipated the importance of this delegation's visit to Alpine in mid-February, and telegraphed Everett Townsend with the news of their impending arrival. "[I] am sure you and other citizens of Alpine appreciate [the] great importance [of] this visit," wired the El Paso congressman, "and what it means toward helping put over our program."[38]

Thomason made it clear to the "father of Big Bend" that he was "leaving nothing undone here [Washington] to get results and am sure you are doing same there." In particular, wrote the congressman, Townsend needed to know that Wirth "is *our friend*," and that "if Mexican authorities are strong for it [the international park] I will co-operate [*sic*]." Among Thomason's plans were "ideas for getting some money." He then counseled the former Brewster County sheriff, "This is big stuff and *we must* put it over."[39]

No one had to remind Townsend of the gravity of the moment as the US delegation stepped from the platform of the Alpine train station on February 17 and shook hands with the longtime park promoter. They and the Mexican commission members, among them such staunch advocates of international cooperation in natural resource conservation as Miguel Angel de Quevedo and Daniel Galicia, drove southward to the future national park and thence to the Rio Grande. Crossing the river at Boquillas, the commissioners drove into the Fronteriza Mountains before exchanging their vehicles for horses.

After some time in the area that one day would become the Maderas del Carmen Flora and Fauna Protected Area in Coahuila, the party resumed their automotive tour to what future park superintendent Ross Maxwell would call "several interesting native villages." Then the US and Mexican commissioners drove from Boquillas westward around the north face of the Chisos Mountains to the border town of Lajitas, fording the Rio Grande once more for the trip south into the state of Chihuahua to the historic community of San Carlos (the largest town in what would become in 1994 the Cañon de Santa Elena Flora and Fauna Protected Area).[40]

As the commissioners left the Big Bend area, they carried with them the radical idea to join the United States and Mexico in the creation of an international park where Mexican and American soldiers had clashed two decades before. Photographs of the commission's tour of the Coahuila and Chihuahua landscape published in the *Fort Worth Star-Telegram* revealed the sense of brotherhood and commitment shared by commission members. The historian John Jameson writes that the officials marveled at the differences across the river in Mexico, where "unlike the overgrazed American side, there was little evidence of erosion in Mexico, and the mountains were covered with virgin stands of pine trees, some as tall as sixty feet and three feet around the base."[41]

Then one of the most tragic events to strike Big Bend (not to mention the international park idea) occurred less than twenty-four hours after the commission dispersed: the deaths of Roger Toll and George Meléndez Wright in an auto accident. The two park service officials were en route from Big Bend to study the Arizona border park sites when a car veered into their lane on the old two-lane highway east of Deming, New Mexico. Richard Sellars, writing with the hindsight of six decades of history, would note in 1997 of the untimely deaths of Toll and Wright, "Although not fully apparent at the time, the loss of Wright's impressive leadership skills marked the beginning of the decline of [park service] science programs." Wright also had a personal interest in the success of the parks along the border, given his own Latino heritage and his ability to convey to the Mexican delegation the opportunity for cultural understanding that these parks could embody. It would be sixty years before the NPS and the government of Mexico would hold similar conversations at the highest levels about joining their two nations along the Rio Grande, and by then the memory of Toll and Wright's contributions had all but vanished.[42]

At the time, however, NPS officials and their Mexican counterparts expressed a determination to continue planning for the international park, using the deaths of Toll and Wright as an incentive. Yet the initiative had lost two of its most ardent advocates, a circumstance that all who wished for a joint park realized within days. Maier wrote to Juan Thacker, one of the Mexican commissioners from El Paso, on March 8 to review the planning to date. Maier reminded Thacker, "Upon my last visit in your office I had a conference with a man from Chihuahua who is interested in securing a nucleus herd of buffalo and elk for a club in the vicinity of Chihuahua in Mexico." The regional director of the ECW program had discussed the idea with Toll and Wright while on the inspection tour of the international park, telling Thacker, "Both of these gentlemen assured me that it will be possible to secure both elk and buffalo from the Yellowstone herds."[43]

Toll and Wright did caution Maier, "It will be highly advisable to consider the matter of undertaking the developing of herds of these species with a great deal of care and forethought." They knew that "in many cases living specimens supplied by wildlife refuge officials have proven a liability rather than an asset . . . since the undertaking of development of herds involves a great many scientific and practical considerations." Toll advised Maier that "the elk and buffalo indicated for distribution during the current year have all been pledged." Yet the Yellowstone superintendent believed that "it will be quite possible to secure specimens during the coming year."[44]

Then Maier revealed to Thacker the scale of the deaths of Toll and Wright for the park service: "Considering the fact that both of these fine men have been unfortunately removed from our midst, I suggest that the individual in charge of this undertaking . . . take up the matter directly with Mr. Ben Thompson . . . who is a wildlife expert, and who was assistant to Mr. George Wright."[45]

The death of Toll and Wright also had personal implications for park service officials engaged in the work of park planning in Texas and Mexico. Amid the correspondence that the park service's publicist, Leo McClatchy, handled that spring was a note from Mrs. Roger Toll, who resided in Denver while her husband traveled the West in search of new parks for the United States. Toll's widow noted that the *El Paso Times* had printed pictures of the international park survey. She wondered whether McClatchy would provide her with copies of the images that included her husband.

The NPS publicist could not locate any of the original pictures, as all of the negatives had been sent to the NPS headquarters in Washington. He did, however, have a clipping from the *Star-Telegram* where "Mr. Toll is seen helping to push the car out of a rut." Then, in a touching statement about the meaning of Toll's work to his peers within the NPS, McClatchy told his widow, "Though I had known Mr. Toll but a brief time, he was extremely courteous and helpful to me on the Big Bend trip, going out of his way to assist me in gathering information."[46]

Officials of the Department of Forestry, Game and Fish in Mexico sustained their own investment in the international park concept throughout the spring and summer of 1936, with the key representative, Daniel Galicia, soliciting of McClatchy any newspaper stories in the United States about the project. Writing in Spanish, Galicia referred in a March 25 letter to the process of "establicimiento del Parque Internacional 'Rio Bravo'" (establishment of the "Rio Bravo" International Park). Galicia then wrote to Wirth to thank the assistant NPS director "for all the courtesies shown me and the members of the Mexican Conference on the International Commission of Parks and Reserves." The Mexican forestry division chief was "very happy to know that you [Wirth] enjoyed the trip that we made in the sierra del Carmen, in the State of Coahuila, in order to establish the Mexican portion of the International Park of Peace between Mexico and the United States."[47]

He also wanted Wirth to know that "we are also working to gather all the necessary data on the formation of the National Park 'Rio Bravo' in Coahuila as part of the Big Bend in Texas." From this Galicia hoped that "soon we will be able to declare it a National Park although we are faced with legal difficulties insofar as the acquisition of the land is concerned." Galicia nonetheless anticipated "another International Conference," along with a visit from Wirth to Mexico "to show you some of the beautiful attractions which we have in my country." He then praised "the enthusiasm and patriotism of my superior Senor Ing. Miguel A. Quevedo," for "these places are now being converted into national parks."[48]

By late June, NPS officials had just begun to recoup the momentum on the international park interrupted by the deaths of Toll and Wright. Wirth discussed with park service director Arno Cammerer the need for another meeting with the IBC. "As you know," wrote Wirth, "after the terrible accident, things were rather left up in the air." Yet the assistant NPS director reminded Maier that "we did make arrangements insofar as the international park at Big Bend is concerned, to meet with the Mexican authorities this fall and go over their proposed boundaries."[49]

Wirth then asked the NPS's Region III director to contact officials in Mexico to see whether "they would have the material ready so as to be able to sit down and decide on the boundary lines and determine the final recommendations to be made to both Governments." Director Cammerer had planned to attend this gathering, said Wirth, who hoped that Maier could coordinate such a gathering in Mexico when the director also could meet with Texas officials regarding the bill to be placed before Lone Star lawmakers for the purchase of lands on the American side of the Rio Grande for Big Bend National Park.[50]

Maier reported back to Wirth that he had spoken with Santos Ibarra, the commission member charged with identification of the Mexican boundary location. From Ibarra Maier had learned that "it has been a little difficult to determine . . . just how they [Mexican officials] intend to acquire their portion of the land." Compounding this situation, wrote Maier, was that "of course their idea of setting up a National Park has been quite different from ours, for the most part, because funds are not available to purchase immense areas." This procedure Maier described to Wirth as "in some cases they declare an area a national park, although there are private holdings within it, and in such cases they limit destruction of all plant and animal life, but do not force such land owners that may be within the area to immediately give up the land."[51]

Yet Maier conceded that the Mexican commissioners "are thoroughly in sympathy with our ideals, and this contact with our National Park Service will probably eventually lead to the same general policies as ours." To strengthen this bond, Maier noted that "when we were in Mexico City a trip for the Mexican officials was planned which would bring them up into Yellowstone and other National Parks in August and September."[52]

In preparation for the fall gathering of the International Park Commission, Maier assigned J. T. Roberts, associate landscape architect for Region III, to join Galicia in Alpine to study "the problem of boundaries for the proposed park." When the two departed for the Rio Grande on September 2, Galicia informed Roberts that his instructions from Quevedo "were to limit the boundaries, as far as possible, to the forested area because of the very limited funds available for use in obtaining land for park purposes." Galicia and Roberts had to leave their vehicle at the river town of Boquillas, Texas, because "the Rio Bravo [was] on a 6 foot rise." Taking a truck from the Mexican village of Boquillas, the party traveled along "the eastern and northern extremities of the Fronteriza Mountains," finding that "the timbered lands were mainly above 1780 meters, or approximately 5300 feet."[53]

Roberts would report to Maier that "for this reason Sr. Galicia first proposed an eastern and northern boundary from Mesa de los Fresnos to Mesa de los Tremblores." From there, wrote Roberts, the boundary line would extend "to Pico Sentinel, then north, including only the face of what we know as Del Carmine, then to Stillman at the end of the Boquillas Canyon." Roberts believed that "this would be similar to establishing the boundaries of the Chisos Mountain area by running a line from Mule Ears to Castillon Peak to Elephant Mountain to Crown Mountain to Lost Mine Peak and so on."[54]

The problem for the NPS architect was that "in this no consideration was given to the wild life or scenic values." He informed Maier that "with some difficulties in conversation I presented these points as we traveled along, and it was finally determined that the park should include all the mountain areas and such adjacent land necessary for the protection of wild life," a decision that Roberts said "will include Pico Etereo."[55]

In order to redesign the Mexican portion of the international park, Roberts told the Region III director that "Sr. Galicia will recommend that the entire area within the original proposed boundaries be established as a game preserve, eliminating at once the value of the land for hunting." The NPS architect noted that Galicia "will then suggest that those owners within the boundaries of this area exchange their holdings for other excess forested areas now held by the Government." Roberts conceded that "the greatest trouble experienced by the department [of forestry, game and fish] is not with the native owners but with those owning 'The Club,' all of whom are citizens of the United States."[56]

Within the acreage owned by these foreigners, "the physical features," said Roberts, "may be described as very rugged, of volcanic origin and heavily timbered above 5300 feet." Among the species of timber were "Ponderosa pine,

Mexican white pine, cypress, and fir, probably pseudopseudo douglasii." Roberts further reported that "below 5000 feet there is a great variety of trees, the most predominant being the oak and wild cherry." He contended that "sufficient water is available, all year, at The Club for a large development, and it may be found that there is an ample supply below the mine."[57]

Roberts indicated that "there are many other places, such as the Laguna and Carbonera, for overnight facilities." This latter locale was, "on the present trails, a three hour horseback ride from 'Casa del Nino' and four hours from The Club . . . at an elevation of 2170 meters (6500 feet)." Roberts estimated that "the distance between The Club and Casa del Nino is 28 kilometers [16.8 miles]," and he claimed that "it is between those two points that the most beautiful scenery was found on this inspection trip."[58]

Other distinctive features included an area "above the laguna, which is about 5 kilometers [3 miles] north and east of Carbonera," which was called "Mesa Escondida where the largest timber of the mountains is found." Roberts also "found a cave described as being 'large enough to hide two hundred men and horses and with water convenient.'" The NPS architect then closed his report by noting that Galicia spoke less enthusiastically of "the eastern slope of the 'Del Carmine Mountains'—that is, the limestone uplift from Boquillas south." Roberts agreed that the area "is barren of trees and has no spectacular geological formations." He concurred in "Sr. Galicia's point of view [that] it is of no value as a National Park and is in fact of interest only as a wild life refuge."[59]

Galicia's caution reflected the sentiments of his supervisor in Mexico City, Quevedo. While dedicated to natural resource preservation, Quevedo also knew of the political and economic realities of life in Mexico that constrained the Cárdenas administration in its negotiations for an international park at Big Bend. As he prepared to attend the commission meeting in El Paso that fall, Quevedo advised Maier in September that he would accept NPS director Cammerer's invitation, "inasmuch as I have numerous problems I desire to clarify."[60]

American promoters of Big Bend National Park, however, saw only good fortune awaiting the deliberations of the international commission. Amon Carter's *Fort Worth Star-Telegram* trumpeted the windfall of publicity and tourism to come to the most isolated reaches of the Lone Star State. "Texans have a right to be enthusiastic about this development," declared the *Star-Telegram* on November 4, 1936, as "already the Big Bend park begins to take rank among the foremost on the national list." Carter's editors could hardly restrain themselves when calculating the benefits to accrue from the "millions of American holiday visitors" about to descend on the "last frontier."[61]

Echoing the prose of Walter Prescott Webb, the *Star-Telegram* reminded its readers that "great mountain ranges on both sides of the river, gigantic abysses, towering peaks and crashing streams complete the region's attractions to the sightseer." Then the paper noted that "the international aspect of the park project enlarges its possibilities to an infinite degree." If possible, "the area in Mexican territory has been even more remote, more inaccessible, than that on the Texas side." This led the *Star-Telegram* to claim that joining the two countries in a venue covering some 1.2 million acres in "an international park freely open to the public of both nations—a sort of free port of recreation and fraternization—is a notable project in international relations."[62]

Four days after Franklin Roosevelt achieved the most sweeping victory in modern times in a presidential election, the director of the NPS arrived in Texas in November 1936 for a series of meetings on Big Bend and the adjacent Mexican park initiative. Historians have noted the energy that surged through the FDR administration in the days and weeks after his capturing of 61 percent of the nation's popular vote, and all but 8 of the 535 electoral votes, for president. Roosevelt and his staff believed that the public had validated their measures for reform, economic recovery, and protection of the nation's natural and cultural resources.

Issues to be discussed at the El Paso gathering of federal officials from the United States and Mexico thus expanded to plans for reforestation along the border (a favorite of Quevedo) and a meeting of NPS officials and the National Park Committee of the West Texas Chamber of Commerce. Headed by Sul Ross's Howard Morelock, the entourage wanted to remind the park service of their own work on the acquisition of land for Big Bend, and of the need to highlight statistics about travel and economic development akin to those of the *Star-Telegram*'s news story of the previous Sunday.[63]

When the international commission on parks and reserves came to order on November 9, the attendees represented the highest levels of natural resource management in both the United States and Mexico. NPS director Cammerer joined with his top assistants, Wirth and George Moskey, Maier of Region III, and Frank Pinkley, the longtime superintendent of Casa Grande National Monument, who also served as the coordinator for the Southwestern National Monuments network. Maier had invited his top assistant, Milton McColm, along with his chief biologist, Walter McDougall; Merel Sager of the surveying parties; and Everett Townsend, representing local interests in the international park initiative.

Daniel Galicia led the Mexican contingent, which included game division chief Juan Zinser, Juan F. Trevino, and Juan Thacker. The IBC likewise sent its highest-ranking members from both countries: L. M. Lawson for the United States and Joaquin C. Bustamante, the IBC's consulting engineer from Mexico. The NPS played for the commission a reel of film on the Big Bend region, followed by a presentation from Maier on the criteria used by both nations to determine the boundary lines of the international park.[64]

It soon became clear to the attendees that the demarcations of the joint initiative would be the most challenging task before them. Maier reported after the meeting that "it will be highly desirable that the east and west boundaries of the Mexican area, as nearly as practical, coincide with those of the Texas area where they join the Rio Grande." The commission members thus "agreed that the point where the Mexican boundary line will touch the River on the west should be the confluence of San Antonio Creek with the Rio Grande." The regional director then noted that "this will throw the Lajitas Crossing and its road for mining and cattle outside the area, which is desirable."[65]

Maier conceded that "while the eastern boundary of the Mexican area will contact the Rio Grande at the present proposed point," he realized that "the American line will be swung somewhat to the north so as to strike the Rio Grande at Los Vegas de Silwell [Las Vegas de Stillwell]." The attendees further decided that "probably only one vehicle bridge across the Rio Grande within the international park, crossing to the Mexican side, will be necessary and advisable for administrative and policing purposes." The future park management would have to consider, however, "that visitors should have free access to both sides, any Customs regulations being taken care of at the checking stations leading into each area." Then Director Cammerer agreed that "it will probably be best not to run a main park road along the Rio Grande on the American side." Instead, the NPS director believed that "this should be left free for open wildlife range down to and across the border."[66]

After a luncheon hosted by the El Paso Chamber of Commerce, the commission heard from the IBC's Lawson, who showed them "very useful aerial surveys and aerial photographs of the Rio Grande." The group then revisited the boundary question, agreeing that "the present crossing at Boquillas for cattle and the mines could continue to operate even after the park is established." A primary consideration was the location of the road from Boquillas to Marathon along the eastern edge of the proposed Big Bend National Park. Several attendees noted that "mining activity on the Mexican side of the Rio Grande is almost extinct and the moving of cattle to the U.S. side is now of little consequence."[67]

Referring to "the small ranches now operating along both sides of the Rio Grande," Maier reported that "it was felt that the two governments, even though acquiring the land, might well extend permits to the owners of the land to remain for the remainder of their lifetimes." Then the regional director observed that "the boundaries of the American and Mexican side were corrected on the map by Daniel Galicia and Merel Sager and new photostats struck off and copies distributed to both delegations for future guidance."[68]

Following the discussions of boundaries and their locations, Conrad Wirth "suggested that on the basis of these lines the President of each country should be approached by the respective Departments and the two Presidents could then make final arrangements for the international aspects and proclamations." One detail that might hinder such collaboration was addressed by Lawson, who "discussed the possible hydrographic considerations along the Rio Grande within, above and below the area in which it [the IBC] and the U.S. Bureau of Reclamation may in the future be interested." Lawson led the commission to believe that "no major hydrographic project along the Rio Grande within the proposed area is now being considered."[69]

Yet several commission members had heard that "there may be a storage reservoir established immediately below the eastern U.S. boundary [of Big Bend]." Maier added in his report that "the present Irrigation Project on the Mexican side along the Conchos River, running into the Rio Grande above the area, may in time consume the major part of the water at present flowing into the Rio Grande proper below this point and through the proposed park," a point that the attendees agreed was "of marked importance." The El Paso conferees concluded, however, "that once the international park is established an adjustment in the operation of the Conchos River irrigation project may be effected by the Mexican government so as to prevent this threatened consumption of the main source of Rio Grande water within the park area."[70]

For promoters of Big Bend National Park, the good news from El Paso coincided with their campaign to lobby the Texas legislature in January 1937 for funds to purchase the private land in Brewster County needed for the park. Milton McColm wrote to Arthur Brisbane of the King Features Syndicate in New York City, to encourage the national journalist to "comment in your column 'TODAY,' on the proposed Big Bend International Park that would link 788,000 acres in Texas . . . to approximately 400,000 acres on the opposite side of the Rio Grande, in the Mexican States of Chihuahua and Coahuila." McColm noted that plans now called for two separate national parks, each "under the supervision of its respective government." Texas thus would have its first NPS unit, while "the International Park, it is believed, would tend to cement existing friendly relations between the two nations."[71]

This latter point, McColm hoped, would appeal to Brisbane's nationwide readership. "Director Arno B. Cammerer . . . has stated," wrote McColm, "that the establishment of such an international park, dedicated to Peace, in which the rank and file of both nations may freely mingle on both sides of the international boundary in their hours of leisure and recreation, and unrestricted by customs and similar regulations, may set an example to other nations." Speaking as if Cammerer's words soon would come to fruition, McColm concluded that the initiative "marks an outstanding step in the recreational field."[72]

McColm's solicitation of Brisbane's support indicated the broad level of interest that the park service hoped to reach with its publicity on the international park. Another approach that the NPS took was to endorse the concept in an article in the December 1936 issue of the journal *American Forest*. The Mexican Department of Forestry, Game and Fish then reprinted the story in Spanish as "El Parque de la Paz de Mexico." This allowed Mexicans to read for the first time in a national publication of the wonders of the proposed international park in Coahuila and Chihuahua, complete with photographs from the February 1936 journey of US and Mexican members of the International Park Commission.[73]

Howard Morelock wasted little time in capitalizing on this new mood of cooperation, contacting Texas state representative R. A. Bandeen with "a tentative draft of a resolution covering the 'Good Will Trip' to Old Mexico." The Sul Ross president wanted to take a group of state lawmakers to Mexico to impress upon them the sincerity of the Mexican government. To strengthen his case, Morelock asked Everett Townsend to review the proposal, which the longtime park advocate did in language revealing the delicate nature of negotiations behind the optimistic public pronouncements.[74]

Townsend cautioned Morelock to avoid use of the term "international park" without references to the specific control that each nation would have over its territory. "We want to breathe as much peace and good-will as possible throughout the whole document," wrote Townsend. He also wanted the Sul Ross president to emphasize that the trip to Mexico "would be for the consummation of this great International Peace Park or play-ground—the first thing of the kind ever attempted between non-related nations." Yet Townsend found himself in the unlikely position of correcting Morelock over the tone of the resolution. "I just know that you can do better than the sample that I have," he wrote. "You must remember that those people South of the Rio Grande love a lot of flowery language," Townsend concluded, "and of course, the Resolution will be made public down there, and we want it to please them as much as possible."[75]

While publicity circulated nationwide in favor of the international park idea, Mexican and US commissioners in April 1937 addressed the boundary issue in separate surveys. A problem soon arose when IBC and NPS officials realized that the eastern and western limits of the international park did not intersect. J. W. Ayres of the Region III office learned when he arrived in El Paso that neither the US nor the Mexican IBC agents had copies of the maps corrected the previous November by Daniel Galicia and Merel Sager. Ayers did report to Maier on April 16 that "Lawson's mosaic map has pencil cross at approximate location to which Bustamante has agreed." He then noted that the American IBC surveyors would travel to Big Bend "to establish a mark at each point consisting of metal disk cemented in rock with six foot wooden monument painted aluminum over it."[76]

The IBC's Lawson wanted these markers "located for latitude and longitude by stellar observation and later tied into existing triangulation system." Ayers met with Lawson's crew in Terlingua, proceeding to the CCC camp in the Chisos Mountains before spending a week on the Rio Grande. Upon completion of their work, the western boundary markers had been placed at latitude 29°14'48", longitude 103°40'17", while the eastern marker was placed at latitude 29°22'09", longitude 102°50'47".[77]

Marking the parameters of an international park proved easier than convincing Texas legislators to fund the acquisition of land on the American side for their state's portion of this historic initiative. As word filtered down to Mexico in June 1937 that Texas governor James Allred might veto the Big Bend appropriation of $750,000, Herbert Maier decided to enlist the aid of Mexican officials engaged in the international park process. Pierre de L. Boal, chargé d'affaires for the US embassy in Mexico City, contacted Secretary of State Cordell Hull on June 7 to advise him of a conversation that had taken place that day between himself and Daniel Galicia. Maier had asked Galicia to contact US ambassador Josephus Daniels for a letter to Governor Allred in support of the bill, adding the benefit of the international park to the larger scope of the Texas governor's action.[78]

Galicia's supervisor, Miguel Angel de Quevedo, also acceded to Maier's request for Mexican support, by writing Boal on June 7. "I beg to inform you," Quevedo told the American official, that "the establishment of the Sierra del Carmen National Park in the States of Coahuila and Chihuahua contiguous to the Big Bend National Park in the State of Texas having been approved in principle by the President of the Republic, these two parks to be combined, at the suggestion of the American Government, into an International Peace Park—the Matter now awaits the conclusion of topographical studies now being made, and the drafting of the (Presidential) Resolution making this area a National Park."[79]

Given the advanced status of study, said Quevedo, he hoped that Boal would ask the American ambassador, Daniels, "to lend his valuable cooperation in asking the Governor of the State of Texas to approve the appropriation" of the funds for Big Bend. Daniels, well liked by the Mexican people for his understanding of their culture and historical realities, and identified by Maier as having a "personal interest in the project," had no time to influence Allred before his veto of the Big Bend bill. Daniels, however, did meet in Washington with NPS director Cammerer to voice his support of the park, and to "hope that it is only delayed" by Allred's rejection of the funding measure.[80]

Solicitation of Mexican support for the Big Bend funding bill prompted Quevedo and his department to publish in *El Diario Official* an *acuerdo* ("accord" or agreement) about national parks in Mexico. Boal sent a copy to the NPS in Washington, as he believed "that this order may have some relation to the establishment and protection of the International Park around the Big Bend area of Texas." Drafted on April 28, signed by President Lázaro Cárdenas; Cabino

Vasquez, chief of the Agrarian Department; and Quevedo, but not printed until June 7 (at the height of the lobbying campaign against Allred's veto), the *acuerdo* declared "unaffectable the National Parks in the matter of ejidial dotations and restitutions."[81]

Recognizing the need to preserve Mexico's forests to avoid erosion, and because "the country requires places or spots where nature appears in its wild state, as living and real examples of what virgin forests and wild fauna are in their primitive state," the Mexican federal government "considers it essential to submit [national parks] to a special system of control (*regimen especial*)." This process would be in addition to "issuing measures tending to insure the utilization (*aprovechamiento*) of the grasses, dead wood and other products (*demas esquilmos*) which neither harm nor destroy those parks, for the exclusive benefit of the ejidos or nuclei of rural population immediately adjacent to them."[82]

To explain the meaning of this paradigm shift in Mexican natural resource policy, the American embassy in Mexico City drafted a statement for officials in Washington. William P. Bowen of the embassy staff suggested that "this provision appears to be a withdrawal of Mexican Federally owned lands of national park character from the right of acquisition by the Mexican peasant under . . . both the Agrarian and idle land laws, and a regulation of the use of certain products of the areas of national park character."[83]

Bowen then asked his Mexican counterparts to explain the history of their country's land laws, so as to place the June 7 *acuerdo* in perspective. His synopsis for State Department officials revealed the painful legacy of the Porfiriato (1880–1910), "during which foreigners and foreign capital were given every privilege in Mexico" by the regime of Porfirio Díaz. After the revolt in 1910, "men of Indian or Mexican blood came into power," followed by "a great wave of nationalism with the slogan 'Mexico for Mexicans'—Mexicans being the Indian population of the country." Bowen wrote that the task of land reform for the revolutionaries was daunting, in that "many of [the Spanish-era] haciendas were of unbelievable size, measured in miles rather than acres, and in many instances were held by absentee landlords." This meant that "the Indian populations of these plantations had been reduced to serfdom and virtual slavery."[84]

Of significance to American policy makers, wrote Bowen, was the fact that "the coming to power of the Mexican, the advance of socialism, and the cupidity of the politician gave rise to the theory that the Spanish landlord, just as Americans, Germans, etc., were aliens and that they had despoiled the Indian of his rights." This concept held "that the land rightfully belonged to the peasants." In "working on that theory," said the American embassy official, "a great number of the vast estates were confiscated by the State—depending, I was told, upon which side of the political fence the owner stood." In so doing, "title was by decree vested in the State, [and] bonds, in an amount which the Government found as due the divested owners, were issued to the landlords."[85]

At this juncture "the former peasant made application to the Government for a parcel of land for which he was to make stipulated annual payments, which payments were to retire the bonds held by the former landowner." Bowen compared this process to "the settlement of the Irish Land Question," and "the system was called restitution of the land to the Indians."[86]

The most challenging issue of the *acuerdo* remained the selection of lands for national park status. Bowen admitted, "I have no knowledge of the idle land laws, but it seems logical that they would be laws relating to lands in Government ownership that have not been 'restored' to the Indians." He also found that "there is no English word 'unaffectable,' but in a breakdown of that coinage, we would get 'not capable of being affected.'" The term *ejido* had a more straightforward meaning ("a public common held by a pueblo or the like"). As to the term "dotation," Bowen claimed that it was "an [endorsement] or the giving of funds (in this case lands) to a public institution." The embassy official read this section "to mean that those areas which have been set aside as national parks, are removed, by this order, from the provisions of the laws governing the endowment of villages with lands for commons." In addition, said Bowen, such status meant "reserving them from the provisions of the laws governing restitution of lands to the peon—that is, they are not to be used for either purpose."[87]

In the case of proposed national parks, Bowen read the language of the *acuerdo* to prohibit release of such lands wherever a park was being surveyed. He then closed with an explanation of the language permitting local landowners to use the natural resources of future national parks. Bowen believed that "the provision in this order is to require that before attempting to use the products they must first consult the Agrarian Department, to determine whether such use will harm or destroy the park, and to obtain permission for such use."[88]

The fall of 1937 was a critical period for Mexico, the United States, and the fate of the international park. As the Texas legislature would not reconvene for another eighteen months, the issue of land acquisition on the American side of the Rio Grande looked unpromising. In Mexico, workers in American-owned oil fields went on strike demanding higher wages; a circumstance that led the following March to the bold move by the Cárdenas administration to nationalize all oil production in Mexico (and endanger both the "Good Neighbor" policy and the international park). Yet proponents of Texas's first national park persisted in their efforts to link the two nations by means of publicity and news coverage.

One intriguing moment in this campaign occurred in October, when Leland D. Case, editor of the *Rotarian*, the magazine of Rotary International, wrote to Leo McClatchy upon receiving word of the international park initiative in the Southwest. Six decades later, Rotary International would campaign aggressively for creation of a park between Mexico and the United States like that of the Waterton-Glacier International Peace Park, an initiative that Rotary had orchestrated in 1932. Rotary had expressed no interest in the Big Bend idea when developing the Canadian-American park, and Case revealed his ignorance of this oversight when he asked McClatchy, "Are there any other international parks in which the United States is concerned . . . ?"[89]

Case had planned an issue of the *Rotarian* devoted to "International Peace Monuments on national boundaries," and McClatchy revealed no sense of irony in his reply. The Region III publicist noted that the "International Peace Gardens" existed on the border between North Dakota and Canada, although this was "strictly a State Park, and there is no international angle."[90]

More appealing to Rotary, said McClatchy, was Big Bend, which "would merge areas occupied by two different races—people with different languages and different customs." The NPS official thought that this "would be a big step in the direction toward which Rotary points—the promotion of international good will." In addition, he told Case, "it would lead generally to a better understanding between Mexico and the United States, and it should tend to cement the existing friendships between those two countries." It was McClatchy's hope that the *Rotarian* would focus on Big Bend. They would be grateful if Case folded that story into a larger narrative about borders in general and their parks for peace.[91]

McClatchy could not know that the last official action taken by either government to ensure creation of the international park occurred on October 16, 1937. On that date, the government of Mexico accepted the boundary markers on the south side of the Rio Grande across from the American markers. Overshadowing the dreams of park advocates was the deterioration of relations between Mexico and the United States, in addition to the looming crisis in Europe that would explode in September 1939 as World War II. Friedrich Schuler writes in *Mexico between Hitler and Roosevelt: Mexican Foreign Relations in the Age of Lazaro Cardenas, 1934–1940* (1998) that "whereas 'experimentation' had been the central paradigm for the period between 1934 and 1936, by 1937 the new central theme would be 'survival.'" The Mexican economy had not improved materially with three years of *Cardenismo*, even as the American economy softened after the first term of the Roosevelt New Deal.[92]

Schuler contends that Secretary of State Cordell Hull "saw Mexico's crisis as an opportunity to extract concessions from Mexico first and help the southern neighbors later." Then, in the months after the nationalization of foreign oil interests, says Schuler, "even the staunchest Cardenas supporters were rethinking their personal commitment when the government failed to pay wages, left rural banks unfunded, and did not stop the rise in food costs." Michael Meyer and William Sherman elaborate on this challenge to Mexico and America by noting that "many United States newspapers expressed outrage, and not a few politicians called for intervention to head off a Communist conspiracy on the very borders of the United States."[93]

No better statement of the chilling effect of oil nationalization on the international park could be found than the cryptic letter of November 21, 1938, from Conrad Wirth to NPS director Cammerer. "There are no new developments in connection with the Mexican side of the proposed park," Wirth reported, other than the approval by both nations of the boundary markers. Yet the NPS could not report to Mexican officials any success in the campaign to raise $1.5 million in private funds for land acquisition, nor in the effort to revive the vetoed Texas legislation for state purchase of the future Big Bend National Park.[94]

Then a minor controversy arose in 1939 when NPS planners discovered that they had no official measurement of the Mexican portion of the international park. Ross Maxwell, the junior geologist for the NPS's Region III, turned to Everett Townsend for help in determining where the Mexican and US officials had traveled in search of boundary sites. When the surveying parties had gone to the South Rim, wrote Maxwell, "Sr. Daniel Galicia asked Mr. Townsend to point out certain landmarks in Mexico that had been selected by the Mexican Government as points of boundary for the park." Relying on Townsend's vast knowledge of the border region, Galicia and his Mexican colleagues sketched out an area of some nine hundred thousand acres that would constitute the southern portion of the international park.[95]

Once the park service learned of the actual dimensions of the Mexican land base, it discovered a discrepancy in the eastern markers for both countries. Wirth informed Region III officials that their reliance on the drawings made at the 1936 El Paso conference by Daniel Galicia had not been followed carefully. He had determined that "the eastern Mexican boundary coming to the Rio Grande at Rancho Stillwell on a tangent from the [promontory] called Pico Eterea" should be relocated "four miles north opposite the mouth of Stillwell Creek." Wirth suggested that Galicia had relied on maps that did not include Stillwell Creek, and concluded that "he inadvertently drew the line to Rancho Stillwell believing it to be at the mouth of Stillwell Creek."[96]

At the behest of the NPS assistant director, junior geologist Ross Maxwell reported that "the apparent misunderstanding as to the erection of monuments near the Rio Grande marking the eastern limits of the Big Bend International Park Project in Mexico and Texas appear to have developed because of the questionable location of the Stillwell ranch." Maxwell's study found that "the Stillwells apparently ranched temporarily anywhere in southern Brewster County, Texas and the adjacent parts of Mexico where they could find grass and water."

This resulted in "old Stillwell ranches at several localities in that area." In particular, said the geologist, "two Stillwell ranches are indicated on the U.S. Geol. Survey Topographic map, the Chisos Mountains quadrangle, within the proposed park," while "several sites were used by the [Stillwells] that are not included in the present proposed boundary."[97]

Upon closer examination of both sides of the river, Maxwell learned that there were as many as three Stillwell cow camps in Mexico, and that there was a Stillwell Crossing not related to Stillwell Creek's entry into the Rio Grande. Maxwell reported to Maier that "the Mexican officials are probably correct in erecting their monument at the Stillwell ranch and we are possibly also correct in placing our monument opposite another of the Stillwell cow camps."[98]

The NPS geologist had more trouble with the designation of the eastern boundary of Big Bend at the mouth of Heath Creek. Calling this location "ambiguous," Maxwell claimed that "the Chisos Mountains quadrangle [map] shows that the drainage designated as Heath Creek separates into about one dozen streams after it passes through Hubert Ridge." Whereas the western branch of Heath Creek entered the river more than one mile above the present boundary marker, Maxwell preferred to locate the monument closer to Boquillas Canyon (where "the lower Heath Creek drainage . . . is approximately correct").[99]

Maxwell then suggested another issue for NPS planners: whether "we should move our monument or convince the Mexican officials that they should move [theirs]." He reported to Maier that "the present location of our monument and the eastern park boundary as described by the new state law provides for a buffer strip at the mouth of Boquillas Canyon which is the chief scenic feature in the area." At present the boundary did not include Stillwell Crossing, "a historical site that was used as a route of travel across the Rio Grande by the Indians, the early Spaniards, and the early Anglo-Americans." By moving downriver to the Mexican marker site, this crossing would be part of any new park land. In addition, Maxwell surmised that "if there should be a road built along the eastern side of the Sierra del Carmen highland the Stillwell crossing would probably be [the] best place to cross the Rio Grande."[100]

Maxwell had concerns as well about the language of the new Texas legislation on Big Bend that called for location of the US boundary across the river from the Mexican marker. Should the NPS adopt this site, said the geologist, "the Big Bend National Park (proposed) would then include virtually all of the Texas portion of the Sierra del Carmen (Dead Horse Mountains)." The park service would acquire "the remainder of the backbone ridge of the Sierra del Carmen highland, Margaret Basin, and the most of Big Brushy Canyon."[101]

Unfortunately for Maxwell, "this area does not include any important scenic or geological features that are not virtually duplicated in that portion of the

Sierra del Carmen already . . . in the park area." The geologist believed that "it is doubtful if it contains any additional wildlife," and as for cultural resource value, "I know nothing about the Archaeology, but I suspect that it is too far from water to be important." Yet Maxwell recognized "a few points that may favor this strip to the park area." One of these was that "the land is not worth much for grazing." In addition, "the difficulties of a boundary survey and a boundary fence will be greatly reduced by shifting the boundary eastward to the flank of the highland belt."[102]

Finally, said Maxwell, "Margaret Basin and Big Brushy Canyon are possible sites for the proposed Longhorn Cattle ranch." The geologist then recommended that Maier review the maps drafted by the US Army Corps of Engineers and the US Geological Survey, and identify "a representative of the National Park Service to meet with Sr. [Galicia] at Stillwell Crossing (Las Vegas to some) and decide in the field on a satisfactory location for both U.S. and Mexican Rio Grande markers."[103]

Maxwell's advice on the international park boundaries appealed to NPS officials, both in the regional office in Santa Fe and at the national headquarters in Washington. Herbert Maier informed the director that attendees of the International Park Commission conference in El Paso had been shown maps that did not locate the eastern park boundary to "include all of the horizon, there being several high points on the Del Carmen crest which would distinctly fall outside the park." Language in the Texas land purchase bill called for acquisition of up to 1 million acres of park land, instead of the projected 788,000 acres defined in the 1935 congressional act.[104]

Arthur E. Demaray, acting NPS director, reviewed the reports of Maxwell and Maier, and noted that "the boundary change suggested in your memorandum of May 27 would add approximately 50,000 acres to the Big Bend National Park Project." As to Maxwell's suggestion for a meeting with Daniel Galicia, Demaray believed that "it may not be necessary to meet the Mexican officials on the ground since it may be possible to agree on the proper location of the boundary markers without further field work."[105]

Maier agreed, deciding to seek the advice of his regional geologist, Charles Gould. "The line should run from Sue Peaks to a point opposite the Mexican marker at the mouth of Stillwell Creek," said the Region III director. He also noted that "since a CCC camp has been approved for the Big Bend for the 14th Period, it probably will be most practical to survey and establish the marker on the American side after the camp has been occupied and a survey party is available." Maier would include the additional fifty thousand acres that this boundary change would affect, as "investigation during the past two years has shown that the point selected at Sue Peaks throws the boundary inside the horizon and leaves out the very valuable area, both scenically and geologically, known as Margaret Basin."[106]

Maier advised against informing Texas officials of this decision. Instead, he told the NPS director, "after the success of the fund-raising campaign can be better gauged, it may be well to take a party including certain important Texas individuals into this area and have them render an opinion so that the suggestion, if it is adopted, will come from them." In like manner, Maier declined Maxwell's suggestion to invite Mexican officials to review the boundary markers on-site. The NPS regional office had agreed to move the American marker downstream to coincide with that of Mexico, and Galicia and his staff "will be advised of the new location of the American marker when same has been accurately located."[107]

Maier and his associates had little clue when they reviewed the boundary-marker issue in early August 1939 that three weeks later the world (and Big Bend) would change forever. The German invasion of the European nation of Poland, while thousands of miles removed from the canyons and cliffs of the Rio Grande, would mobilize the US government and shift the emphasis from the social welfare programs of the New Deal to military preparedness.

For Mexico, the effect would be similar, if not on the scale of American industrial production. Schuler writes that "suddenly, the U.S.-Mexican border became the southern front of U.S. territory that required protection and defense against a possible Axis invasion." Within thirty days of German expansion into Eastern Europe, says Schuler, "the absence of a viable Mexican air force and a national Mexican air-defense system motivated U.S. military planners to take over the defense of Mexico." This blend of American interventionism and economic centralization for the war effort rendered obsolete any plans for an international park far from the capitals of Washington and Mexico City.[108]

Lane Simonian defines the implications of the wartime emergency for natural resource preservation, and for Miguel Angel de Quevedo's department. "With the push for heavy industrialization that began during the 1940s," he writes, "conservation ceased to be a concern among most high-level government officials." Simonian believes that "only a few retained Quevedo's conviction that forests should be protected for their biological value."[109]

The final blow came in the fall of 1940, when outgoing president Cárdenas abolished Quevedo's department and scattered his staff to other agencies like the Agrarian Department. It had not helped, says Simonian, that "Quevedo did not favor Cardenas's land reform program because he believed the peasants would expand their fields at the expense of the forests." Meyer and Sherman add that Cárdenas's "last two years were characterized by severe economic difficulty." Food prices in 1940 were nearly 50 percent higher than when Cárdenas took office, wealthy Mexicans refused to invest in the Mexican economy, and foreign capitalists looked elsewhere for lucrative investment fields. Schuler summarizes these complex forces by concluding, "As far as Mexican foreign relations were concerned,

Mexican history between 1934 and 1940 was a grand dialogue between the domestic push for capitalist economic development and the reverberations of international war."[110]

Hindsight suggests that the two nations had their best chance to make history at Big Bend in the tumultuous days of the 1930s. The momentum for creation of an international park would not return until the last decade of the twentieth century, when Big Bend's first Hispanic superintendent, José Cisneros, would build on the work of the preceding six decades and make the international relationship a cornerstone of his leadership. More typical of the desultory nature of the partnership between Mexico and the United States were the events of 1940, such as those outlined in a memorandum of George L. Collins, acting chief of the park service's land planning division, to Conrad Wirth. The assistant director was to meet with the new interior undersecretary, Alvin Wirtz, and Big Bend was one of the agenda items.

Summarizing the work of the NPS and Mexican officials since the heady days of 1935–1936, Collins could only report, "Aside from evidence of considerable interest in the project on the part of the Mexican officials, nothing is known as to what progress has been made toward the establishment of the Mexican national park." Wirth's supervisors likewise had to temper the enthusiasm first displayed by Harold Ickes for the international park by 1940, as seen in correspondence between the acting secretary and Cordell Hull. The secretary of state had received a letter from Albert W. Dorgan of Castolon, "who proposes the creation of a Pan American Peace Park in the Big Bend section of Texas." The interior official apologized for not being able to accommodate Dorgan's wishes, as "the immediate problem is that of land acquisition."[111]

Horace W. Morelock, the son of the Sul Ross president, tried to fashion a new paradigm for the international park in a letter of August 10, 1940, to Ickes. The younger Morelock had read a story in a recent issue of the *Saturday Evening Post* in which critics of the interior secretary had disparaged his efforts to expand the acreage of the Cascade Mountains National Park and Olympic National Park in the state of Washington. Praising Ickes as "not a man to let a minority opinion prevail against your own good judgment," Morelock nonetheless worried: "Is it possible that you are overlooking a far better bet in Texas?" The Austin resident cautioned Ickes that "right now the burning issue before our people is that of self-defense." Only "slightly less important," said the park advocate, was "continental solidarity."[112]

Citing a recent trip of Cordell Hull to Cuba, Morelock claimed that "those people lying south of the Rio Grande are willing to meet us half way if we will only extend the hand of friendship to them." He humbly declared, "In my opinion the establishment of the BIG BEND INTERNATIONAL PEACE PARK on the

Texas-Mexican border would do much to win the friendship of Mexico and other Latin American nations." In so doing, said the observer of his father's efforts to create a national park in Brewster County, "we are giving all, asking nothing," offering "a gesture motivated by no material or monetary motives."[113]

Morelock then focused on Texas's own problems with Big Bend, which he hoped that Ickes could cure with such a proclamation. "The state wide drive to raise funds for this park," said Morelock, "has been delayed for many reasons, principally because of the war scare." He reminded the interior secretary, "Your department seems to have established the general rule that the Federal Government will not furnish funds to pay for national park acreage." Yet Morelock believed that Interior "could well afford to appropriate one million dollars for the purchase of this park site, and its returns in good will and friendship would bring more gains to this country than all the Pan-American conferences ever held."[114]

Echoing the prose of his father, Morelock appealed to Ickes's sense of history (if not his vanity) by commenting, "That American statesman who is foresighted enough to put this project through to completion will find that his name was 'not writ in water' but in letters of everlasting bronze." After a decade of negotiations, surveys, meetings, and publicity, Morelock subconsciously revealed the lost momentum of the international park initiative when he pleaded with Ickes, "Why not put your shoulder to the wheel?"[115]

A year after the onset of World War II, the Interior Department could not offer Morelock (or anyone else advocating creation of Big Bend National Park) the hope of joining Mexico and the United States in a park for peace. Undersecretary Wirtz spoke for Ickes when he told Morelock, "I believe that the State of Texas could make no more significant contribution to the solidarity of the Americas than by doing its share toward the establishment of this international park now."[116]

The most striking indication of the change of attitude forged by war came in December 1940. Walter McDougall, chief biologist for Region III, arrived in Alpine to learn that "three Mexican officials were in town and wished to spend the next two days in the Big Bend area." The party, consisting of J. Pedrero Cordova, the Mexican commissioner for the IBC; Joaquin Bustamante, the IBC's consulting engineer; and their translator, W. C. de Partearroy, had requested the assistance of Everett Townsend, whose ill health forced him to decline their offer. As the biologist had the best perspective on park issues, McDougall accompanied the Mexican officials to the Chisos basin and the canyons of Santa Eleña, Mariscal, and Boquillas. The NPS biologist noted that "while their trip prevented me from doing most of the things I had planned doing in the Big Bend, I think it was well worthwhile to change my plans in order to accompany them."[117]

McDougall then warned Region III director Minor Tillotson of the new order of Mexican priorities in the Big Bend region. "The only unpalatable thing about the trip," he reported, "was the fact that the Mexican gentlemen were most interested in the canyons because of the possibility of building dams in them." After six years of discussions, meetings, conferences, and surveys, McDougall was surprised to discover that they did not know that "the Park Service does not want any such dams." The biologist concluded in his report to the Region III office, "I did not tell them this, however, since I saw no reason why I should discuss matters of policy with them."[118]

This posture toward Mexican involvement in Big Bend would prevail for decades after 1940. Yet the Mexican officials who had appeared on Townsend's doorstep that winter faced their own agenda of economic development and international diplomacy. The degree of enthusiasm and energy expended in the 1930s for the international park had subsided, replaced with fitful moments of interest, indifference, and tension. A letter written to Townsend within days of the Mexican IBC visit to Big Bend revealed the power of the dream that a partnership on the border could instill even in those officials bent on identifying multipurpose water project sites in the canyons of the Rio Grande. Cordova wanted Townsend to know that "we have just returned from our trip to the Big Bend region, and are still under the spell of the days spent in that area." The IBC commissioner told the former US customs agent, "I shall never forget the night we spent at the [CCC] Camp in Chisos Mountains, where due to Mr. [McDougall] and the Officials in charge, we were treated with the utmost courtesy."[119]

Cordova, whose job took him throughout the Rio Grande basin, believed that the site "where this camp is located is one of the most beautiful I have ever seen." He now knew "that it is just one of many forming what in a very near future will be known as the Big Bend International Park." Then Cordova, perhaps speaking for many who shared Townsend's dream of peace along the Rio Grande, closed by writing, "I wish to take advantage of my recent visit to that area in order to congratulate you for your untiring efforts in that connection." The IBC commissioner believed that "in a very short time your dream will come true for the benefit of the numerous visitors the International Park will have."[120]

CHAPTER 5

The River Becomes a Border—Big Bend in an Age of Unity and Change

If the hard times of the 1930s had inspired the best of Mexico and the United States, wars hot and cold in succeeding decades complicated efforts to sustain the neighborliness of the "Last Frontier." The two nations drifted apart more often than they shared a vision of one landscape and one people. It was true enough that the imperatives of World War II, followed by the tensions between Russia and the United States known as the Cold War, distracted park service officials from the goal of a binational park. There was no better example of how quickly the dream had faded than the one that would appear in the 1940 draft master plan of Harvey Cornell, NPS's regional landscape architect. "Very little study was made," wrote Cornell to his superiors in San Francisco, "of the possible park development in the adjoining area in Mexico." Cornell concluded, "The most interesting portion of the proposed park is in the vicinity of the Sierra del Carmen and the Fronteriza Mountain ranges." This left little room to consider the remarkable landscape that so many observers from Mexico and America had seen when they joined in promotion of Big Bend just a few years before.[1]

As the Civilian Conservation Corps assumed the task of preparing Big Bend for its inclusion in the NPS system, the park service in March 1941 sent a team of inspectors to review their work. John H. Veale, assistant regional engineer, accompanied project supervisor Ross Maxwell and other staff members on a survey of the water supply and sewage disposal facilities in the Chisos basin. They viewed the cabins under construction, noting the work in adobe brickmaking. Maxwell spoke at some length in a report to the regional director about the process of adobe construction. The NPS's regional geologist commented that CCC crew members "are using a weathered calcareous shale which is obtained from near Terlingua at the same site from where most of the adobes in the buildings at Terlingua were made."[2]

Maxwell conceded that "this clay is mixed with sand and the results appear excellent as compared with most adobes." Yet the geologist worried that the crew was "attempting what is almost 'the impossible,' an adobe brick with perfectly square corners, straight surfaces, and sharp edges that can be laid in a wall as perfectly as high-grade brick."[3]

The comments of the review team, especially Maxwell's criticism of the adobe-brick process, prompted the Santa Fe regional office to consult with associate architect Lyle Bennett. J. E. Kell, acting regional chief of planning, reported to the director that Bennett considered Maxwell's assumptions "entirely incorrect as it was intended that the adobes should have 'sound' faces rather than 'perfect' faces." Kell reminded his superior that "the first adobes made showed disintegration of one-half inch or more of the faces and that many had lost the original faces entirely from disintegration and internal stresses." Bennett wanted adobe that had "some chipping of edges and bulging, roughness, or irregularity of faces" because "that is the natural character of adobe brick." The associate architect noted to Kell that the NPS's southwestern region already had "received criticism from various sources because of the 'perfection' of masonry work and the amount of waste rock." Bennett contended that "too much cutting of stones is going on in an attempt to arrive at some preconceived perfection of line and surface."[4]

The NPS had instructed its CCC crews at Big Bend and elsewhere that "a stone veneer was not sound construction because it produced a weak wall," and that "this pattern is neither economical for natural stone nor does it bring out the most desirable natural qualities of real stone." Bennett had to admit that "it is still evident that the square and chisel are being overworked in an effort to force a naturally irregular material into an unnatural regularity, thereby losing some of the best qualities of the material."[5]

Bennett wanted Kell to know that "disregarding the fact that we are trying to reproduce . . . a Mexican hut of very honest construction," the NPS should remember that "the people who will rent these cabins will be more pleased with a structure which has character, informality and softness in line and texture." Visitors preferred "a general atmosphere inducing relaxation, in contrast to hard, precise, sharp, and perfect lines and contours of a more sophisticated structure."[6]

Senior NPS engineer E. F. Preece spoke more critically about the use of adobe at Big Bend. In his report of April 28, 1941, he found fault with the park service's strategy of "spraying the walls with a paint or preservative coating of some sort." This, said Preece, "has been proven so definitely unsatisfactory that it is difficult to understand why we continue to try to do something which we know will not work." Preece complained that "for years now this Service has been using every kind of material to preserve adobe ruins," only to realize that "there is not a single record of even mediocre success and an attempt to paint the adobe bricks at Big Bend will meet with no better success." The senior engineer thus recommended that "this proposal be completely abandoned."[7]

As to the adobe brick controversy, Cornell told the NPS director that Bennett had offered more elaboration of his thoughts. Bennett admitted, "I cannot defend a job which is so far from the results intended as regards appearance." Yet the associate architect contended that "it is questionable whether more supervision by this office would have greatly improved results unless someone with the experience to understand and execute the kind of work desired were available to devote full time supervision to the job."[8]

Cornell concluded that future construction work at Big Bend needed "the continuous direction of a supervising architect," with an example being the "arrangement followed at the Painted Desert Inn, Petrified Forest National Monument." He also reminded the NPS director that "the successful adaptation of the provincial Mexican style of architecture, with the colorful blending of native materials into a natural setting, should not be too difficult to accomplish."[9]

This debate did not stop Paul V. Brown, chief of the region's division of recreation land planning, from conducting his own inquiries about facility development in the future national park. One issue that concerned Brown early in the process was reference in the region's files to "a possibility of a selection of one of the canyons within the proposed park boundary for water storage." Writing on April 15, 1942, to Earl O. Mills, planning counselor for the National Resources Planning Board in Dallas, Brown noted that a publication of the University of Texas for the IBC referred to "a Big Bend Dam Site in Boquillas Canyon." Brown also found mention in the minutes of the first meeting in January 1940 of the "Lower Rio Grande Basin Committee" of a "Rio Grande Water Reservoir possibility" in the same location. Further confusing Brown was any reference in NPS files to a decision by Mill's office "recommending that the National Resources Planning Board undertake a fact-finding study of the Lower Rio Grande Drainage Basin."[10]

Brown's work on the Big Bend master plan led Southwest regional director Minor Tillotson to praise his findings to the NPS director in Washington. On April 28, 1942, Tillotson sent to park service headquarters Brown's report, along with his own recommendations for the Texas NPS unit. Tillotson's first consideration was "promotion of the International aspect of the area." This should begin, said the regional director, with "early establishment of a contiguous National Park south of the Rio Grande."[11]

From there the NPS and Mexico should consider "the park area on each side of the river as a single unit without too much regard for the political boundary and, as Mr. Brown states, in such a way that the two areas will serve to complement rather than to compete with each other." This would lead, in Tillotson's estimation, to "free interchange of travel between the two sections of the International Park just so far as Customs and Immigration regulations can be modified to permit." Along with this would be "maintenance of the 'border' atmosphere of old Mexico" and "retention of certain typical Rio Grande trading posts and eating places."[12]

The regional director then encouraged Washington officials to preserve "the spirit and atmosphere of early-day Texas" at Big Bend, with "the park to be essentially a saddle and pack horse area, rather than one through which the automobile will be the principal means of transportation." For Tillotson this meant "emphasis on the development of trails and camping places rather than on high standard roads and hotels," with accommodations akin to "ranch house and frontier days type." Finally, Tillotson suggested that the NPS plan accommodations for two seasons of visitation, with summer visitors in the Chisos basin and "the Rio Grande for the winter visitors."[13]

Brown's own narrative about planning for the new national park revealed the power of the border, the need for better relations with Mexico, and the imperatives of World War II on the park service's imagination. The regional recreation-planning chief noted that "Mexican music and the colorful characteristics of Mexico definitely have influenced the music, the dance and the art of this country." In addition, "the economic and political relationship of the two nations as well as the blending of cultural sympathies is becoming more and more of vital importance."[14]

As Brown considered Big Bend to be "in the very heart of this land of romance and frontier lure," he hoped that the NPS would make it "the particular park of the National Park System where the Mexican and Texan scene may be experienced in reality by the vacationist." He believed that this interpretation of a shared cultural frontier was inevitable, as "the area will always reflect the Mexican and Spanish influence and will serve to introduce the two people to one another." Brown speculated that "when international highways connect at the park, as should be anticipated in our planning, the gateway function of the area will be greatly enhanced."[15]

The lure of the exotic for visitors, said Brown, required the NPS to "contemplate and encourage" development of accommodations south of the Rio Grande. "The planning theme," Brown continued, "must be towards retaining that unique atmosphere which is conducive to appreciation and understanding of the wide-open spaces." He also suggested that NPS planners think of "the simple primitive relationship of man to rugged lonely landscape," of the "inter-dependence and friendship between a rider and his horse," and of the "ever-welcome mountain landmarks that keep the explorer from being 'lost.'"[16]

Wartime exigencies also revived the issue of water-storage reservoirs on the Rio Grande within the boundaries of the future national park. Brown and Tillotson had traveled to El Paso in May to meet with L. M. Lawson of the IBC. Among the topics discussed were "the possibilities of dam construction and power development on the Rio Grande in the Big Bend area." Although there originally had been a dam projected in or near Boquillas Canyon, the tentative plan now would place this farther downstream near Sanderson. In so doing, the IBC would "take advantage of the inflow to the river between Boquillas and Sanderson, to shorten the length of transmission lines necessary, and to locate the dam site at a point where it would be more accessible to rail and other transportation."[17]

Tillotson then received in late August a copy of Confidential Bulletin No. 112, issued by the National Resources Planning Board. This contained what the regional director called a description of a proposed dam on the Rio Grande at the Big Bend area south of Marathon, Texas. Tillotson inquired of Lawson whether "tentative plans have again been changed or if the description of the project mentioned in Bulletin No. 112 is erroneous." The IBC commissioner eased Tillotson's fears by reporting that his survey crews would work south of Sanderson to the juncture of the Rio Pecos and the Rio Grande. He also noticed that the National Resources Planning Board had sought a comparison in cost of a dam near Boquillas with the preferred site at Del Rio.[18]

Pressure for increased access to natural resources to support the war effort extended to criticism of NPS policies prohibiting production of *candelilla*. Drew Pearson, a nationally syndicated columnist for the *Washington Post*, wrote a column in the *Dallas News* of October 26 entitled "Gas Masks or Parks?" Pearson, whose "Washington Merry-Go-Round" columns were read by millions weekly, noted that "to make a scaling compound for gas masks, the War Department requires a certain wax obtained from the *candelilla* plant, found only in hot, arid regions." The columnist had learned from Charles T. Wilson, whom he described as a "New York millionaire," that the latter had leased property in the Big Bend area "for exploitation of the plant." This included construction of a factory near Marathon, Texas, with Wilson's employees sent out to "gather the weeds which heretofore nobody had been interested in except the burros."[19]

Wilson then claimed that "officials of the State of Texas intervened saying the property was desired as part of the Big Bend National Park," with "Wilson and his wax gatherers . . . ordered off the premises." Pearson complained that "so now the deer and antelope, instead of gas-mask wearers, will have the benefit of the candelilla."[20]

By June 1943, the state parks board announced that enough deeds had been executed to permit local park promoters to hold a transfer ceremony at Sul Ross State College. Texas governor Coke Stevenson recognized the significance of the moment on September 5. The governor had plans to visit the Mexican states of Coahuila and Chihuahua with Luis Duplan, the Mexican consul from Austin. "With Mexico contemplating setting aside a similar area on the other side of the Rio Grande," Stevenson remarked, "it should become an International Park to help increase the already existing good feeling between the two republics." The governor "sincerely [hoped] that nothing will ever happen in this Big Bend territory that will, in any way, cause friction between the two countries."[21]

Minor Tillotson of the Southwest Region expressed similar thoughts at the deed-transfer ceremony. "This, the twenty-seventh national park in the United States," said the regional director, "will take its rightful place along with Yellowstone, Grand Canyon, Yosemite, and others." Tillotson predicted that "in some respects, it will outshine others since it will be international in scope—and Mexico is expected to act soon." The NPS official further hoped "that the time is not far off when the presidents of the two republics can meet at the park for a joint declaration."[22]

To promote the occasion, Isabelle Story, editor in chief of the NPS, drafted a press release recounting the wonders of Big Bend. Her statement included the benefits accruing to the state of Texas for its work in acquiring 697,684 acres of private land. To familiarize newspaper readers across the country with Texas's first national park, the NPS noted that "Boquillas, in the southeastern part of the park, lies in the latitude of Daytona Beach, Florida," a reference to the popular tourist attraction on the Atlantic Coast.[23]

Story reiterated the praise of Big Bend's natural beauty and wilderness that suffused NPS publications and reports of the 1930s. Yet the park service's chief editor had to caution William Warne, director of information for the Interior Department, that the final press release reflected the realities of race relations on the border. "Since the State of Texas has expressed disapproval of statements concerning the 'Mexican atmosphere' of the area," wrote Story, "we have regretfully deleted a proposed paragraph on that phase of the park."[24]

This last remark by Story revealed sentiments still echoing throughout Texas regarding Mexico's nationalization of oil late in the 1930s, and the history of border relations since the Texas revolt of a century before. The park service also faced the rising tide of political conservatism that accompanied wartime mobilization. Regional director Tillotson discussed with the state parks board the need to "make the actual acceptance ceremony as simple as possible." Tillotson worried that "if we made a big 'to-do' over the acceptance ceremony and had the Secretary, the Director, members of their staffs, and others gone to Texas for this ceremony, we would all of us rightly have been subject to public criticism for expenditure of the time and money involved during war times."[25]

Tillotson reminded the parks board's Frank Quinn that President Franklin D. Roosevelt could not have attended, but that "we are all of us anxious—as I know you are—to have him take a prominent part in the formal dedication of the park." Thus the "more informality we can have in connection with the acceptance ceremony, the greater will be our chances to have a real celebration at the dedication ceremony."[26]

Tillotson cautioned Quinn that this meant waiting until the close of the war, "at which time I believe under the approved plan there would be an excellent chance of getting the President of the United States, the President of Mexico and the Secretary of the Interior to be present in person somewhere in Texas, preferably in the Big Bend National Park, at a formal dedication ceremony." Then the regional director reminded Quinn of the prosaic reality of land acquisition. Congress, through the intervention of Texas representative Ewing Thomason and Senator Tom Connally, had approved funds for the "administration, protection and maintenance of the Big Bend National Park during the present fiscal year." Without all land parcels deeded to the federal government, the NPS could not expend these funds. Yet Tillotson promised the parks board secretary that he would "have established the positions involved and to secure approval of the appointment of those selected to fill such positions, so that they may been entered on duty without delay immediately [when] the park is established."[27]

Use of water resources in the future NPS unit also required attention, as A. M. Mead of San Benito, Texas, pressed the state's congressional delegation to build a dam and reservoir on the Rio Grande within the park's boundaries. "Now, as the Big Bend is a State and Nations Park," wrote Mead, "wouldn't it be grand to have a Big Lake in it, for boating, bathing, hunting and fishing." Mead even suggested a means for constructing such a facility. "Listen," he told Congressman Milton West of Brownsville, "a big dam across the Santa Elena Canyon, on the Rio Grande River, would do this job and the lake would catch all the flood waters and hold them in storage for Mexico and this Valley." Mead also suggested that "we could work those Nazi prisoners on this job and get the job done, and would have plenty of water for this Valley at all times."[28]

C. E. Ainsworth, a consulting engineer for the IBC, worried more about the contracts that his agency had with local ranchers to measure rainfall and operate stream-gauging stations on the Rio Grande. "This office has need for all available rainfall records from the Big Bend Park area," Ainsworth informed Tillotson, and the IBC wondered when Elmo Johnson and Albert W. Dorgan would no longer be able to provide the stream commission with this data.[29]

Tillotson then called on the park service to locate the main visitors' complex on the Rio Grande near Boquillas at the Daniels Ranch property. "Here there is ample room for development and expansion together with plenty of water for irrigation, operation of air conditioning system, etc." The regional director still held out for an architectural design "on the lines of an Old Mexican Hacienda and every effort should be made to maintain the Mexican atmosphere of the place." The Chisos basin, by comparison, would get only lodges for summer visitors. "This entire development," wrote Tillotson on March 29, "should maintain the general atmosphere of a typical old Texas ranch layout," with "corrals . . . provided as the starting point for saddle horse and pack trips." Campgrounds could be built in Pine Canyon, said the regional director, and at Castolon, Boquillas, Hot Springs, or San Vicente.[30]

When the NPS constructed its food-service facilities on the river, said Tillotson, they "should be in the form of a typical Mexican restaurant somewhat along the lines of that formerly operated at Boquillas by Maria Sada." Visitors also could avail themselves of souvenir shops within the park, said Tillotson, "especially those of Mexican manufacture," and "there should be no ban on the sale of such foreign made articles as are manufactured in Mexico." Presaging an idea promoted in the year 2000 by park superintendent Frank Deckert, Tillotson told NPS officials, "I can also foresee a large business to be done by the operator in articles of clothing typical of the country, such as cowboy boots, bright colored shirts and neckerchiefs, ten-gallon hats, Mexican sombreros, charro costumes, *huarachos* [sic], etc."[31]

Tillotson's admiration for the visitor services provided over the years by Maria Sada struck a chord among NPS officials designing concessions at Big Bend. One week after noting that Sada had left the area to run a restaurant in Del Rio, Texas, Tillotson reported to Newton B. Drury, the NPS director, that "she has now returned to the Big Bend in order to 'collect some accounts due her.'" Sada had taken up residence upriver at San Vicente, writing to Tillotson for permission "to reestablish her former location now owned by the Government at Boquillas." Tillotson told Drury that "since there is absolutely no other place in the area where a visitor can secure a meal, it seems to me that it would be a distinct advantage from our standpoint to have her provide such service."[32]

The regional director preferred that Sada relocate on NPS property, advising her to reoccupy her old establishment. "Personally," wrote Tillotson to Drury, "I should like very much to see her remain in the area with her little store and eating place until such time as National Park Concessions takes over and thereafter have her remain as an employee of the company conducting a typical Mexican restaurant in keeping with the border atmosphere." The regional director offered both Sada and W. A. Cooper special-use permits to allow them to provide visitor services when the park opened on July 1 to the public.[33]

Sada's permit reflected one of the most enduring dichotomies of the creation of Big Bend: the NPS's desire to tell an authentic border story, along with the other features of natural and cultural resource management, even as the NPS faced pressure to avoid references to its partnership with Mexico. The Women's International League for Peace and Freedom, based in Washington, DC, called on NPS director Drury in December 1943 to invite Mexican officials to any ceremony opening the national park. Mrs. Josue Picon, chair of the US Section, Committee on the Americas, told Drury that such a gesture might "encourage our Mexican friends to hasten plans for the giving of a tract of land on their side opposite the Big Bend."[34]

Then in May 1944, Zonia Barber of Chicago wrote to Harold Ickes "to ascertain whether the contemplated Mexican Park on the other side of the Rio Grande is ready and willing to join the Big Bend Park in forming an International Park." Barber reminded Ickes that, "realizing the influence Symbols have on human action, as Chairman of the Peace Symbol Committee of the Women's International League for Peace and Freedom, I am urging that the new International Park be named 'Big Bend–(name of the Mexican Park) International Peace Park.'" Ickes should recall also, said Barber, that "each of us who has spent much or little time in Mexico realizes the necessity of using every available opportunity of expressing through action the 'Good Neighbor' policy" of President Roosevelt.[35]

While the operating permit for Sada and the pleas of the Women's International League for a peace park designation occupied the time of Tillotson in 1944, the more critical feature of border relations was the signing in May of the US-Mexico treaty dividing the waters of the Rio Grande. Director Drury sent Arthur Demaray to a meeting in Washington on April 17, where the associate NPS director spoke with representatives of the US State Department, the US Bureau of Reclamation, the US Geological Survey, and the Office of Indian Affairs.

These agencies negotiated their roles in any future use of Rio Grande waters pursuant to the clauses of the 1944 treaty. Demaray asked his colleagues to support "a provision in the supplementary legislation which would provide that no dam or other structure for the storage or transmission of water be authorized affecting lands within the Big Bend National Park without first securing specific authority of the Congress."[36]

The last issue of border relations to reach the desk of top-level NPS officials in May 1944 was correspondence from Walter P. Taylor, unit leader of the US Fish and Wildlife Service's office at Texas A&M College and author of the survey that spring of the ecology of Big Bend. Taylor wanted Hillory Tolson to inform his colleagues in the Chicago headquarters of the park service of an article by Glenn Burgess on the international park idea that appeared in the Chihuahua newspaper *Tiempo*. "From a Rotary dinner held a short time ago in the city of Chihuahua," said the Alpine Chamber of Commerce manager, "came the idea of constructing a large international park within the limits of the states of Chihuahua and Coahuila, at the place where the Rio Grande River makes a rather big bend." Burgess told the Rotarians that the state of Texas stood ready to endorse the concept, and that "President Avila Camacho had accepted in principle the proposition of granting an equal amount of land by Mexico."[37]

The chamber manager conceded that "the idea of constructing the huge international park is nothing new," as "it dates from 1930, in which year was begun the construction of the highway" that ran from Dubuque, Iowa, southwest through Alpine and on to Presidio, Texas. Burgess suggested to the *Chihuahuenses* that "Mexico, in addition to contributing its share of land, should construct a road which starting from Ojinaga will pass through San Carlos (today, Manual [*sic*] Benavides), and will end in the city of Chihuahua."[38]

The benefit of such a route, said Burgess, would be "a circuit which will connect Ciudad Juarez and El Paso, Texas, besides crossing the entire park on the North American side." Burgess speculated that no fewer than four hundred thousand tourists would come annually to Big Bend, "attracted by this new drive—very high mountain peaks, deep canyons, woods, forests, and water falls—all of it located in the most beautiful part of the Rio Grande River."[39]

Plans for a postwar world reached into the Big Bend country with the continued interest of President Franklin D. Roosevelt in good relations with Mexico. Writing in October 1944 to President Manuel Ávila Camacho, apprising the Mexican leader of authorization that June of Big Bend National Park, FDR claimed that "in the United States, we think of the Big Bend region in terms of its international significance." Roosevelt hoped that "the Mexican people look forward in the same spirit to the establishment of an adjoining national parks of both countries." This the American president believed exemplified "the cultural resources and advancement, and inspiring further mutually beneficial progress in recreation and science and the industries related thereto." Roosevelt had "followed the progress of the conversations between the representatives of our respective governments regarding the establishment of international parks."[40]

Encouraged by the symbolism that this initiative offered in peacetime, FDR sought Camacho's advice about the task of unification of the shared landscape of the two nations. "I do not believe," said Roosevelt, "that this undertaking in the Big Bend will be completed until the entire park area in this region on both sides of the Rio Grande forms one great international park." Seeing a future beyond war, FDR asked of the Mexican leader, "I would appreciate your views regarding my hope that early in the postwar period such a park, formed of suitable areas on each side of the boundary in the Big Bend region, might be dedicated." In so doing, the binational partnership "might mark the initiation of a joint program of park development for the benefit and enjoyment of our peoples." Six months later, Roosevelt died without visiting the Big Bend.[41] For the next half decade, the park service and Mexico devoted their attention to the return to peacetime, and also to the conflict known as the Cold War.

When the United States and Mexico met formally in the fall of 1955 to dedicate Big Bend National Park, much had changed in both countries since the presidential administrations of FDR and Lázaro Cárdenas. Mexico ushered in a period from 1940 to 1960 commonly referred to as the "Mexican Miracle" because of the sustained and unrelenting modernization that took place in the country. For the first time in modern Mexican history, the nation elected presidents with no direct experience in or ties to the military. With the change in leadership came a shift of emphasis. Mexican presidents who followed in the wake of World War II stressed economic gains for the nation over a redistribution of wealth and social mobility for the masses. As a component of the nation's newfound resolve to improve the country's productive capacity and economic condition, the republic experienced significant demographic shifts.

Big Bend's accomplishments reached their apex on November 21, 1955, when Douglas McKay, secretary of the interior, gave the keynote address at the park's dedication. Standing before a crowd of 1,100 visitors and dignitaries from the state of Texas, the Republic of Mexico, and the NPS, McKay looked out over the landscape and declared the ceremony "a proud and memorable occasion." With the US and Mexican flags flying together in the breeze, the interior secretary apologized for the absence of "that great son of Texas and noble American, Dwight D. Eisenhower." Eisenhower had spoken two years before at the dedication of Falcón Dam, southeast of Big Bend on the Rio Grande. There he had emphasized his administration's commitment to "friendship between our two countries." The multipurpose water project, built by the International Boundary and Water Commission and the US Bureau of Reclamation, reminded the president in his first year in office of how "neighbor nations can and should live: in peace, in mutual respect, in common prosperity."[42]

The president had suffered a heart attack in the summer of 1955, but McKay conveyed Eisenhower's wish to praise "this, the seventh largest of all our twenty-eight national parks." The former Supreme Allied Commander in World War II wanted the audience that day to know, said McKay, that he valued Big Bend's creation "not alone because of his very deep and sincere appreciation of the priceless value of our national parks, nor because Big Bend is in his native state."[43]

More important to the career soldier was "the fact that this park was conceived as a symbol of international peace." McKay recalled that Big Bend "was formally established on June 12, 1944, while our soldiers were fighting to establish a beach head in France." Unfortunately, said the interior secretary, "when peace finally came after that terrible war, it proved only temporary." Instead, "plans for this dedication ceremony had to be shelved while sons of Texas joined other American boys on the bloody battlefields of Korea."[44]

With conflict in the Far East resolved, McKay could convey to the attendees the president's belief that "people of all nations seem now to look more to their hearts than to their armed might in developing plans for a peaceful world." The interior secretary found it "altogether fitting, then, that in this era of heartfelt hope, we should dedicate this great gift from the people of Texas to the people of America." In a reference to Cold War tensions still affecting world affairs, McKay reminded his audience that "the pooling and mutual sharing of great scenic treasures along those borders [between the United States, Canada, and Mexico] is an inspiring example to the troubled peoples behind the iron and bamboo curtains of the way free men and women can live in peace and friendship."[45]

As if to emphasize the challenge of peace in the postwar era, the interior secretary noted that "the land is peaceful now, and always shall be, but it was not always so." From the volcanic eruptions of eons before, to the warfare between Indian tribes and the Spanish, to the "cattle rustlers and outlaws" of the nineteenth century, Big Bend had a cultural legacy that marked it as unique in the NPS system.[46]

The twentieth century had a different story to tell, thought McKay, as "peace came to this wild country when free men settled down and learned under democracy to live with one another as neighbors." The interior secretary cited Captain Everett Ewing Townsend as one of "the early teachers of the virtues of law and order and the principles of good neighborliness." To the longtime rancher and public servant, said McKay, "all of us are forever indebted for the part he played in paving the way for the establishment of Big Bend National Park." Townsend's foresight, and that of Horace Morelock and Amon Carter, declared McKay, was evidenced by the fact that "only 28 of the 181 areas in the National Park System can bear that proud title [of national park]." The interior secretary also praised the citizens of Texas, who "did not ask Uncle Sam to acquire the land."[47]

Once the NPS opened the gates to Big Bend, "it was not easy or comfortable to visit this beautiful wilderness area. Yet from a base of 850, visitors to Big Bend will approximate 500,000, according to our National Park Service experts." Such visitation patterns could threaten the serenity of the Chisos basin, said the interior secretary, and "to permit this to happen would be a desecration." Yet McKay comforted his audience by intoning, "It shall not happen. That I can promise."[48]

Then McKay offered a breathtaking synopsis of the planning process that the park service had in mind for Big Bend. "The rugged beauty of the Chisos Mountains," he declared, "will be preserved by restraining over-development." The former automobile dealer from Salem, Oregon, conceded that "of course, the facilities now here must be improved and modernized." Yet "park planners feel . . . the construction of roads and the developed area in the Basin has progressed just about as far as it can without harming the scenery." Instead "future plans contemplate the establishment of an attractive village in an oasis near the river in the vicinity of Hot Springs."[49]

Here the park's principal visitor accommodations would be concentrated, said McKay, with "motels, cabins, stores and other visitor's facilities . . . created and operated by park concessioners." Once the NPS installed "roads, water and sewage facilities and public campgrounds," it then would build "a spur road [to] take visitors to the spectacular Mariscal Canyon area." Yet another development was contemplated "for the Santa Eleña Canyon area with provision for expansion to meet the growing needs of the future."[50]

This grand scheme for Big Bend formed part of the larger Mission 66 initiative, so called "because we hope to reach its objective in 1966 when the National Park Service will celebrate the golden anniversary of its establishment by Congress." McKay claimed, "In my long career as a public official [including service as mayor of Salem, Oregon, and governor of Oregon], no duty has been more rewarding or brought me more personal satisfaction that that of exercising stewardship over the parks in which our people find enjoyment."[51]

He declared Mission 66 "one of the most important developments in the entire history of the National Park Service," as he had discovered upon taking office in 1953 that "the Park Service was attempting to take care of almost 50 million visitors in a park system developed to handle about half the number." Since the peak of CCC and New Deal construction, "the demands of World War II, the Korean War and the cold war forced curtailments all along the line."[52]

McKay then placed Big Bend's Mission 66 improvements within the context of system-wide efforts to rejuvenate the park service. The NPS budget had increased under the Eisenhower administration some 40 percent (to $45 million), making Big Bend's $1 million allocation for the 1956 fiscal year 8 percent of the entire NPS increase. McKay emphasized that "we have encouraged concessioners to make substantial improvements toward improving and expanding the facilities they operate." He also noted proudly that "we have added new land to the system every year." Mission 66 reflected what the secretary called "aggressive action . . . to put the park system in shape to meet future demands which are clearly foreseeable."[53]

Mindful of the congressional mandate "that the park areas must be preserved for the benefit and enjoyment of the American people," McKay seized the opportunity at Big Bend's dedication to remind his audience that "the thought of rationing use of our parks is repugnant to me." Americans, however, "must face the hard truth that visitor enjoyment is impaired by masses of people who crowd to the same spot to see the same view at the same time." Warning that "rationing the beauty of our national parks might be the only solution if we stood still," the interior secretary nonetheless concluded that "we can reject such a suggestion only because we are moving forward" in parks like Big Bend.[54]

One person who beamed most proudly during Big Bend's induction ceremony was Virginia Madison. A longtime advocate of all things Big Bend, Madison was more nuanced in her thinking. A graduate of Sul Ross State College in Alpine, she paid attention to change and contingency in history, open to possibilities that history might reveal. She wrote about place names and stories, and in 1955 she penned the area's history, simply entitled *The Big Bend Country of Texas*. Where Carlysle Raht had once identified the Southern Pacific Railway as "a dead line [between El Paso and San Antonio] which no Mexican bandit has had the intrepidity to cross," Madison, however, reimagined the area as a place that linked not only nations and peoples' daily life but also peoples' common destinies.[55]

Madison also viewed cogently the same area and the same historical event as one of "the people from both sides of the tracks" (the title of one of her chapters). She found that in 1955 the place was "a strange conglomeration of new and old, wealth and poverty, success and failure, mystery and hard reality." She arrived at the same conclusion reached by other historians: that the United States' original political mission was to establish a US-Mexico border, "to divide—to keep apart two nations, different in culture, heritage, and teachings."[56]

In her study of the Big Bend, distributed during the formal opening ceremony of Big Bend National Park, Madison's outlook was at once hopeful and forward-thinking. Her text spoke to opportunity in a land of freedom, and fulfillment of those dreams in a dynamic and interconnected world. Alluding to faint and lingering underpinnings of the Lone Star State's complicated past, she emphasized the contributions of *all* in shaping the area's history and present. Wrote Madison, "The well-developed industries in the Big Bend country today are a tribute to the population groups, who despite different heritages, have managed to surmount a thousand obstacles to learn to live and work together peaceably."[57]

Should visitors read Madison's work, she hoped that they too would come to know how fortunate Mexico and America were to have this national park. "With its marvelous flora and fauna," she wrote, "and its Western spirit, mingled with the romance of Mexico," Big Bend exuded "a personality all its own." Calling the park "the ideal winter climate" along the Rio Grande, Madison echoed the sense of wonder that Everett Townsend felt sixty-plus years before. "After viewing the magnificent scenery, through the Window and through the South Rim," wrote the Sul Ross graduate, "visitors understand why the phrase, *tierra desconocida* (unknown land), still applies." Not for nothing did Madison conclude, "It weaves a spell—this *tierra desconocida,* the Big Bend country."[58]

In the early years of the 1960s, Douglas Evans, chief naturalist at Big Bend, analyzed the visitation patterns of the park in anticipation of changes in the interpretative program. As late as 1959, he wrote, Big Bend hosted some 70,370 patrons; a number that was hard to verify, since Big Bend did not charge admission, and there were no automobile counters installed at the entrance stations until the late 1960s. By 1963, Big Bend's visitation estimates had grown some 62 percent (to 114,232). Evans speculated that "if this rate of increase continues, we could expect 185,000 visitors in 1968 and 300,000 by 1973."[59]

The chief naturalist viewed these figures from the vantage point of 1965 as "conservative," assuming that "visitation will certainly be affected by the completion of the new interpretative roads, new lodge, campgrounds, trailer facilities, and museum facilities" that he studied. He also believed that once "the new road, now being constructed northward from Muzquiz, Coahuila toward Big Bend is completed, the number of park visitors will certainly soar above all predictions made thus far."[60]

At the west end of the park, said Evans, the NPS should consider expansion of visitor services at the old army compound of Castolon and the mouth of Santa Elena Canyon. "Plans for the future," he wrote in 1965, "include sleeping and dining facilities, saddle horses, campgrounds, trailer facilities, and picnic areas." NPS staff could explain to visitors "United States Cavalry operations during the Mexican Revolution of 1910–1920, and of an isolated Mexican-border trading and ranching center."[61]

Evans suggested that the park service use the Alvino residence to "illustrate the way of life on a Mexican border farm." The interpretation could include "a small demonstration garden of vegetables and melons" growing next to the house. Then, in a statement filled with irony, the chief naturalist noted that "the candelilla wax processing system will be restored nearby." Museum exhibits to be housed in the old Castolon store also would have on display candelilla wax, which Evans characterized as "an important means of livelihood."[62]

In retrospect, the realities of the Big Bend landscape fit perfectly the goals of Stewart Udall and other champions of natural beauty and ecology. In April 1966, the interior secretary accompanied Lady Bird Johnson on a one-day raft trip through Mariscal Canyon on the Rio Grande, a visit designed, said Evans, to focus national attention on wilderness preservation. Joined by ninety reporters and photographers, the First Lady came to the Marfa air station on April 2 to spend three days in West Texas, one of which would be devoted to Big Bend. The El Paso Natural Gas Company paid the costs of her visit, recalled Evans, who drove to Marfa to escort Lady Bird, Udall, and NPS director George Hartzog to the park. "A cottage in the Chisos was 'redone' for her," Evans remembered, and the raft trip included "35 NPS trainees from the Albright center [at the Grand Canyon] in twelve Navy rafts." Lady Bird "was in the lead boat," said Evans, who paddled for her and Udall, and "she asked to be pulled ahead of the press" to gain some privacy. Evans mused that "the media were 'fish out of water,'" with several rafts capsizing on the ten-mile journey from Talley Ranch to Solis.[63]

Garner Hanson, president of National Park Concessions Inc. (NPCI), recalled in 1997 that his organization catered the event, and that Superintendent Perry Brown "saw the visit as a challenge to preservation." Several Greyhound motor coaches traveled down the rutted dirt road to the Talley put-in, while Lady Bird's press secretary, Liz Carpenter, wanted a "big Bonfire" at the Chisos campground for effect. That evening, recalled Evans, NPCI arranged to have "a fiesta for her at the Rio Grande Village, complete with recorded coyote sounds." All of this graced the nightly television news and the headlines of the nation's newspapers, not unlike the coverage generated thirty years earlier when Texas historian Walter Prescott Webb promoted Big Bend's charm and peril in his own river trip through Santa Eleña Canyon.[64]

One of the ironies of the visit in 1966 by Lady Bird Johnson was its focus on the need for more wilderness designations in the United States. Two years earlier, her husband, President Lyndon B. Johnson, had signed the landmark legislation known as the Wilderness Act. Big Bend appeared to the reporters covering the raft trip to be nothing but wilderness, as several interviewees recalled the difficulties of getting film footage out of the canyon area each day for shipment to the television networks. Yet 1966 also represented another defining moment for resource management within the NPS and other federal organizations: passage of the National Historic Preservation Act. This required public agencies to identify and research the historic significance of structures and neighborhoods, with the goal being protection via listing on the National Register of Historic Places.

A young graduate student in history in the 1960s at Texas Tech University, Jerry Rogers, would later become director of the National Historic Landmarks Program of the NPS in Washington. Rogers, a native of West Texas and the field superintendent at the time of the NPS's Southwest Support Office in Santa Fe, recalled how Big Bend National Park had fared in matters of cultural resource management before and after passage of the National Historic Preservation Act. "Big Bend was typical of other great scenic national parks," Rogers noted, in that "drawing visitors was more important." For Big Bend, "the great crime was bulldozing San Vicente," a small community of Mexican people on the US side of the Rio Grande.[65]

The legacy of this and other efforts to remove evidence of human habitation at Big Bend bothered Rogers and Curtis Tunnell, director of the state of Texas's Office of Historic Preservation. Tunnell complained in public meetings that "the National Park service gave lip service to archaeological resources [at Big Bend]," said Rogers. It helped Big Bend little that Rogers's supervisor, NPS director George Hartzog, created the Office of Archaeology and Historic Preservation. "Then the battle of George Wright and the 1930s biologists to gain equal status with scenery recurred with cultural resource management."[66]

In 1968, the US Congress passed the Wild and Scenic Rivers Act. While it would be another decade before the Rio Grande flowing through Big Bend would receive such a designation, interest in rafting gained momentum from the publicity surrounding Lady Bird Johnson's April 1966 river trip. Hartzog called Lady Bird Johnson the NPS's "greatest saleswoman" because of her active and spirited involvement with the country's park sites. Dozens of White House staffers and members of the press corps espoused Lady Bird's Make America Beautiful campaign. In one of the more memorable episodes of the visit, a women's club presented the First Lady with a memento of her travels. One scholar recorded, "The women of Alpine present this painting to you, because no other First Lady has contributed so much to the nation. Because of you we can truly call our country America the Beautiful. We hope that every time you see this painting you will think of our Big Bend National Park." The First Lady proudly responded that she would hang the painting at her and her husband's ranch in Johnson City.[67]

If the First Lady's river trip through Big Bend revealed the brilliance of its environs in all their raw and natural form, Supreme Court Justice William O. Douglas helped publicize the work of the NPS in providing hospitable accommodations for park enthusiasts. Once considered by FDR to be his vice-presidential running mate, Douglas settled into his Supreme Court position an unabashed friend to environmental causes. At a time when the debate over purist standards of wilderness advocates challenged and sometimes drowned out inroads made by the park service, the sojourn of Douglas through Big Bend in the mid-1960s helped bring attention to improvements made by the national parks system.[68]

Highly critical of Texas land developers, Douglas quoted chapter and verse from the Wilderness Act of 1964, calling for more land to be preserved for future generations. In a polemical work, the Supreme Court justice took issue with Texas developers, writing, "The voices of conservationists are more and more being heard in Texas. Committees and clubs are being formed. Under White House influence, conferences on *Beautiful Texas* have sounded clarion calls to action." Upon arriving in Big Bend, Douglas spoke fondly of the easy access and public facilities adjoining the park. "One who takes the twenty-mile auto trip from park headquarters to Boquillas finds spacious campgrounds, particularly attractive for wintertime use." He continued, "The Park Service has . . . installed a pumping station, irrigated a goodly bit of river bottom, planted cottonwood and mesquite, and installed drinking fountains, rest rooms, and cooking facilities in the form of metal braziers standing on stems about waist high. . . . Some family campsites have a roof without sidewalls—a ramada—that provides some shade. There are, of course, alcoves for trailers—and picnic tables."[69]

Douglas spoke in appreciation of a new aesthetic that combined the amenities and a welcoming convenience provided by the NPS with unsurpassed access to a world beyond. The Chihuahua Desert revealed, in his words, "a complex of life that is unique in the American outdoors." Douglas wholeheartedly believed that "there will in time be a Mexican Park, physically united with Big Bend for recreational uses; and it will open up to wide use the spectacular Sierra Madres Mountains to the south and the Sierra Fronterisa and the Sierra del Carmen to the southwest," the latter bisected by the Rio Grande. The Supreme Court justice acknowledged that "the Mexican mountains are today only scenery for Big Bend visitors, but they offer scenery extraordinary." Moved, as so many observers have been since the earliest days of human habitation in Big Bend, Douglas wrote in 1967, "The Sierra del Carmen show crimson cliffs in a lowering sun; and the distant Sierra Fronterisa are washed by the shadows of fleecy clouds in midday and a thickening purplish cast as the day wanes."[70]

There could not have been a better contemporary spokesperson than Douglas, who at once extolled the virtues of strong federal leadership and regenerative New Deal measures of preservation. He alerted readers, "This is a fragile land and can easily be destroyed even by those who walk reverently" upon it. He continued that "the philosophy of Adam Smith is so dominant in Texas that opposition to the establishment of other like national parks is fierce and unrelenting." Taking heed in the struggles to establish Big Bend, he reminded his audience, "The land in Big Bend National Park was so worn out by owners, who pounded and despoiled it, that 'bailing them out' through government acquisition became attractive by entrepreneurial standards."[71]

In the late 1960s, NPS resource planner David J. Jones would come to Big Bend to gauge the future of resource planning and comment on the challenge that facilities expansion posed. "The establishment of Big Bend as a National Park has not entirely solved the problem of consumptive use," claimed Jones in a 1967 natural sciences research plan. "Recreation has replaced the previous forms of land use," he suggested, "but it, too, places demands upon natural resources." In Jones's mind, "three developmental determinants established long ago are critical factors."[72]

These he labeled as "encouraging a highway in Mexico to connect with the park ending at Boquillas; concentrating visitor-use facilities in the Chisos Basin; [and] developing visitor-use facilities at Rio Grande Village and Castolon to avoid over-concentration of visitors in the Chisos Basin during the heavy travel season." The NPS faced "a crucial problem . . . [in] making the decisions now that will control how we accommodate the one million visitors anticipated annually some 60 to 100 years from now." This would include "providing them [with] an enjoyable and quality park experience with minimum impact upon the biological and esthetic well-being of the land."[73]

Like every other federal agency involved in natural resource issues, the NPS had to adjust its planning process after passage in 1969 of the National Environmental Protection Act. In January 1972, a group from Temple, Texas, calling itself Americans Backing Better Park Development demanded that the park service consider its "Alternative to the Master Plan and Wilderness Proposal for Big Bend National Park." Bob Burleson, president of the association, echoed David Jones's cautions about the 1965 master planning strategies. The 1972 document, said Burleson, "would authorize projects that in the long run will result in over-development in the form of high-speed highways, excessive automobile and commercial traffic, an international river crossing to Mexico, and excessive water use and impact in the Chisos Mountains Basin." Burleson's group realized that "all parks cannot be left forever undeveloped, and that some segments of public pressure on the National Park Service will tend to call for increased development in the future." But the group warned that "over-development, in the long run, will be a much greater sin than under-development."[74]

The organization, which Burleson claimed had over one thousand members in chapters throughout Texas and in Los Alamos, New Mexico, agreed with the NPS that "the Wilderness proposal is realistic and large enough to protect the most important values in the Park." Burleson called the "Chamber of Commerce-type groups" that opposed the plan "misguided." What they sought, claimed the association, "is an influx of automobile tourists, the 'pie in the sky' road link with Mexico, motels and campgrounds for the 'swelling millions' of tourists that they envision will contribute heavily to the Alpine-Marfa economy." Burleson's associates believed that visitation would increase with "a really quality experience," given that "the beauty of the Big Bend Country lies in its mood of remoteness, of silence, of vast and untouched space, of its blend of desert and mountain wilderness."[75]

While criticizing the tone of the master plan as "vague," Burleson agreed with its goals "to reduce human impact in the Chisos basin, remove the horse concession to some other point in the park and to concentrate development in the future in the area of Panther Junction, Nugent Mountain and Rio Grande Village." But the "consensus" of the association was that "the proposed Master Plan will continue to allow excessive impact and development in the Chisos Basin, and that its emphasis on the proposed international park and bridge crossing into Mexico is highly dangerous to the long-term survival of the highest values of the Park."[76]

Writing some forty years after the initial conversations with Mexico about the international park, Burleson and his group regarded the Muzquiz-Boquillas road as "the most dangerous proposition that Big Bend National Park will ever have to face, exceeding in gravity even the anticipated large increases in automobile visitation to the Park from the United States of America." The road was "fraught with such danger to the park," said Burleson, that "we were shocked by the great emphasis placed upon this proposal in the Master Plan and by the enthusiasm with which the Park Service has embraced a proposal that threatens the ultimate destruction of the most valuable features of the Park."[77]

Burleson warned that "the National Park Service was not created as an instrument of foreign policy, and is ill-suited to the role." Unaware of the four decades of negotiations over the international park, the association claimed that "anyone acquainted with the history of Mexico and its present problems of population growth vs. economic growth will at once recognize the dangers of mixing Big Bend National Park with foreign policy."[78]

Burleson argued that "the Mexican government is obliged by political expediency to remain committed to The Revolution, one of the cardinal tenets of which is that the rural landholdings should be broken up and re-distributed to the former peons." This had given rise to "the Ejido Program, under which tracts of land are worked cooperatively, almost communally, both for livestock grazing and for row-crop agriculture." The *ejidos* created near Boquillas and Santa Eleña, claimed Burleson, included "a vast grassland area, and an important source of commercial timber, as well as active mines." The association president warned that "all of these are local economic interests which will have to be reckoned with by the Mexican government if it should ever actually be *serious* about an international park."[79]

Burleson then noted the policies of the Mexican government in the 1960s to shift its population from the central valleys to the northern border. "The lack of money, jobs and space in Mexico," wrote Burleson, "and the ease with which the border is illegally crossed and employment obtained, has caused tremendous buildups of population in Mexican cities along the border where international crossings are maintained and cities have grown up." Given these realities, the association claimed that "Mexico has no genuine interest in withdrawing lands from economic use and creating on its soil a 'national park' of the type that we have in Big Bend."[80]

Burleson believed that "economic self-interest" tied the chambers of commerce in West Texas to Mexico's plan for a highway to Boquillas. Since "the Mexican government cannot be expected to take away the property and livelihood of the local miners, ejido-dwellers, and ranchers without gaining for the area some economic benefits," Burleson claimed that "this must come from the proposed commercial uses of the new road and river crossing." He warned that "the population of Boquillas can be expected to increase perhaps a thousand-fold in the event that there is an automobile linkup and river crossing." "Who wants a Villa Acuna across from Rio Grande Village," asked Burleson, "among the tourist traps and vice parlors?"[81]

Instead, wrote the association president, the NPS "should stick to its business of providing quality park experiences within our own national park system, and leave the economic development of northern Mexico to the Mexican government." The park service would do better to encourage development at the La Linda bridge-crossing outside park boundaries. The local economy would not suffer, and "both tourism and commercial use would be greater on such a road . . . because it would be less restricted."[82]

Public debate about the master planning process for Big Bend led NPS officials in March 1973 to send another team to assess the interpretative needs of the park. Aram Mardirosian and Bill Ingersoll of the NPS's Denver Service Center went to Big Bend with Bill Brown of the Southwest Region and discussed the issues surrounding the master plan with park staff. The team tried to reconcile the vision of park use outlined by Doug Evans in the mid-1960s with that of the environmentally conscious planning of a decade later. The Denver Service Center review team also commented at some length on the park's distinctive historical resources, noting the need for more recognition of the cultural heritage of the Big Bend country. The team liked what it found at the Castolon compound, especially the presence in the grocery store of historical detail that "gives the place the look of an old country store." The team called on park officials to provide "formal furnishing plans" at Castolon, as "Big Bend is a marginal area, and there are virtually no social histories of that time and place." They believed that "the first decades of the 20th century are just long enough ago so that furnishings are beginning to interest collectors."[83]

Then the team commented at length on the invisibility of Mexican culture at the compound. "Big Bend is curiously free of Mexican food," wrote the reviewers, "although there is hardly any place in the park where you can't see Mexico." They suggested that "a small Mexican kitchen in the other wing of the [Garlick] house could sell tacos and burritos or something similar." The team believed that, "interpretively, the Mexican kitchen would underscore the fact that Big Bend is not as overwhelmingly Anglo as the visitors are, [and] that the ecology of the Chihuahuan Desert ignores the international boundary." Their plan for a Mexican restaurant "would certainly not be aggressively modern, but then it wouldn't be historically pure either, just a comfortable sort of bridge across the river, linking the past and the present."[84]

By 1975, the NPS had prepared a revised master plan that incorporated much of the debate and thinking about Big Bend since the early 1970s. The 1975 plan did recognize criticisms about the Muzquiz-Boquillas road, suggesting instead the La Linda bridge alternative. "Such a route would also provide much better access into the Sierra del Carmen-Fronteriza Range," said the planners, and could become "a principal feature of Mexico's proposed companion park." The planners preferred to leave border crossings at Santa Eleña and Boquillas as they were, as "the residents of the Mexican agricultural villages along the park boundary use both park roads and concession services in the Rio Grande Village and Castolon areas."[85]

Should the NPS be permitted to implement these ideas, concluded the 1975 planning document, the park service could make great strides to preserving the wilderness conditions that had prevailed centuries ago. Echoing the words of Walter Prescott Webb four decades earlier, the planners wrote that "Big Bend National Park provides an opportunity for a desert experience unequalled in quality or quantity in its region and the Nation." As had previous generations of NPS planners and scientists, the 1975 document called for "sound land-use practices, effective water utilization, and establishment of a companion park in Mexico" as the "major priorities for the continued qualitative use of the park."[86]

Then park planners reminded NPS officials that "every encouragement should be given to the development of the park in Mexico by that government." They believed, as had commentators as diverse as Roger Toll, Everett Townsend, and Daniel Galicia in the 1930s, that "physically, the outstanding resources in the Big Bend National Park landscape are matched, and in some cases excelled, by the outstanding resources in Mexico south of the Rio Grande." The "facilities, developments, and wild areas for the two parks," wrote the NPS team, "would be planned to complement one another, to heighten the visitor's understanding of the region's plant and animal life and wildlife, and to better interpret the relationships between the Rio Grande watershed and all the people who inhabit it."[87]

Trapping and poaching shared space in Big Bend with yet another historic resource problem: trespass livestock from Mexico. A 1984 review lamented the fact that NPS programs to restore the denuded grasslands and eroded stream banks now confronted an increase of illegal grazing. "Some of the trespass is deliberate," the report stated, while "some is accidental, but with no real efforts made by the Mexican people to prevent the activity." This the reviewer attributed to "a definite lack of an adequate feed source on the Mexican side of the river caused by severe overgrazing and a prolonged drought." The reviewer had observed that "many animals are literally starving to death." The report did note that "the problem along the park boundary which borders ranches in the United States is similar but not nearly as significant as along the river." This condition occurred because of "livestock crossing into the park through downed or damaged fences."[88]

As with the master planning process, the 1984 natural resources review offered cogent solutions to problems of long standing in the park. No fewer than eleven recommendations revolved around the hiring of more staff to round up trespass stock, remove fire dangers, catalog cultural resources, conduct backcountry patrols, and execute more effective law enforcement. The Rio Grande Wild and Scenic River needed its own staff so that Big Bend rangers "could spend additional time on duties and responsibilities in the park."[89]

In like manner, the park would benefit from a full-time employee serving as "liaison with neighboring Mexican states and communities to help mitigate resource threats which originate in Mexico." "The price will be high to protect those things for which the park was established," concluded the reviewer. Yet "it is a price well worth paying," as "continued impacts and damage to the park's resources cannot be allowed to continue." Ignoring these features of resource management "will mean that our mandates have not been fulfilled, and that future generations will be denied the right to experience this park in an 'unimpaired' state."[90]

CHAPTER 6

Guardians or Warriors? Rangers in the Cold War Years

The essence of national park designation is features of natural or cultural significance not found elsewhere in America. For Big Bend National Park, the existence of 124 miles of the Rio Grande coursing along its southern boundary meant issues of planning, operations, maintenance, interpretation, and law enforcement rarely encountered in the vast NPS system. Then the presence of an international neighbor along that river further distinguished Big Bend from other units of the park service. From the end of World War II, through the "Sunbelt boom" and Cold War of the 1950s and 1960s, the violence of the drug wars of the 1970s, and the efforts of the late twentieth century to restore the civility first apparent in the era of the New Deal and the Good Neighbor Policy, Big Bend National Park had to fashion policies and procedures about the use of the Rio Grande that had no equivalent anywhere in the NPS network. Finally, the restoration of cordial relations with Mexico in the last two decades of the twentieth century, aided by the passage in 1994 of the North American Free Trade Agreement (NAFTA), allowed the dream of Franklin D. Roosevelt and Lázaro Cárdenas to reappear in the form of discussions about collaboration where once there was only violence and war.

Upon reflection at a distance of seventy-five years, a student of Big Bend could surmise that park management would have been a challenge, even without the presence of the Rio Grande. Big Bend's isolation, distance, and aridity; the attitudes of local communities and ranchers; and the fluctuations in funding that beset all NPS units would have taxed the patience and imagination of every superintendent and staff. Yet the Rio Grande possessed its own ecology, cultural life, and policy imperatives, such that the fate of Big Bend over the years often hinged on the success or failure of its managers to understand the river and its users (both Mexican and American).

Those policies included ones concerning efforts to rid the landscape of historic cultural resources, the production of candelilla wax (itself a legal product until the close of World War II), trespass livestock, and immigrants seeking a better life north of the Rio Grande. At century's end, the NPS finally had come to grips with the need for careful attention to the river's realities, with the hope of shared use of the Big Bend landscape more promising, and the memory of border conflict a feature left to history.

When the first superintendent at Big Bend, Ross Maxwell, assumed his duties in the summer of 1944, much had changed in the relationship of the United States and Mexico since the days when the NPS geologist had hiked with Everett Townsend along the Rio Grande and into Mexico. Lane Simonian writes that after 1940, "Mexican policymakers did not provide conservation agencies with enough human power to enforce land use restrictions in nature reserves." First with President Manuel Ávila Camacho (1940–1946), then with his successors for the next four decades, Mexico "promoted the expansion of agribusiness to provide the underpinnings for industrialization itself."[1]

World War II brought to Mexico, as it would for the United States, a bonanza of factory and farm production that had to be sustained in order to avoid relapses into the depths of depression. For Camacho, says Simonian, this meant that "Mexico should industrialize to meet its domestic needs so that it could break its cycle of dependency in which it exported cheap raw materials and imported expensive manufactured goods." Given such imperatives, says Simonian, "the Mexican government was a principal agent in the country's environmental decline."[2]

This shift of emphasis at the dawn of the park's existence suggested that neither nation would address the binational resource in the same way as their predecessors of a decade earlier. Julio Carrera, director of the Maderas del Carmen protected area in the state of Coahuila, noted in a 1999 interview that "after 1940, the United States and Mexico turned to other issues." From his thirty-year perspective of natural resource management and research at La Universidad Antonio Narro in Saltillo, Coahuila, Carrera declared that "the politicians looked for urban development," while "the structure of natural resources in Mexico placed [the bi-national park concept] under some economic agency."[3]

One example of this policy's affecting the Rio Grande and Big Bend was the signing in May 1944 of the treaty between Mexico and the United States regulating usage of the waters of the border streams. Carlos Marin, chief engineer for the International Boundary and Water Commission in El Paso, recalled in a 1998 interview that the treaty allocated to Mexico one-half of the streamflow in the Rio Grande below Fort Quitman, Texas. "Mexico's policies on irrigation can be variable," said Marin, as "water has been a sensitive issue between the US and Mexico." Hence usage of water and land resources would occupy much of the thinking of both nations during and after World War II, leaving dreams of a national park on hold.[4]

What did exist on the border in 1944 was a world inhabited by people like Maggie Smith. As the wartime operator of J. O. Langford's Hot Springs resort, Maggie (a native of Uvalde, Texas) and her husband, Baylor, returned in 1943 at the behest of the Texas State Parks Board. John Jameson writes that park officials "were concerned that the vacant site would fall prey to vandals during the transition from state to national park." Etta Koch, the administrative assistant at Big Bend from 1946 to 1955, had come to the river in 1944 in search of a cure for the tuberculosis that she had contracted in her native Ohio. When her photographer-husband, Peter Koch, traveled around the country in the winters showing his films of Big Bend, Etta and her three daughters moved into one of the cabins at the Hot Springs.[5]

She remembered in a 1996 interview that among the qualities that appealed to the NPS about Maggie Smith was her ability to speak Spanish. "Mexicans came over to her store to trade," recalled Koch, and they would make "clothes out of flour sacks, and were very particular about the choice of sacks" at the Hot Springs store. Koch also spoke of attending a wedding in Boquillas with Smith. "It was a 'pretty wedding,'" Koch noted, where "men and women sat on opposite sides of the dance floor." Then "someone had a baby in the middle of the dance," recalled Koch, and as "Maggie was a midwife, [she] delivered it." Smith also gained fame along the river for delivering sacks of candy to Mexican children on Christmas eve, an event in which Koch once participated while staying at the resort.[6]

Some of the most distinctive stories of the first years of the park's relationship to the Rio Grande and Mexico came with the memories of Curtis Schaafsma, the young son of park ranger Harold Schaafsma. Curtis, later to become the state archaeologist for New Mexico, and whose wife, Polly, would write extensively about petroglyphs in the Southwest (including the NPS's Petroglyph National Monument near Albuquerque), visited Big Bend each summer between 1948 and 1953 to stay with his father. Through the eyes of a youth (Curtis first arrived at Big Bend at the age of ten), the Rio Grande was a place of wonder and mystery. "It is hard to explain how wild the river was," recalled Schaafsma in 1996.[7]

One day in the summer of 1948, Harold and Curtis joined NPS ranger Stan Sprecher and Bobby Cooper (son of W. A. Cooper, storeowner near Persimmon Gap), to navigate Santa Elena Canyon. They took one large automobile tire's inner tube and "walked five hours from Lajitas to the Rio Grande without water." Curtis remembered nearly fifty years later that "none of the 1948 party had been down the river before." They entered the river above Santa Eleña Canyon and floated "to the rock fall, then up Fern Canyon on the Mexican side." Schaafsma noted that "maidenhair ferns grew out of the rocks," impressing him as "an Eden." Two years later, Schaafsma and several other park rangers rode the river through Mariscal Canyon in war-surplus life rafts. "Mariscal Canyon was a marvelous trip," said Schaafsma, "but the River Road was very rough in those days to get to Tally [the entrance point to Marsical Canyon]." Schaafsma believed that "this was the beginning of proper river trips."[8]

Beyond the experience of navigating two of Big Bend's canyons, Schaafsma made mental notes of the communities along the river that stayed with him for five decades. "People on the Mexican side," said Schaafsma, "were growing crops and running stock." He recalled "an active town life in San Vicente and Boquillas." The mines in the Sierra del Carmen "sent ore trucks through Boquillas to Marathon," he remembered, and he also recollected his own experience in catching rides on the trucks from Marathon to park headquarters at Panther Junction. "These were huge six-by-six transport trucks," said Schaafsma, necessary for the carrying of silver ore. He also mentioned in 1996 that "life in Boquillas was 'real Mexico,'" as he met "river runners, cowboys, rangers, and all wore pistols."[9]

Then Schaafsma recalled that "the Mexicans were equally rowdy." He detected "much tension because of the untrustworthiness of the *federales*," even though the latter limited banditry. This degree of law enforcement was necessary, as "few people went south of Boquillas because of violence." Schaafsma had scant memories of the town of San Vicente but did recall that "Castolon was really neat." He saw farms irrigated at Cottonwood Campground, and "the Castolon store was where farmers shopped." The latter establishment "had very little for tourists," even though it operated year-round. Schaafsma also spoke of the Greene brothers, Aaron and Wayne, who were "river riders" for the US Department of Agriculture's Bureau of Animal Husbandry. The Greenes, said Schaafsma, "kept cattle with hoof and mouth disease out of the United States." They also would "kill trespass stock, of which there were quite a few," with the animals coming through the park on trails that ran from Lajitas to Stillwell's Crossing.[10]

As the decade of the 1950s unfolded, Big Bend's reputation as a border park would attract young rangers eager to serve in a rugged wilderness setting. One of these was Joe Rumburg, whose year at the park (1950–1951) was part of a long career that included service as director of the NPS's Southwest Regional Office in Santa Fe (1974–1976). Rumburg came to Big Bend to be the district ranger at Castolon, discovering that "the big problem on the border was candelilla [wax] harvesting." Speaking from retirement in 1996, Rumburg recalled that "Mexican *forestales* [forest service officials] ran candelilla harvesters across the river." The Mexican government then "bought wax from the harvesters, [and] sold it either in Mexico or the United States for profit." Local residents told Rumburg that "candelilla was used in wax records, and also cosmoline." He knew that the wax "was used by the military as packing for rifles," as it was "the equivalent of a vacuum seal." From his perspective at Castolon, Rumburg encountered "no trouble with illegal immigrants." He conducted no river patrols, instead joining the animal-husbandry bureau in removal of trespass stock. "There were few law enforcement problems," Rumburg concluded, with "wax running . . . the only real [challenge]."[11]

Serving with Rumburg in 1950 at the Boquillas district was Bob Smith, who recalled forty-six years later how he and Rumburg constituted the entire NPS presence along the river. Boquillas, Texas, that year offered Smith "an old ranch house" with "a white-washed adobe wall between [there] and Aaron Greene's." Nearby, said Smith, "was an old structure that had been a restaurant at Boquillas station," perhaps the famed Chata's frequented by NPS and Mexican officials in the 1930s. Burros would cross the Rio Grande "to drink at the Boquillas spring," recalled Smith, and "there was a gas engine to pump water into a tank on the roof of [his] house." In the one hundred-plus degree heat of a Big Bend summer, "the water was very hot," allowing Smith to take hot showers in the open. His porch "was screened by ocotillo branches," and the "roof was made of carrizo cane."[12]

One of Smith's first encounters with law enforcement on the river occurred when he and Rumburg "went on big roundups of hoof-and-mouth searches, riding from Boquillas to Santa Elena." Smith recalled that he, Rumburg, and the Greene brothers "stopped at an abandoned ranch to corral stock for blood tests" and to prepare them for auction. Unfortunately, said Smith, "the stock had venereal diseases and had to be disposed of." On another occasion, the district rangers joined with chief park ranger George Sholley on a search of Santa Elena Canyon, where they found wild burros on park land. "George shot and killed three or four burros," Smith remembered, "and asked the others to shoot the rest." Sholley also would fly in fixed-wing aircraft belonging to the US Department of Agriculture in search of animals, while the "hoof-and-mouth riders covered areas of four to eleven miles each day."[13]

Yet another detail of Smith's patrols was the search for candelilla wax camps. "In May 1950," said the former Castolon ranger, "candelilla wax sold for twenty-two cents per pound." He noted that "Mexicans could not bring wax into the US, but once here it could be sold." The following year, "wax sold for fifty-four cents per pound," and "the *forestales* wanted their cut of wax production." He remembered that Maggie Smith would purchase wax from Mexican producers, and "so did Raymond Fisk of San Vicente."[14]

As had Schaafsma, Bob Smith marveled at the distinctiveness of life in the Mexican villages across the river from Big Bend. Smith once was asked to go to Boquillas to purchase liquor for a party held by NPS staff in the Chisos basin, as this was the closest place to do so. "There were lots of goats running through town," he recalled, while "children were poorly dressed and barefoot." To Smith, Boquillas "looked like a slum area." He noted that "the locals had a little garden between the Rio Grande and town." Boquillas itself consisted of "only thirteen adobe units," and "there was a tower and cable used to transport ore."[15]

Smith then recounted an incident where a young girl, bitten by a rattlesnake, had been brought across the river to the ranger's office. Smith took her to Alpine (a distance of 120 miles), only to be "later told that Alpine doctors did not like indigent patients." Then when a knifing occurred at Boquillas, Smith "did nothing because of his earlier experience." Someone else transported the wounded man to Alpine, and Smith then was advised "to take people to Alpine" again.[16]

Into this contested landscape came Lemuel "Lon" Garrison, who served for two years as park superintendent (1952–1954). A veteran of eighteen years in the NPS, Garrison would write in his 1983 autobiography that the Rio Grande during the Cold War had become highly militarized. "With 127 miles of common boundary," said the superintendent, "we obviously had many Mexican contacts." While the park service described the region as "a 'friendly' and undefended boundary," Garrison observed that "the United States has established a powerful force of police." At the border crossings, "the usual Immigration and Border Patrol rules applied." Yet near the river, said Garrison, "our park patrol rangers . . . were the action force." It was they who "would make notes and report problems to the Border Patrol and the U.S. Customs."[17]

This transition of park rangers from guardians to warriors also affected the potential for creation of the international peace park. "The idea was still inviting," said Garrison, "but it would require a lot of political maneuvering." While he spent only two years in Big Bend, Garrison came to learn that "Mexico is a proud nation." He wrote forty years after his interactions with Mexican officials and local residents alike, "A Fronterisa National Park must be truly representative of Mexico and not just another border community as an American tourist attraction." Garrison could not forget that "Mexican people must use it and be proud of it." Unfortunately for both nations, said the superintendent, "this was not possible at the time."[18]

As the 1950s advanced, and the NPS invested monies in facility development under the aegis of Mission 66, park officials had to resolve the question of their relationship to the river. Chief ranger George Sholley's demolition of the Hot Springs caused no small amount of tension on both sides of the Rio Grande. This included placing the NPS in the awkward position of asking Maggie Smith to leave. Monte Fitch, chief ranger from 1957 to 1959, recalled four decades later that "Maggie Smith was in on everything happening on the river." Fitch claimed that "she smuggled guns into Mexico," and that she "could tell stories that were unbelievable."

By contrast, said Fitch, "George Sholley was not loved on the river," nor did the ranger venture across it very often.[19]

When the park service closed the Hot Springs concession, writes John Jameson, "fifteen hundred people signed a petition to allow Maggie to stay, but to no avail." Smith and her husband then left to operate stores in the town of San Vicente (until it too was bulldozed), and then on the western edge of the park in Study Butte (where she died in 1965). Russell Dickenson, chief ranger at Big Bend in 1955–1956, would note in a 1997 interview that "Maggie Smith was still in business" when he arrived, and that she was "an independent western woman . . . [who] tolerated rangers because they were no threat." Dickenson, who in 1980 became director of the park service, recalled that "her trade with Mexicans was the basis of her business," and that "she spoke Spanish well." For Dickenson, "the border was its own world," and Smith symbolized all that was good and bad about it.[20]

Dickenson's year at Big Bend was marked by the enthusiasm with which he and his rangers addressed the persistent candelilla wax trade. There had been talk of Big Bend being incorporated in plans for civil defense against foreign aggression (primarily fears of Communist invasion in the Cold War). Should a nuclear attack or conventional invasion occur, Big Bend would serve as a military training and surveillance center. Dickenson, a veteran of World War II, was told by Superintendent George Miller "to carry the fight against wax camps." The chief ranger recalled that "rangers' shirts were covered with sulfuric acid from blowing up vats." The Mexican wax producers used tubs made from "fifty-five gallon barrels . . . cut in half" that "could handle .45-caliber shot." Dickenson and his rangers would use Primacord, an explosive that they acquired from the military, to "explode the vats." His theory was that "veterans knew how to use explosives."[21]

Keeping with the combat motif, Dickenson further stated that he and the ranger staff "used 'search-and-destroy' tactics for trespass stock." When NPS staff "saw horses on the US side opposite villages like San Vicente, the rangers would warn villagers." If the Mexicans did not gather up their animals, "these would be shot" as well. Dickenson's logic was that "Big Bend had a small force." Aerial surveillance identified the camps, and two-to-three-man teams "used the element of surprise, coming in at daybreak." What Dickenson often found were "primitive" conditions, and he and his rangers burned any supplies left behind by the wax workers.[22]

In contrast to the military-style raids on the wax camps, said Dickenson, was the sporadic interaction between the park and the Mexican communities. Echoing Bob Smith and other rangers of the 1950s, Dickenson recalled that "the villages were primitive." Rangers would cross the Rio Grande at Boquillas to purchase "Boca Negra whiskey," and "there was a one-day fiesta when Panther Junction and Boquillas got together for a barbecue." Dickenson recalled no "cross-river transportation," and "no visitors went to Boquillas unless they could drive." He did note that "there was individual boating and rafting," but that "Big Bend did not issue permits." There were no outfitters in the 1950s, and for those individuals who floated the Rio Grande, "World War II rubber rafts were the most common." Superintendent Miller did recognize the need for some level of visitor protection on the river, asking his chief ranger to train the rangers in search-and-rescue techniques.[23]

Monte Fitch's tenure as chief ranger at Big Bend echoed the experiences of Dickenson, only with a larger staff and more financial resources as a result of Mission 66 development projects. When he came to the park, "rangers shot everything that crossed the river." Then Superintendent Miller decided to halt the shooting of animals, "as this had made people destitute." In addition, the park generated "bad public relations" from the campaign to rid feral and trespass stock. Candelilla production, however, continued to face ranger attacks under Fitch. "Candelilla was harvested by permit in Mexico," he recalled in 1997, and the park service had "no authority to cross the river."[24]

Fitch and his patrol crews found piles of candelilla "as big as haystacks," with the plants "torn out by the roots." He then learned that "it was legal to bring candelilla across the river and sell to Marathon and Alpine." Fitch "ordered blocks of [the explosive] TNT, and packed it into the camps." The park service then "detonated the drums, and also confiscated the [pack] burros." Fitch would find that "mostly Santa Elena and Mariscal Canyons were isolated enough for wax camps." He also discovered that "there were a lot of arms and ammunition going to Mexico, and also lots of illegals [Mexican nationals] heading north."[25]

At decade's end, the Rio Grande seemed to new rangers like Eldon Reyer, Chuck McCurdy, and Bill Wendt to be, in the words of Karen Reyer (the daughter of former superintendent Lon Garrison), "wild and wooly." McCurdy, who served as the ranger for the Maverick district in the late 1950s, remembered forty years later the work of Aaron and Wayne Greene on the hoof-and-mouth patrols. "Aaron Greene had been ten years old," said McCurdy, "when Mexican raiders had crossed the Rio Grande in 1916." Greene told him four decades after the fact that he "remembered fleeing to safety." This made the Greene brothers "very cagey about relations with Mexico," a circumstance exacerbated by "incidents with the hoof-and-mouth disease campaign."[26]

For McCurdy, "there was very little law enforcement, except for candelilla camps and trespass stock." He knew that "tanks [for the wax] were made at Lajitas by Rex Ivey, a car dealer in Alpine." Ivey would charge twenty-five dollars for his tanks, "which were floated down the Rio Grande to Santa Elena Canyon, then carried up the [Mesa de Anguila]." McCurdy also learned firsthand of the rigors of rafting the Rio Grande, as he joined photographer Peter Koch on one outing. On another occasion, the Maverick district ranger used a "two-man sur-plus air force craft . . . to go through the [Santa Eleña] canyon after a flood to look for damage and bodies." He found it "hard to get through the rock slide," and heard from local *Hispanos* that "there was a 'bull' in the water between Laji-tas and Santa Elena that rose up and ate people."[27]

McCurdy would in later years find the level of tension on the border trou-bling, preferring to dwell on his commitment to cultural understanding. After the flood of 1958, he learned from the "head of the [Santa Eleña] *ejido* . . . that they needed medical supplies." McCurdy then approached the Red Cross to pro-vide these necessities, while he solicited the aid of the Civil Air Patrol to bring them to the park. From there the Red Cross conveyed the medical supplies and food to Santa Eleña in rubber army rafts.[28]

McCurdy also recalled the efforts of river ranger Rod Broyles and his wife, Phyllis, to bring some semblance of decency to the trespass stock removal pro-gram. Both of the Broyles spoke Spanish, and Phyllis would offer evening instruc-tion in the language for any park staff who demonstrated an interest. "They wrote brand names in Spanish on paper," remembered McCurdy, "and told the people that the NPS would round up the stock." Once impounded, "Mexicans came to the corral at Maverick [district] to pick up their stock." Local Mexicans came to view the Maverick and Castolon districts as "a customs and check sta-tion," and "when locals wanted questions answered, they were put on the radio to Phyllis Broyles."[29]

McCurdy contrasted this effort at cultural accommodation with stories told to him by Wayne Greene, who recalled working with Joe Rumburg in stalking a wax camp. "Joe took out his revolver," said McCurdy, "and looked at the escap-ing Mexicans." Their flight had made "Joe so angry," said Greene, that "he was going to shoot the Mexican 'like a duck in a rain barrel.'" Wayne then "hit Joe's arm as he fired," propelling the bullet harmlessly away. The second story of bor-der tension that remained with McCurdy involved Wendell Bryce, a ranger who claimed descent from Ebenezer Bryce, owner of the land that became Utah's Bryce Canyon National Park. Bryce and McCurdy came upon a wax camp where McCurdy "found a Mexican with his ten-year-old boy." He recalled that "they did not run, and the family crossed over" the Rio Grande. At that point he "took the man in, and his family was crying." McCurdy later learned that the wax worker "was processed at La Tuna [the federal prison] in El Paso."[30]

Yet a third border incident that defined the complexity of the border for McCurdy was the campaign to stop the smuggling of cotton across the river from Santa Eleña to Castolon. "The Castolon cotton ranch was suspected of receiving cotton from the Santa Eleña *ejido* without passing through customs," said McCurdy. Park rangers asked Wayne Greene to "cross the river one night to sprinkle fluorescent powder on the cotton, so that it could be traced." No more problems emanated from the Mexican cotton fields after Greene's espionage.[31]

Border issues by 1960 were central to the thinking of Superintendent George Miller and his assistant, Hank Schmidt, who served as acting superintendent that year between Miller's departure and the arrival of his successor, Stanley Joseph. For Schmidt, the river area was as wild as any park where he had worked for the NPS. This included Arches National Park in southeastern Utah, a place that inspired seasonal ranger Edward Abbey in 1968 to write his book *Desert Solitaire*. "The River Road had only carried ore trucks," Schmidt remembered in 1996, "and had to be improved for visitors." He also found "no motorboating on the Rio Grande," and "few rafters."[32]

It was Superintendent Miller who "came up with the idea of permits for rafters." Float trips by Schmidt led him to conclude, "The Rio Grande is not a 'boating' river; it is for rafting." At first the river was used primarily by people from El Paso and Alpine. Then "tourists came unprepared," said Schmidt, requiring NPS staff to warn them of the dangers of the river, most significantly the need for plenty of drinking water.[33]

For Assistant Superintendent Schmidt, as with his predecessors in park management, matters of wax making and trespass stock absorbed much of his time. "The candelilla problem was west of the Hot Springs," he recalled, "in the lower foothills of the Chisos." He and the rangers found "regular trails to the candelilla." Compounding this, said Schmidt, was the fact that "Jim Casner was buying candelilla wax for a nickel a pound," even though he was "a big booster of the park." With trespass stock, Schmidt went to Boquillas to discuss the issue. There he learned that "Mexico was different, and NPS staff were welcomed." Schmidt later remembered that "the towns were very poor," and that "a Lions' Club in Marathon . . . took Christmas groceries to Boquillas." In addition, "park staff gave their old clothes to Boquillas." He also noted that "drugs were no problem for Big Bend in the 1950s." Yet he did recall that "Mexicans would come for [the hallucinogen] peyote between Boquillas and the foothills of the Chisos." The Mexicans followed "an old road from Boquillas west to the Chisos" to harvest peyote, which they then sold across the river.[34]

Bill Wendt would recall his exposure to the river in 1959 as the Santa Elena subdistrict ranger as the start of a career in international park affairs. Upon his arrival at Big Bend, Rod Broyles issued Wendt "a pistol and ammo without law enforcement training." He then acquired along the border what he called "*campesino* Spanish," a skill that would serve him well on duty. "Santa Elena," recalled Wendt in 1996, "was part of the '*ejido* system' of colonizing empty areas of Mexico." He realized that "there was just enough land to make farming pay." His duties included "a lot of first aid," as well as patrol with Mexican customs officers "who were rotated out every sixteen days." "Fight victims" received medical care at the Santa Eleña subdistrict, and Wendt remembered repairing "a Mexican customs official who had shot off his own finger in target practice."[35]

"Law enforcement at Santa Eleña was lonely," Wendt remembered. He worked with the Greene brothers on river patrols, where "they shot and burned trespass animals in the hoof-and-mouth season." Wendt faced the same issues as his predecessors with candelilla wax. "There was a lot of candelilla trade in the park," he noted, "and it generated cash money." Wendt came to realize that "it is an individual decision by staff to work with the border," and that he had to resolve international issues with little guidance from park administration.[36]

The border that Stan Joseph encountered in his three-year tour as superintendent (1960–1963) reflected two decades of NPS efforts to control trespass stock grazing and candelilla production (both legal before 1944). In a 1996 interview, Joseph would remember that on his arrival, Hugh White, the mayor of Alpine and owner of a motel, and others introduced him to Glen Garrett of the Texas governor's Good Neighbor Commission. This group had formed when "lodging and accommodations were denied to Mexicans." While this gesture indicated goodwill among local merchants, by 1960 "the peace park idea had quieted." Whatever discussions had existed in the 1950s to establish an international peace park like Waterton-Glacier would not surface for another generation. Local personalities like Paul Forschheimer "wanted a joint educational program between Big Bend and Mexico," recalled Joseph, while the venerable rancher Hallie Stillwell "said that the Hot Springs had to be restored."[37]

Then Joseph accidentally learned of the scale and scope of the candelilla wax controversy while visiting with Jim Casner in his automobile dealership. "Casner Motor Company supplied sulfuric acid for the candelilla trade," said Joseph, because "Mexico put a 100 percent tax on the export of candelilla." Mexicans would process the wax in the park, then haul it back by mule south of the border. The day that Joseph met with Casner, the Chevrolet dealer received a telephone call that a rail car in the Alpine railyards was leaking three thousand gallons of sulfuric acid. Casner had to leave to oversee the cleanup. Joseph later learned that Casner had asked permission to harvest lechuguilla in the park, pursuing the idea all the way to the office of Interior Secretary Douglas McKay (himself a Chevrolet dealer from Oregon), but to no avail.[38]

Superintendent Joseph's exposure to the border itself would remain in his mind long after his departure. Early in his tour, Joseph and his wife crossed over to Boquillas on the tram. "Boquillas was a fluorspar center then," he recalled, and "smugglers crossed by signal lights." When local residents "got the flu, the NPS asked the Lions' Club of Alpine to give inoculations and blankets," as well as "polio shots." Joseph found that Santa Eleña "was very similar, but was less

developed [than Boquillas] with fewer bars, [and] no fluorspar mining." Santa
Elena farmers "pumped water out of the Rio Grande into ditches," said Joseph,
while they crossed the river to Castolon to collect their mail. "The contrast
between Castolon and Santa Elena was stark," a situation compounded by the
presence nearby of Texas Rangers. The latter "questioned the NPS's jurisdiction in
the 'wetback period,'" a derogatory term for the 1950s concern for immigrants
swimming across the Rio Grande to avoid detection. Joseph also recalled that
"smuggling was known," and that the Rangers "felt that they had to use force to
stop the well-armed mule trains."[39]

Joseph's assessment of the border's role in park operations held true until the
end of the 1960s, when the US Congress in 1968 passed the Wild and Scenic
Rivers Act. While it would be another decade before the Rio Grande flowing
through Big Bend would receive such a designation, the interest in river use by
rafters gained momentum with publicity surrounding Lady Bird Johnson's 1966
trip. By decade's end, Jim Milburn, then the director of Big Bend's concessions
for National Park Concessions Inc. (NPCI), would join with Glenn Pepper on
one of his first float trips on the Rio Grande. Milburn, to become in the late
1990s president of NPCI, recalled in a 1997 interview that Pepper "had an old
school bus, and filled his rafts with propane tanks." When Milburn first came to
Big Bend in 1963, he saw that "there was no volume of river traffic." This Milburn attributed to the fact that "access to the river was bad."[40]

With the rise in the 1970s of environmental consciousness, and the initiative
to create protected wilderness areas in the United States, devotees of river rafting
acquired more reason to promote wild-and-scenic status for Big Bend. Yet that
decade also witnessed what might be called the low point of border relations, with
the rise of narcotics traffic, more incidents of trespass stock and wax production,
and ever-growing migration of Mexicans north of the river to seek employment.[41]

With no small sense of irony, NPCI president Garner Hanson recalled in a 1997
interview that the 1970s witnessed the apex of the "wild West" promotion. For
NPCI, the park, and tourism officials in Brewster County, the "outlaw, *bandido*, and
cowboy image drew visitors." Even the "wax trade and drugs . . . added to the mys-
tique of Big Bend," recalled the longtime park concessions president. That perspective would attract and repel NPS employees, compounding the ongoing problems
of managing a large park unit with limited resources. Rob Arnberger, superintendent at Big Bend from 1990 to 1994, noted in a 1996 interview that he first had traveled to the park in 1973 "on a narcotics detail." As a young law enforcement ranger
(and the son of a prominent NPS official), Arnberger knew something of the cultural
complexity and environmental challenge posed by Big Bend.[42]

Yet Arnberger, like so many of his park service peers in the 1970s, recalled that
he thought he had "entered the macho world of the border" to work with customs

agents. "There had been shootings and drug smuggling," said Arnberger, who thought that he had returned to "the Texas Ranger days." Even though the United States remained ensnared in the conflict far away in Vietnam, Arnberger found at Big Bend "army units that dug foxholes and waited for drug smugglers." In a way, Big Bend had reverted to the tension and ethnic distrust that had marked the border in the first decades of the twentieth century. This time the improvement of transportation and communications masked the real issues of poverty, distance, isolation, and violence that would fester as the decade advanced.[43]

In 1971 the NPS selected as superintendent Joe Carithers, whose legacy at Big Bend would be the deterioration of park operations and the collapse of good-neighbor relations with Mexico. Until his removal by Southwest Region director John Cook in 1978, Carithers oversaw a park that several of his staff remembered as riddled with "paranoia," in the words of Mike Fleming, who worked from 1981 to 1996 in the park's Science and Resources Management Division. Jim Liles, chief ranger at Big Bend from 1977 to 1983, recalled in 1997 that the border's effect on Carithers was palpable. "Joe Carithers was consumed by the smuggling of drugs," said Liles, as he "had a propensity for the romantic aspects of Big Bend." The controversial superintendent "lived in the past," said Liles. He had "been with the last cavalry unit at Fort Riley [Kansas], and saw himself as 'an old cavalry guy.'"[44]

Liles learned that Carithers had admired "Big Bend's role in the 1916 Mexican Revolution, and the arrival of the air corps at Johnson's Ranch." In addition, the superintendent "liked the border raids and the Indian wars." While on duty, said Liles, "Joe was involved in a continual struggle with outlaws." Carithers "wore a gun, and got all excited when customs agents were 'on the chase.'" During his tenure at Big Bend, "customs took over patrol functions, and hassled people at night." This behavior Liles attributed to the fact that "Joe had little park management experience." He had worked previously for the National Parks and Conservation Association, and then had been selected in the late 1960s by NPS director George Hartzog "to head the NPS's Operations Evaluation Office in Washington."[45]

Getting a firsthand look at the level of tension in Big Bend during the Carithers administration was Steve Frye, hired in 1975 as a seasonal law enforcement ranger. Frye would serve one year at Big Bend, leaving for a career that had led by the time of his 1996 interview to the position of chief ranger at Glacier National Park. He recalled that "the drug trade was significant in 1975, and the NPS did not solve the drug traffic." In Frye's estimation, "there was a hell of a lot of drugs coming across the border." Stationed at the Castolon ranger district, Frye would learn that "dealers 'leaked' information to rangers about mule trains crossing the river." They then "would cross at another site."[46]

While Frye and his fellow rangers made "some major busts of El Caminos [a popular Chevrolet automobile modified for use as a pickup truck] with false beds filled with marijuana and some cocaine," the real concern was that "dealers had 'central distribution points' in Mexico." In shipping their cargo north through the park, the dealers sometimes engaged in arguments "that spilled over into the park." Frye, like ranger Bob Smith a generation before him, would recall that he "drove a youth from Santa Elena to Alpine who had been shot in the stomach for cheating a dealer."[47]

His most dramatic moment in border law enforcement, however, occurred when he joined the other Castolon rangers to cross the river into Santa Elena. While there one day, Frye "saw the *federales* haul someone down the street and shoot him." Their explanation to the terrified citizens was that "he was a drug dealer." This prompted in Frye an "overriding concern" about "how cheap life was." He also recalled that "there was a reward in Mexico for a US law enforcement officer's badge." The amount varied between $100 and $125, which Frye characterized as "a year's income" along the border. He was "not sure that the Mexican outlaws would carry out these threats," as it seemed like "a 'cat-and-mouse' game."[48]

In matters of resource protection on the border, Frye heard "a lot about candelilla theft," though he "never made any busts." Another resource utilized by local residents was what Frye called the "sale of bat guano." Finally, Frye engaged in the long-standing Big Bend tradition of impounding trespass stock along the river. He joined "the first roundup on horseback of Mexican cattle in years." The crew included "DEA [Drug Enforcement Administration], customs, and other agents." Frye, sitting in a coffee shop on a July day near the Canada-US boundary, still could recall vividly a border far to the south, where the search party "swept up the River Road area near Boquillas, and rounded up 100–125 horses, cows, and bulls." From there, park rangers took the animals to the US Department of Agriculture's corrals in Presidio, a distance of over one hundred miles, where local Mexican ranchers had to go to reclaim their stock.[49]

This degree of anxiety about drugs, contraband, and trespass stock contributed to a series of incidents at Big Bend that led in 1978 to Carithers's dismissal. Jim Liles was told of Carithers's "unwarranted fear . . . that the outside world was dangerous." Both Carithers and his assistant superintendent, Gene Balaz, "feared going down to the river and into Mexico," said Liles. Rick LoBello, a young ranger in the late 1970s at Big Bend, heard from veteran rangers that "there was concern over terrorist attacks on NPS sites in 1976 during the Bicentennial," the two hundredth anniversary of America's creation. LoBello and other staff received training to respond to such situations.[50]

Then a tragic incident marred the reputation of Big Bend even more: the shooting on the river of an undergraduate student from Sul Ross State College in a failed drug operation. Liles and Frank Deckert would recall twenty years later that the young man had been arrested by law enforcement officials for making his own illegal purchase. Then the US Customs Office enlisted his aid as part of his plea agreement to help capture drug dealers on the Rio Grande. One night, an undercover customs agent and the college student, who had no experience with clandestine activities, met with drug dealers along the road to San Vicente Crossing. Earlier, other customs agents had positioned themselves in the brush near the river. As the drug deal unfolded, the agents near the water exchanged gunfire with horseback riders who had appeared out of the dark.[51]

When the shooting began, in the words of Deckert, "one of the drug dealers spooked, pulled out a pistol, and shot and killed the Sul Ross student." The next day, Deckert flew to the area by helicopter with customs agents to take aerial photos as they re-created the crime scene. As if to add insult to injury, recalled Liles, soon after this incident the popular late-night television talk-show host Johnny Carson invited onto his *Tonight Show* a "major drug dealer turned informant" to reveal secrets of his trade. "Carson asked if he would say where the border was the easiest to cross," Liles remembered, "and the informant said Big Bend National Park." Not surprisingly, said Liles, "all of this made Carithers paranoid."[52]

The superintendent's anxieties reached their peak when stories surfaced of an encounter on the river between NPS rangers (including Carithers) and Mexican herders with trespass stock. Several park employees of the 1970s recalled how the superintendent believed, as Deckert learned in October 1975 from chief ranger Al Trulock, that "the Mexicans had automatic weapons, and that a 'revolution' was imminent." Sul Ross professor Keith Yarborough echoed this observation, recalling in 1997 that "Carithers had hand grenades and automatic weapons" of his own. The superintendent also liked to travel around the park wearing a sidearm, and Gene Balaz, assistant superintendent at Big Bend from 1976 to 1978, mentioned a ranger known as "Two-Gun" because he "put extreme pressure on wax camps to run them off."[53]

Carithers's behavior would attract the attention of NPS officials in the Santa Fe regional office and headquarters in Washington, DC. John Cook, in 1976 an associate director of operations at headquarters, learned of "a shooting of Mexican nationals by Big Bend rangers," and he sent a Washington official to the park to investigate. The following year, when Cook became director of the NPS's Southwest Region, Carithers shocked regional officials when he waded out into the Rio Grande, firing his pistol at Mexicans fleeing with their trespass stock.[54]

Two decades later, Cook would recount in an interview how outraged he and his staff (including Hispanic officials like Southwest Region personnel director José Cisneros) became. Cook sent his deputies to Big Bend to investigate, and then flew to the park with Cisneros in 1978, where they removed all supervisory personnel except chief naturalist Frank Deckert. Carithers then was offered a "desk job" in Santa Fe. He refused, leaving the park service soon thereafter.[55]

For Cook, the regional staff, and park employees, the departure of Carithers did not end the difficulties that the border posed. Cisneros, who would return to Big Bend in 1994 as its first Hispanic superintendent (and also as the first native Texan to hold that position), remarked rather acidly that "Big Bend in the 1970s was a 'plantation,' with Anglo leadership and Mexican American employees living in trailers." Cisneros agreed that "there were problems with drug interdiction," but believed that "Big Bend was a 'virtual armed camp.'" LoBello remembered that Mexicans came to the park's visitors' center for their *permisos* (authorizations to cross the river), and that "this caused some tensions" with the Anglo staff.[56]

For Balaz, Carithers's temporary replacement as superintendent, stopping the drug traffic consumed most of his time. "Dope deals were being done in park campgrounds," recalled Balaz, while "backcountry roads and the River Road had been the route for carnuba wax smugglers." In addition, "marijuana came across [the river] on horseback." Since the Southwest Region, in Balaz's estimation, "offered little support," his park "had to go it alone." Balaz coordinated an "interagency interdiction force," using officers from the newly established DEA, even though Balaz (a seasoned park ranger) considered them "primarily office people."[57]

He was surprised that "the Border Patrol did not want to deal with drugs," and thus accepted the customs office's offer of "eight officers . . . to put pressure on transfer points." Balaz noted that "the interdiction force needed manufactured housing, utilities, and a radio network." Beyond that, the team required a "working relationship with the National Park Service," all of which Balaz extended to them, with the result that "drug incidents fell 75 percent after one year of action."[58]

Robert Haraden, the new superintendent, came to Big Bend in 1978 facing a host of issues related to the border. Stopping in Santa Fe to meet regional director John Cook, Haraden would recall two decades later that Cook "wanted to reduce the law enforcement image." For the regional office, Big Bend's rangers "came on too strong, and there was a shootout at the park." Cook wanted Haraden to rebuild Big Bend's infrastructure that had suffered during the Carithers years, yet continue the campaigns against "drugs, cattle, 'wetbacks,' etc."[59]

The issue that surfaced even as Haraden acquainted himself with Big Bend was the designation of the park's stretch of the Rio Grande as a "wild and scenic river." Discussions had begun on this designation in the last six months of Balaz's tenure as acting superintendent, accelerating as Haraden took command of the park. Liles recalled that his first major task upon arrival at Big Bend in 1977 was to respond to "a notice from the Texas governor's office to start the Wild and Scenic River program." US representative Bob Krueger (D-TX) had been a major sponsor of the designation, while "the Texas Explorers Club pushed protection of the lower canyons [of the Rio Grande]."[60]

From Liles's perspective, "the whole WSR [Wild and Scenic River] issue was political." He believed that "Krueger was persuaded by river constituents [landowners] to shelve the [1978] wilderness proposal for Big Bend in exchange for not opposing the WSR." Aiding in this strategy, said Liles, was the realization that "the governor would support the WSR if the wilderness designation were dropped." Liles attended what several park officials and local residents recalled as a "bad public meeting" in Marathon. There NPS regional planning chief Doug Faris and others learned of the bitter reaction that echoed the late 1970s land-use movement known as the Sagebrush Rebellion.[61]

When Haraden left Big Bend in 1980 to assume the superintendency of Glacier National Park, he would lament that "it became a disappointment when the park service did not buy land away from the river." There would be "no place to camp along the wild and scenic river," even though "the WSR idea was to preserve unique rivers." Then Haraden recalled a revealing feature about border relations in the 1970s: "There were no negotiations with Mexico." He recalled that "there had been talk of a 'peace' or 'companion' park with Mexico," and he had attended several meetings with Mexican officials on this matter. But by 1980, the border with Mexico was to the United States a zone of conflict as it had been in the early twentieth century, when few could imagine the dream of a park for peace.[62]

CHAPTER 7

An Old Tale for a New Time—
Ghosts, Dreams, and Walls

As the Republic of Mexico and the United States entered into a new century, advocates of transnational cooperation between Big Bend National Park and the adjacent Mexican states of Coahuila and Chihuahua confronted once more their history as friends and as enemies. For two decades (the 1980s and 1990s), accommodation and shared experiences shaped a variety of initiatives, both public and private. The hopes of Presidents Lázaro Cárdenas and Franklin D. Roosevelt, now some seventy years gone, for the desolate reaches of the river with two names (Rio Grande / Rio Bravo), seemed almost within reach. Then the tragedy of violence far away—the terrorist attacks of September 11, 2001, on Americans in New York City and Washington, DC—led to calls for closing the avenues of travel and commerce between the United States and Mexico; this despite the fact that the 9/11 incidents had been perpetrated by people from the Middle East. For the next decade and more, advocates of a world where "nature has made us neighbors" labored yet again to scale what the historian Samuel Truett calls the "fences and walls [that] are prominent features of human landscapes."[1]

The decade of the 1980s began with the arrival of a new superintendent for Big Bend National Park, Gilbert Lusk. In an interview with journalist Alan Weisman, Lusk spoke of his curiosity about the international character of his new posting. Further research led the superintendent to conclude that "we've never taken the time to understand Mexico." Among Lusk's first steps was to change the longstanding policy toward confiscation of trespass livestock. Whereas Mexican ranchers had to travel one hundred miles upriver to Presidio, then pay $250 per head to reclaim their cattle, Lusk ordered his staff to charge a first-time fee of $25, raising it to $75 for further violations. Then Lusk called in 1981 for Spanish-language training for his ranger corps, and the hosting each October of an "International Good-Neighbor Day Fiesta." Villagers from fifty miles up and down the Rio Grande joined with park staff and families to share barbecue, music, and sporting events. This celebration would endure beyond Lusk's tenure, ending only when the border closed in 2002 for reasons of national security.[2]

With better relations on the river under way, Superintendent Lusk then traveled in 1981 to Saltillo, the capital of the Mexican state of Coahuila. There he hoped to meet with the governor to discuss more formal ties between his park and its southern neighbors. Lusk would recall a decade later that he waited in the lobby of the governor's office for eight hours, only to learn that they would not meet that day. Undaunted, the superintendent sought out partnerships with Mexican and American officials like Marco Antonio Girón, then a staff member of the Mexican Ministry of Urban Development and Ecology (Secretaría de Desarrollo Urbano y Ecología [SEDUE]). Girón would tell Weisman that he had written a proposal to his superiors in Mexico City to protect the resources of the Maderas del Carmén from "poachers, cattle ranchers, and the lumber industry." Should Mexico decide to acquire this land, said Girón, it could become "a Mexican counterpart to Big Bend National Park in the United States, so as to share and work in harmony, with both parks benefitting the region."[3]

Responses such as those of SEDUE's Girón would lead by 1985 to initiation of the Border States Conference on Parks, Recreation, and Wildlife. In contributing to the endeavor, Lusk had followed the guidelines established two years earlier with the signing of the United States–Mexico Agreement on Cooperation for the Protection and Improvement of the Environment in the Border Area. Dennis Vasquez, a ranger at Big Bend in the early 1980s who would return a decade later to serve as chief of interpretation, wrote in 1994 that this strategy "provides a forum for scientists, researchers, and resource professionals from the border region in both countries to present papers and exchange information." Vasquez believed that "many doors had been opened and many alliances have been built as a result of these conferences." The fall fiesta and the border meetings became mainstays of park outreach. This supported Lusk's belief that "our strategy was broad enough to allow us to build on success and not have minor failures along the way derail the entire process."[4]

Two other issues on the border challenged Lusk and his peers as they sought to be the "good neighbors" that Franklin D. Roosevelt had envisioned. In 1981, Washington officials of the park service announced their rejection of the park's General Management Plan (GMP) for the Rio Grande Wild and Scenic River. This decision left river operations and funding in limbo until the mid-1990s, when Superintendent José Cisneros and his staff prepared a new management document that incorporated the concerns that had burdened the first endeavor.

Then, in 1987, the reputed Mexican drug dealer Pablo Acosta (a native of the village of Santa Eleña) was captured and killed in his hometown by US and Mexican agents (including park service rangers). In each case (the WSR denial and the Acosta raid), the strain on the "good neighbor" initiative threatened to undo the hard work of Lusk, the park staff, and their colleagues in Mexico. Yet a decade later, the call for better relations along the river would result in the most ambitious effort to unite the two nations since the heady days of the 1930s.

The WSR planning team, directed by John Murphy of the NPS's Denver Service Center, submitted their findings in November 1981 to headquarters. They had noted that the original idea of an expansive river corridor could not be achieved. The WSR designation instead would be "only the river area from the United States/Mexico international boundary in the center of the river to the gradient boundary at the edge of the river on the United States side." Its length ran from the Chihuahua-Coahuila state line to the Val Verde county line. Segments of this 195-mile stretch of the Rio Grande from Talley to Solis (the area known as Mariscal Canyon), from the Boquillas Canyon entrance to its exit, and from Reagan Canyon to San Francisco Canyon below the park boundary line would become the "wild" portions of the Rio Grande. "The remaining sections," said the authors of the 1981 report, "shall be designated as SCENIC." Staff from Big Bend National Park would supervise this resource, while two public-access points would be negotiated with private landowners below the park boundary—the La Linda community and Dryden Crossing.[5]

In studying the river for its wild and scenic qualities, the park service learned much about its character and its challenges. Water quantity would be affected by conditions upstream along the Rio Conchos in Mexico. During periods of "storm-related stream-flow rises," said the report, "high concentrations of fecal coliform bacteria can occur as the adjacent land surface is washed by rainfall runoff." The authors also expressed "some concern about water quality degradation related to the fluorspar process plant at La Linda, Mexico." They also witnessed "mercury pollution emanating from an area of abandoned mercury mines in the Terlingua Creek drainage on the west side of Big Bend National Park."[6]

Yet the "most significant water quality problem in the area of the Rio Grande," said the report, "is the presence of DDT and its metabolites." Park service planners had discovered that "concentrations of these compounds in excess of the levels recommended by the Food and Drug Administration have been found in Rio Grande fish near Presidio, Texas." The agency believed that this came from Mexican irrigation return flows to the Rio Conchos, and "high levels of DDT residues seem to be concentrated in the area where the Rio Conchos joins the Rio Grande."[7]

Another resource issue confronting the river planning team was that of air quality. "Preliminary information from Big Bend," wrote NPS staff in 1981, "indicates that the area experiences decreased visibility in some directions, probably as a result of high-altitude particulates originating from industrial facilities in El Paso, Texas; Carlsbad, New Mexico; and perhaps from northern Mexico." In addition, park planners noted emission of particulates from the DuPont Chemical Company's fluorspar mill at La Linda. Then the report prophesied that "impaired visibility and acid precipitation are potential air quality problems for the future," although both problems would result from activities distant from the Rio Grande Wild and Scenic River.[8]

The NPS's acknowledgment that it could not control any land along the riverbank also restricted planning for wild and scenic status. To halt the designation process, a group of private landowners formed the Texans for the Preservation of the Rio Grande. When that failed, said Dudley Harrison, county judge for Terrell County, they approached lawmakers in Austin and Washington to compel the park service to accept the limitations found in the 1981 report. By March of the following year, the NPS would instruct its regional office in Santa Fe to cancel implementation of the WSR plan, leaving the river with little funding and staff. Then, in 1986, Congress amended the Wild and Scenic Rivers Act to permit "study" rivers like the Rio Grande to have an "interim boundary" that ran one-quarter mile from their average high-water mark.[9]

Jim Carrico, who served as superintendent in the late 1980s, recalled a decade later that "the Rio Grande WSR was not negotiated ahead of time." He attributed its problems to the lack of public hearings, noting that "all action occurred at high levels." Carrico's agency had exhibited "some arrogance," which the former superintendent believed "contributed to the 'backlash' now toward the [federal] government." It did not surprise Carrico that the interior secretary in the early 1980s, James Watt, refused to press Congress for resolution of the Rio Grande Wild and Scenic River boundary controversy. Watt, an advocate of the Sagebrush Rebellion, and President Ronald Reagan took a dim view of expanded federal presence on private property. It would fall to Cisneros and his successor as superintendent, Frank Deckert, to revitalize planning for the WSR, and to establish better relations with local landowners as part of the new planning process.[10]

The second feature of 1980s border management that confronted efforts at peace and friendship involved the smuggling of narcotics from Mexico into the United States. Marty Ott, chief ranger at Big Bend in the mid-1980s, recalled in a 1997 interview that "drugs were an absolute real problem" for park law enforcement when he accepted his assignment, returning to a park where his father in the late 1950s had been chief of maintenance. Ott noted that "some folks chose to ignore the problem," while anxiety among others "created a sense of being overrun." The Reagan administration had promoted an antidrug campaign (the

Just Say No initiative), and the park service found itself on the defensive at Big Bend as it had been a decade earlier during the Nixon-era War on Drugs.[11]

With trade in narcotics escalating along the border, the most prominent trafficker in the Big Bend area, Pablo Acosta, became what Ott described as "an embarrassment to Mexican officials." Alan Weisman had conducted a lengthy interview in Ojinaga with Acosta. Like many struggling farmers and ranchers in northern Mexico, Acosta had found that the lure of wealth generated by the sale of marijuana and heroin in the 1960s proved too strong to resist. Yet by the mid-1980s, Acosta "could no longer be tolerated." The Federal Bureau of Investigation sent agents from its El Paso office to inform Ott in 1987 of an impending raid on Acosta's headquarters in the village of Santa Eleña.[12]

The FBI and other law enforcement officers landed in helicopters on the American side of the Rio Grande, watching as their Mexican counterparts "ran into a firefight of one hour." One agent was wounded, and darkness threatened the operation. Then Ott received word that Acosta had been killed, and the FBI asked him to pick up the body. Ott went to the nearby general store in Castolon, where he purchased every sack of ice, and flew across the river to transport the corpse to an American coroner. The chief ranger recalled more than a decade later the scene in Mexico when he landed, as "nearly all the residents of Santa Eleña were lying down in the street." Jim Carrico would add that he wondered at the time "how Santa Eleña people judged this, as Acosta was a 'Robin Hood' who gave money to the poor."[13]

The death of Acosta did not foster discontent among the residents of Santa Eleña and other border communities along the Rio Grande. Instead, it contributed to a growing sense that better relations with Mexico meant good business. In 1988, the park added a staff position (the "international cooperation specialist") to coordinate work with Mexican agencies and townspeople. Ramón Olivas joined with Bill Wendt (himself a former Big Bend ranger from the late 1950s) to develop collaborative training programs for employees of Mexican resource agencies involved with border areas. Olivas also established conferences for officials of both nations and, in the words of Dennis Vasquez, "served as the coordinator for the Big Bend 'Good Will Ambassador' program with local Mexican communities." Then, in October 1988, NPS regional director John Cook met with Eliseo Mendoza Berrueto, governor of Coahuila, to sign "an agreement of good will acknowledging the benefits of cooperative efforts between the USNPS and the State of Coahuila in the areas of resource management." One month later, the park service and the Mexican office of SEDUE embarked upon a plan to develop "protected areas," which included training, technical assistance, and scientific research.[14]

The efforts of the Mexican affairs specialist drew the attention of NPS officials in Washington. In 1991, they asked Olivas to join Howard Ness to expand into other border parks of the American Southwest. This collaboration, known as the Mexican Affairs Office, would be housed on the campus of New Mexico State University. Vasquez remembered in 1994 that "as the environmental movement began to grow throughout Mexico," Big Bend National Park had become better known among Mexican public and private agencies and university officials as a well-established protected area, and also as a resource for training and support materials.[15]

Olivas would relocate to Las Cruces and apply his knowledge of border resource areas to NPS units in Arizona and New Mexico. Yet a sense developed at Big Bend that the Mexican Affairs Office's gain was its loss, as diplomacy and broader binational issues replaced the local momentum that had promised much for Big Bend. Vasquez would write in 1994 that "no 'sister' park had been established, no solutions to cattle trespass had been achieved, and longstanding law enforcement problems and resource management concerns had not been resolved."[16]

To address this perceived decline in cross-border relations, Superintendent Rob Arnberger instructed his staff in 1989, in the words of Vasquez, to restore the "grass-roots" approach initiated earlier that decade by Gil Lusk. "The programs would be designed to achieve specific products for Big Bend," said Vasquez, "as well as to continue nurturing neighborly relations." Among the first initiatives was identification of employees who were sensitive to cultural diversity, who had a language proficiency in Spanish, and who were "knowledgeable in the Hispanic culture." Arnberger wanted "an understanding of the entire staff of the importance of the constructive relations with our Mexican neighbors and an appreciation for cultural differences." The park then created its own "Mexican Affairs Team" to serve as key contacts with the small rural villages adjacent to the park to coordinate any number of activities that might come up in the villages, from organizing health clinics to providing mechanical support for community water systems.[17]

Vasquez did note that "poor communications and inconsistent actions over the years have been the source of persistent difficulties." Educational outreach programs could "carry a message about the function and goals of the USNPS," as well as "highlighting the significance of the natural and cultural resources which we share with our neighbors." The park's chief of interpretation realized that "generations of rural villagers have lived across the river from Big Bend National Park without hearing this message." Even controversies surrounding trespass livestock, drug traffic, and border crossings became part of the dialogue. "While these topics may have a negative connotation," wrote Vasquez, "the park has not shied away from these open discussions." Instead, the regular official visits by Big Bend National Park staff to adjacent Mexican communities had opened lines of communication and helped create a sense of community.[18]

One unique feature of the renewed efforts at local collaboration was establishment in 1989 of the joint US-Mexican firefighting unit known as Project Diablos. Three years of wild-land fires in Big Bend had placed the park's resources in jeopardy, a condition exacerbated, said Vasquez, by Big Bend's remoteness. "Through standard channels," wrote the chief of interpretation, "response time by qualified fire crews is a minimum of 12 to 30 hours." The park recognized that "there existed a pool of potential firefighters nearby, across the Rio Grande who were well suited for arduous fire-fighting duty in the extreme heat and rough conditions of the Chihuahuan Desert."[19]

Turning to the Mexican villages that had supplied so many workers for American ranchers and government agencies in the past, Big Bend recruited some twenty men to become wild-land firefighters. "When the idea was posed to some of the men," recalled Vasquez, "they responded enthusiastically, stating that if they were given the opportunity they would work like 'diablos' [devils] to prove their worth." Such a venture required the approval of the US Immigration and Naturalization Service, as well as the US Social Security Administration. The program operated for several years, until budget cuts in the mid-1990s eliminated the use of Mexican firefighters in the park (to be reinstated after the terrorist attacks of September 2001).[20]

Changes on the American side of the Rio Grande in the late 1980s and early 1990s toward interaction with Mexico elicited a positive response from officials of that nation's government. Gloria Uribe, a former staff member of the natural resource agency SEDUE (later renamed the Secretariat of the Environment, Natural Resources, and Fisheries, or the Secretaría de Medio Ambiente, Recursos Naturales y Pesca [SEMARNAP]), recalled in a 1999 interview in Ciudad Chihuahua that during this time Mexican resource policy "shifted from forestry to desert studies." The Mexican National Institute of Ecology also turned from forest concerns to wildlife. "Environmental issues became more important to plans of management," said Uribe, "like air and water quality." This redirection of a century-old policy, much studied by historians such as Christopher R. Boyer, occurred as university professors from the United States received attention with an agreement signed in 1992 in La Paz. "Sister cities and sister parks were promoted," said Uribe, and in Chihuahua in particular, "some people saw the need for conservation." With the signing in 1994 of NAFTA, work on protected areas and binational strategies for management accelerated. Chihuahua joined for the first time with its eastern neighbor, the state of Coahuila, to address the decades-old dream of an international park along the Rio Grande. Mexican planners, recalled Uribe, "tried to shift from urban programs to protected areas." Resources to accomplish this objective were not easy to find, leading the planners to conclude that "only communities can save these areas." Those resources did appear, however, in limited form with NAFTA, as international agencies and nongovernmental organizations included the Big Bend–Mexican park idea in their agendas.[21]

Alfonso LaFon, professor of natural resources management at La Universidad Autónoma de Chihuahua, recalled in a 1999 interview that his home state's willingness to work with Coahuila and the Mexican federal government helped overcome the obstacle of outside support for resource protection along the Rio Grande. "In the late 1980s," said LaFon, "the World Bank began funding some studies" in Chihuahua. Then NAFTA "pushed increasing the protected areas." One strategy was "political," through the use of "decrees, and management of the land." Mexican authorities also had to work with *ejido* residents to educate them in better use of the land.[22]

Yet another issue facing LaFon and other resource officials in Mexico was the country's change of leadership every six years (known as the *sexeño*). Fortunately, said LaFon, the 1990s witnessed "the continuity of natural resources planning and NPS training." Officials like SEMARNAP director Julia Carrabias promoted a mixture of "conservation, research, administration, and education" to strengthen the presence in the Mexican government of environmental consciousness. Carrabias would work in the 1990s with her American counterpart, Interior Secretary Bruce Babbitt, to create and maintain international relations at their intermediate levels. Said LaFon, "Making permanent relationships and education programs between the NPS and protected areas helps overcome policy."[23]

Reference to "policy" limitations on improved border relations included the issue of electrical supply from the United States to Mexico, and the termination of the unofficial practice at Big Bend of issuing *permisos*. The former involved plans by the governor of Coahuila, Eliseo Mendoza Berrueto, to designate the protected area of Maderas del Carmen. A draft NPS memorandum of September 1990 regarding the international park concept noted that the governor's agenda included "drawing tourism and upgrading the quality of life for the residents of Boquillas and adjacent communities." Mendoza called for rehabilitative work in Boquillas, the installation of a potable water system, open-air restrooms, a visitor center, and the transmission of electricity through Big Bend National Park.[24]

Daniel L. Roth, a graduate student in the public affairs program at the University of Texas at Austin, writes in his 1992 master's thesis of the opposition by American environmental groups to the electric transmission line across the Rio Grande. "The Audubon Society and the Sierra Club," says Roth, "met with the governor of Coahuila to support solar energy as a source of power for the area." These groups feared that the line would endanger the nesting of the peregrine falcon, while other organizations believed that the volume of electricity would allow the Mexican government to invite urban growth. Even "leftist group leaders and some farming groups" in Mexico, writes Roth, "have recently opposed land reforms in Mexico, which may affect the *ejido* system, which in turn may affect park management."[25]

In the matter of permission slips for border crossings, Vasquez noted that "for over 20 years, the USNPS staff at Big Bend National Park issued immigration permits on behalf of the USINS [US Immigration and Naturalization Service] to Mexican nationals living adjacent to the park." Vasquez wrote that while the park service "had no official authority or jurisdiction in conducting this activity, it was done in the interest of providing a service to park neighbors who otherwise would have to travel over 100 miles to secure permits to travel within the United States." In October 1994, "this longstanding program was discontinued for a number of reasons," the most compelling being "the increased workload that the permit program entailed and the decrease in staff size." Vasquez conceded that "the discontinuance of the immigration permit function at Big Bend National Park has had a serious impact on [the] ability of Mexican nationals who have a right to travel in the United States to secure immigration permits."[26]

The year 1994 also marked a turning point for Mexico's commitment to the decades-old dream of an international park. On November 7 of that year, Mexican president Carlos Salinas de Gortari announced establishment of the two protected areas across the Rio Grande: the Maderas del Carmen (Coahuila), and the Cañon de Santa Eleña (Chihuahua). The former consisted of 514,701 acres (208,381 hectares), while the latter comprised 684,706 acres (277,209 hectares). In extending the status of protection over this 1.1-million-acre area, the Mexican government gave the NPS and Interior Department the opportunity to develop strategies for collaboration in matters of resource management, scholarly research, and ecotourism initiatives.[27]

Julio Carrera, a longtime natural resource official for the state of Coahuila, became director of the Maderas del Carmen region, while Pablo Dominguez of SEMARNAP assumed direction of the Chihuahua protected area. Dominguez spoke in a 1999 interview in Ciudad Chihuahua about the benefits of partnership with the United States. "On maps of the World Wildlife Fund," said Dominguez, "there are very few disturbances to Cañon de Santa Eleña land." His hope was to "make some kind of deal on correct use of natural resources without eliminating the historic land uses." In collaboration with La Universidad Autónoma de Chihuahua, SEMARNAP had developed a program of management that explained the region's unique natural and cultural resources. It also offered options for visitor services that did not conflict with the "consensus of people."[28]

Given his concern for international relations, as well as his commitment to the protection of cultural resources, Superintendent José Cisneros made it a signal feature of his management to advance the cause of the binational park. In July 1996, Cisneros escorted a party of Mexican and American natural resource officials to the international peace park at Waterton-Glacier National Park, on the border between Montana and Alberta. Writing three years later in the journal *Environment*, Cisneros and his chief of interpretation and visitor services, Valerie J. Naylor, concluded that "the group was impressed with the international peace park designation and with the collaboration between the two parks." Cisneros, his American colleagues, and the Mexican officials left Waterton-Glacier after four days of study believing that "such a relationship was possible in the Big Bend region." In February 1997, SEMARNAP sent to the US Department of the Interior "a proposal for the establishment of protected natural areas of binational ecosystems in the Big Bend area." This region then would become the model for other shared park sites on the Mexico-US border.[29]

Mexico's gesture required consideration by entities other than Big Bend National Park or the NPS, but the statement indicated to Cisneros that the dream of a borderless park was closer to reality than at any time since the 1930s. The superintendent remarked in retirement in 2000 that his goal had been to move border issues to the forefront of the conversation about Big Bend's future, a strategy that Cisneros believed had borne fruit as the park expanded its general-management research under his successor, Frank Deckert. Flora, fauna, and people did not recognize the artificiality of the boundary line, noted Cisneros, nor did history show any benefit to keeping people apart in the Big Bend country. He applauded the efforts of Rotary International to provide for the binational area of Big Bend (including the NPS unit, Texas's Big Bend Ranch State Park, and the Mexican protected areas) what it had secured for Waterton-Glacier in 1932: the status of an international peace park.[30]

In their 1999 article for the *Environment*, José Cisneros and Valerie Naylor spoke of the actions of the World Conservation Union "encouraging nations to collaborate in the management of trans-boundary ecosystem[s]." The former Big Bend superintendent marveled that "today, Big Bend National Park, the adjoining Protected Areas for Flora and Fauna in Mexico, and nearby state lands protect more than two million acres in the heart of the Chihuahuan Desert." If his successors could sustain the dream of Lázaro Cárdenas, Franklin Roosevelt, Everett Townsend, and many advocates of peace on the border, said Cisneros, "the ecosystem will be the ultimate beneficiary of coordinated bi-national efforts." On that day, Big Bend would have risen above its many challenges of nature and history, thought Cisneros, and would represent what is often said of national parks—the best idea that America ever had.[31]

Hopes ran high on both sides of the Rio Grande in the year 2000 for acceleration of the dream of binational collaboration in the Big Bend country. That year and in 2001, Mexico and the United States sent representatives of their natural resource agencies to the Protected Area Coordination Meeting. Attendees agreed that environmental concerns required immediate action. Among these were studies of fish and amphibian habitats, water quality and quantity, birds and raptors, fire management, and the eradication of tamarisk.

Tom Alex, the archaeologist at Big Bend National Park, called on his colleagues to support cultural resource surveys in the Maderas del Carmen, and to promote new programs in interpretation and environmental education. The US Geological Survey also volunteered to include the Rio Grande / Rio Bravo section of Big Bend in its Border 21 Mapping Project, an initiative to collect data on all manner of natural and cultural resources. The superintendent at Big Bend, Deckert, asked as well whether the group would endorse a plan to extend the Wild and Scenic River status westward, from Lajitas to the boundary of Coahuila and Chihuahua.[32]

As the two nations conversed about goals for improving the natural landscape of their shared border, another initiative gained momentum at the start of the twenty-first century—this time within Mexico itself. Patricio Robles Gil, a photographer of Mexican wildlife, approached Cementos Mexicanos (CEMEX), an international corporation, to discuss the potential for preserving the natural beauty of the protected areas. Robles Gil convinced Lorenzo Zambrano, chief executive officer for CEMEX, that his company could take a bold step as a corporate citizen by investing in the preservation of Mexican biodiversity, an idea as old as the forestry work of Miguel Angel de Quevedo.

In a 2014 interview, Alejandro Treviño Espinosa of CEMEX addressed the company's decision to purchase 400,000 acres (200,000 hectares) of the Big Bend region known as the Maderas del Carmen. Zambrano and other CEMEX officials recognized how long it had been since their country and the United States first had discussed resource preservation along the Rio Grande / Rio Bravo. The purchase of so large a property, which included over one hundred miles of riverfront, would allow CEMEX to "study its complexity," said Treviño, and to allow the land to "rest" in order to be restored, a condition that the CEMEX official called "re-wilding" of the landscape.[33]

The purchase of the Maderas del Carmen had occurred because the Mexican government no longer prohibited the ownership of large tracts of land by private corporations. While substantial portions of the Carmens had been divided into smaller plots under the *ejido* system, the region's real challenges had come from the persistent exploitation of its resources for a century and more by big-game hunters, miners, loggers, and candelilla-wax processors. Called "the first of its kind in Mexico," the El Carmen Project began with what Amy Leinbach Marquis identifies as "a massive species inventory, black bear tracking projects, and big horn sheep reintroductions."[34]

Building on the work of such Big Bend naturalists as Ernest G. Marsh Jr. and C. H. Mueller in the 1930s, Walter Taylor in the 1940s, Rollin Baker and Alden Miller in the 1950s, and Roland Wauer in the 1960s, Bonnie and Billy McKinney left their longtime employment for the Texas State Parks and Wildlife Division to direct the team of El Carmen Project researchers. Bonnie McKinney wanted not merely to study the area in the summertime but to live there twelve months of the year. For the next decade, her team of Mexican and American scientists identified ninety-one species of mammals, 299 species of birds, nine species of owls, and sixty-five species of reptiles and amphibians. They also removed over two hundred miles of fencing within the El Carmen boundaries and undertook riparian restoration that included the replanting of native cottonwoods. In so doing, McKinney wrote in her 2012 study of the project, CEMEX and her team had rendered the Maderas del Carmen "not a park, but a vast ecosystem," something that for decades American scientists had wanted for the Big Bend region.[35]

Restoring the natural conditions of the Maderas del Carmen could advance through the first decade of the twenty-first century because of the generosity of CEMEX. For the remainder of the Big Bend country, whether in Mexico or the United States, events far away in New York City and Washington, DC, in the fall of 2001 conspired to delay, if not halt altogether, the collaborative endeavors of the previous two decades. On September 11, terrorists from Middle Eastern nations attacked the iconic twin towers of the World Trade Center in Lower Manhattan, as well as the Department of Defense's Pentagon building in the nation's capital. Nearly three thousand Americans died that day in the worst assault on US soil since the bombing of Pearl Harbor six decades earlier.

Amid demands to secure the nation's borders, the administration of President George W. Bush (himself a former governor of Texas) decided to restrict access along America's southern boundary with Mexico. Joe Sirotnak of the Big Bend National Park staff would recall a decade later in an article for the *George Wright Forum* that the "closing" of the border contributed directly to "radically changing the human landscape in this remote area." For Sirotnak, 9/11 meant "crippling the fragile economics of the small Mexican border towns" and "eliminating significant cultural and educational opportunities to Big Bend visitors." Equally tragic for the NPS wildlife specialist was 9/11's severe hampering of efforts at binational management of resources.[36]

By May 2002, the United States not only had "closed" its border with Mexico; it also had established a new cabinet-level agency (the Department of Homeland Security) that subsumed all or parts of twenty-two federal offices tasked with protecting the country from external threats. No longer could visitors to Big Bend cross the Rio Grande at Boquillas to patronize its shops and restaurants. Even more problematic was the rerouting of customs and immigration traffic from

Mexico far to the west at Ojinaga/Presidio. In June 2003, the NPS attempted to bring together public and private organizations for a river trip through Boquillas Canyon. There the Mexican Comisión Nacional de Áreas Naturales Protegidas (National Commission of Natural Protected Areas) described its efforts, in the words of Joe Sirotnak, "to control salt cedar, an exotic invasive tree, and facilitated discussions on project expansions on both sides of the river."[37]

Parallel with the park service's efforts to keep the border "open" for scientific research were the steps taken by Rotary International to sustain its commitment to an international park in the Big Bend region. Ernesto Enkerlin, president of the Comisión Nacional de Áreas Naturales Protegidas, met in Ciudad Chihuahua with Rick LoBello of the El Paso Rotary chapter to declare his interest in the decades-old concept. Other meetings in that border city echoed these sentiments, leading the park service to send John King, superintendent of Big Bend, to Austin in January 2004 to meet with regional NPS officials on the matter of the international park. Then King called on staff members of Texas governor Rick Perry, who had succeeded George W. Bush in that office.

Sounding like the Mexican officials in the 1940s who saw little reason to work with their American counterparts during the Cold War era, the governor's representatives told King that he was "upset with Mexico over water allocation issues and is not [favorably] disposed to working with them on things until such time as the water dispute is cleared up." The Rio Grande had for the first time in living memory dried up in the summer of 2001, and a group of investors known as Rio Nuevo Limited had campaigned with the Texas legislature to allow them to pump up to sixteen billion gallons a year from the state's water reserves. King had spoken against the plan, telling attendees of a state senate subcommittee hearing in Alpine that the water plan would "cause irreparable harm," with wildlife migrating through his park in search of new sources of water.[38]

Perry's dislike of opposition to water diversions in the Rio Grande constituted but one concern for advocates of better relations between the United States and Mexico in the Big Bend country. Two studies appeared in 2004 to compound the challenges to binational collaboration in science: the Big Bend Regional Aerosol and Visibility Observational Study (BRAVO) on air quality, and the GMP for the Rio Grande Wild and Scenic River section of the border. The BRAVO project had been conducted by the Colorado State University (CSU) Cooperative Institute for Research in the Atmosphere. The CSU researchers concluded that while Big Bend faced very real deterioration of its viewshed and air quality, the blame could not be placed only on large power plants (Carbón I and II) in northern Coahuila. They did note that "late spring episodes" of haze and pollution along the Rio Grande came from "concentrations of carbonaceous compounds ... due to biomass burning in Mexico and Central America." Dust particles also "contributed an equal amount of the spring haze" in the park, said the BRAVO report.[39]

The park service's own research staff concurred in this assessment of air quality problems in the Big Bend region. The park had not drafted a general management study for a generation, in which time entities like the Environmental Protection Agency had become more diligent in monitoring air standards. Big Bend had earned what the Clean Air Act of 1977 called Class I status, a reference to the EPA's "most stringent air quality classification, [which] protects national parks and wilderness areas from air quality degradation." The vaunted clarity of the Rio Grande skies, praised so highly by Robert T. Hill on his 1899 expedition, had shrunk to less than 5 percent of the river's 150-mile corridor, inflicting on Big Bend "at times . . . the dirtiest air in terms of visibility impairment of any western national park."[40]

The GMP report detailed the challenge to resolve the issue of air quality by noting that both the United States and Mexico shared responsibility. "Air quality is often degraded," said the 2004 report, due to emissions of air pollutants transported from industrial and urban Texas Gulf Coast centers, heavy industries (e.g., smelters and steel mills), and power plants in northeastern Mexico. The last source, said the GMP, constituted "the most current threat to visibility degradation," as the Carbón plants near Piedras Negras, Mexico, "are designed to use a relatively high sulfur, high ash coal."[41]

Scientific evidence of the "binational" sources of pollution for Big Bend captured the attention of the regional news media. King traveled in the winter of 2004 to the Texas state capital to speak to the Friends of Big Bend National Park chapter. The question on many minds was how to address the air quality concerns of the border. King spoke to a group that had raised funds to buy and donate equipment to track environmental phenomena like air quality. The superintendent noted that 55 percent of the pollution came from American border locales, and 38 percent from nearby Mexico. Even more startling was King's reference to degradation caused by emissions from as far away as the Ohio River valley, and perhaps the East Coast of the United States. When added to the drought of the early 2000s, reducing stream flows in the Rio Grande and Rio Conchos basins, and the closure of the border by Homeland Security forces, King could only conclude in his remarks to the Austin Friends group, "Big Bend is a park in peril."[42]

Undaunted by warnings of chronic problems without solutions, public and private organizations on both sides of the Rio Grande worked for the next two years to establish the Joint Declaration of Sister Park Partnerships. Built on the 1997 "Letter of Intent for Join Work in Natural Protected Areas on the United States–Mexico Border," the new agreement recognized lessons learned since 9/11. King traveled to Monterrey, Mexico, in April 2006 to speak before the First Annual Workshop of the El Carmen–Big Bend Conservation Corridor Initiative. Where

King a mere two years earlier saw only trouble ahead for his park, he now realized that "existing geometric political boundaries don't define ecological boundaries."[43]

King reflected in particular on the accomplishments over the past half decade by CEMEX to reintroduce bighorn sheep, antelope, and elk. Grasslands restoration had proceeded to provide for wild game, while water reclamation projects sought "to reverse the long-term effects of mining and timber harvesting." The Big Bend superintendent referred as well to CEMEX's efforts "to acquire additional lands on both sides of the border, to negotiate conservation agreements with private landowners, and to forge partnerships with public land managers." King praised the Mexican corporate endeavor highly, concluding, "What they have done and are doing is nothing short of remarkable."[44]

The occasion of King's address in Monterrey produced a working document of principles and strategies that would have made all champions of binational cooperation proud. Echoes of Miguel Angel de Quevedo, George Meléndez Wright, Everett Townsend, and dozens of NPS and Mexican natural resource officials could be heard in the discussion groups of the two-day workshop. In staking its claim for a new vision built on an old dream, the El Carmen initiative report called for "a vision for the year 2016." The attendees imagined that they would gather once more on April 29 of that year "to celebrate the achievements that have taken place in the last ten years after the first annual workshop that took place in Monterrey, Mexico in 2006."[45]

They wanted most of all to be remembered for creating "a model, a source of pride between our two countries." The landscape would be "re-wilded," with "big animals" and abundant water sources. Exotic species would be removed, and a "green wall that unites U.S. and Mexico" constructed. Schoolchildren from both nations would be "required to take [a] one week stay in a wilderness area." For all citizens, there would exist "a plan for people to move freely between countries in 10 years (2026)." Other border zones could use the El Carmen–Big Bend model, where "communities have been involved in [the] project from the start." Should all these conditions prevail, concluded the workshop attendees, one day the visitor "can hear the lobo/wolf howl" again.[46]

The "re-wilding" of the Big Bend region would encounter another obstacle in the fall of 2006, when the US Congress passed Public Law 109-367, known as the Secure Fence Act. The nation's lawmakers charged the Department of Homeland Security with construction of facilities to intercept "unlawful entry by aliens into the United States" through a series of "additional checkpoints, all-weather access roads, and vehicle barriers." While Big Bend National Park would not see any of the seven hundred miles of iron fencing built by the US Army Corps of Engineers in sections from San Diego to Brownsville, the shadow of national security (already present in the park) would only grow longer.

Yet advocates of the ideas espoused at the El Carmen–Big Bend workshop persevered, with US representative Ciro Rodriguez (D-TX) introducing House Resolution 483, which reminded the El Paso congressman's colleagues that "together with two Mexican protected areas, Big Bend is now part of the largest transboundary protected areas in North America, serving as a model for international cooperation." Martha King, wife of John King, organized an "arts cooperative" that imported arts and crafts from the Boquillas merchants for sale in the park and surrounding communities. Proceeds from the marketing of these crafts, along with private donations, raised enough money to install a solar-powered electric generator and wind-powered well pump in Boquillas.[47]

Construction of the border fence also drew the attention of scholars of the Big Bend's ecological and cultural dynamics. Sharon Wilcox and Brian King wrote in 2008 of a concept that scientists call "bioregionalism." According to Wilcox and King, "Protected areas should be demarcated not by the political boundaries of particular countries but by the ecosystems that most require protection." Sounding much like the Mexican and US scientists of the New Deal era, even as they looked at twenty-first-century realities, Wilcox and King identified the Big Bend area as "the site of a new model of land-conservation in Mexico, based upon public-private partnerships facilitated through commercial ownership and involvement."[48]

Earning particular praise was CEMEX, as it had created "the first certified wilderness on private land in Latin America." King and Wilcox called on their fellow scholars "to assess how protected areas typically engender conflict over space, land tenure, and livelihood production possibilities." Emily Levitt concurred in their findings in her 2009 article "Park Lands and Politics on the West Texas/Mexico Border." The El Carmen Transboundary Megacorridor, wrote Levitt, "integrates smaller spaces into one overarching territory." CEMEX could claim such achievements as "species reintroduction across international borders, joint water conservation, and fire prevention efforts."[49]

Advocates for a reopened border in the Big Bend country could take heart from the academic arguments of Wilcox and King and Leavitt. Yet they faced the realities of a Congress and electorate that supported more constraints on travel along the Rio Grande. William Wellman, who became superintendent at Big Bend in 2006, would write to Rick LoBello the following year that conditions were not auspicious for Rotary International's wishes for a peace park. Wellman agreed that "it has been discussed for many years and most likely will one day be a reality." Yet the superintendent cautioned LoBello, "With the current national debate over border security and immigration, I fear you may have a difficult task resurrecting the project at this time."[50]

Undaunted by such conditions, Wellman supported the plans of a group calling itself COLINDA (an acronym for Consortium of La Linda"). In a 2008 memorandum to Raymond Skiles of his Science and Resources Management Division, the Big Bend superintendent responded to questions about the NPS's position on the reopening of the La Linda Bridge on the park's east side. Skiles had noted that this was "the only Congressionally authorized crossing we have between Amistad [Dam] and Presidio," a distance of some 385 miles. CEMEX and other Mexican organizations had gathered in Monterrey that year to endorse the COLINDA initiative, a project of the US-Mexico Binational Working Group on Bridges and Border Crossings. Wellman agreed with Skiles that an open bridge would ensure "the safety of tourists[,] . . . the binational scientific cooperation called for under existing international agreements, and the security and public safety of communities and citizens on both sides of the international border."[51]

Two additional initiatives had surfaced in the years 2006–2008 that demonstrated the dedication of US and Mexican scientists to preserving the Rio Grande / Rio Bravo corridor. In the fall of 2007, the US Fish and Wildlife Service announced its intention to restock the river with a native fish—the Rio Grande silvery minnow—that had become extinct. Once found throughout most of the Rio Grande's 1,500-mile journey from southern Colorado to the Gulf of Mexico, the silvery minnow had survived only in central New Mexico (5 percent of its habitat). The last silvery minnows reported in the Big Bend area had been seen in 1960, becoming victims of a severe drought in the previous decade.

Another attempt at solving the ecological challenges of the river corridor came in 2006, when the Mexican government unveiled plans to protect a thirty-foot wide swath of the Rio Bravo, from Ojinaga to Nuevo Laredo. Calling this the "green wall," the government wished to restrict roadbuilding and vehicle traffic through the desert and canyon country south of Big Bend and its environs. One day the corridor would be part of a "Río Bravo del Norte Natural Monument," connecting the protected areas of Cañon del Santa Elena, the Sierra del Carmen, and the lands in between known as the Ocampo Protected Area.[52]

Momentum shifted late in 2008 toward more interaction between Mexico and the United States, with the election that fall of Barack Obama as the American president. The Democratic candidate had signaled a desire to improve relations with the two neighbors, something that had eroded significantly in the years after 9/11. That winter the border area became the focus of the World Wildlife Fund, as this nongovernmental organization conducted its Rio Grande Workshop at Big Bend. Joe Sirotnak recalled how the attendees at this "binational meeting" had journeyed far "to discuss and identify restoration priorities and targets for the Rio Grande."[53]

Much like the El Carmen initiative of two years earlier, the workshop participants "developed a single vision statement for the river to be considered as a guide by each country." The partners formed two teams (science and policy) "to identify and investigate conservation challenges and possible solutions." Eager to advance the cause of research in the Rio Grande / Rio Bravo corridor, the teams met again to tour the Rio Conchos watershed in the state of Chihuahua, then to observe the work of a grassland restoration project in the state of Coahuila.[54]

Once the Obama administration had entered office, officials of Mexico and the United States moved quickly to formalize the conversations about the border that had been the domain of private entities for nearly a decade. President Obama accepted Mexican president Felipe Calderón's invitation to visit Mexico City in April 2009 to discuss a variety of shared concerns. US representative Ciro Rodriguez followed this initiative in July with the introduction in Congress of House Resolution 695. The El Paso Democrat called for renewed efforts to establish the decades-old dream of an international park in the Big Bend area. Reminding his colleagues that America once reached out in 1932 to Canada in similar fashion with the Waterton-Glacier International Peace Park, Rodriguez proclaimed, as had so many before him, that "there is a desire to conserve and educate others about the significant natural and cultural resources that span the border of the United States and Mexico."[55]

Soon thereafter, Mexico's natural resources secretary, Juan Rafael Elvira Quesada, met in Mexico City with US interior secretary Kenneth Salazar to advance the cause of conservation in the Big Bend region. While attending the North American Leaders Summit in August, Salazar and Elvira agreed to report to their respective governments within six months about their efforts. "Building upon our shared history of ecosystem and species conservation," said the cabinet secretaries, "the plan will develop a model of bi-national cooperation for the conservation and enjoyment of shared ecosystems for current and future generations."[56]

Calderón had just established the Ocampo Protected Area, located between Cañon de Santa Elena and the Maderas del Carmen. This action would allow the two nations, in the words of Elvira, "to consolidate environmental cooperation . . . and could eventually constitute a symbol of the new era of . . . bilateral cooperation in the conservation area." A unified zone on the Rio Grande / Rio Bravo would mean protection of more than 268 river miles and three million acres (14 percent of the entire US-Mexico border) in what Elvira and Salazar called "one of the most biologically diverse regions of the world."[57]

The community of natural scientists in Mexico, as it had since the days of Lázaro Cárdenas and his progressive approach to national parks, found the Salazar-Elvira announcement to their liking. A nongovernmental organization called the Sierra Madre Group had joined forces with CEMEX to promote the El Carmen–Big Bend Conservation Corridor Initiative. They included "leading NGO's, respected conservationists and local ranchers," with a focus on "guaranteeing the permanence of the ecological corridor in order to ensure its vital role in interconnecting different protected areas and mountain ranges." Other partners included the World Wildlife Fund's Living Planet campaign, which identified the Chihuahuan Desert as "one of the 20 most important eco-regions in the world."[58]

Conservation International had found the Big Bend area to be "a global hotspot due to its extraordinary levels of endemism and serious levels of habitat loss." The Wildlife Conservation Society had placed the border on its map of "The Last of the Wild," a designation of "lands that currently represent the largest, least-influenced wildlife areas in the world." All of this attention, hoped the Sierra Madre Group, would "address one of the greatest challenges mankind faces today: the conservation of wilderness."[59]

By October 2009, the government of Mexico had occasion to announce even more protection of natural resources in the Big Bend region. Working in concert with the Nature Conservancy, Mexico created a contiguous conservation area that it called the Río Bravo del Norte Natural Monument. As CEMEX had done at the start of the decade in the Maderas del Carmen, Juan Bezaury, associate director of external affairs for the Nature Conservancy, proclaimed this "the first time that the Mexican government has used the natural monument classification to designate a river as a protected area."[60]

The decree also extended by 137 miles the existing Wild and Scenic River status that the NPS supervised. Nature Conservancy officials in both countries hoped that this would offer "an incentive for the U.S. National Park Service to nearly double that protected area and match Mexico's mileage all the way down to the Amistad National Recreation Area." Additional benefits included giving "far-ranging species like mountain lions, black bears and desert bighorn sheep the space they need to roam." The conservancy's Bezaury concluded, "This sets the stage for official protection of additional Mexican rivers in the future."[61]

Following in the spirit of international cooperation, the Ninth World Wilderness Congress met in Mérida, Mexico, in November 2009, with Canada joining Mexico and the United States. President Felipe Calderón addressed the convention, noting that "this agreement will allow for the exchange of successful experiences, monitoring, and training of human resources, as well as the financing of projects that will protect and recover wild areas." Federal land managers no longer would be restricted in their collaboration with state or provincial managers across the Canadian and Mexican borders with the United States.[62]

Ernesto Entrekin-Hoelflich, director of the Mexican Commission for Natural Protected Areas (Secretaría de Medio Ambiente y Recursos Naturales [SEMARNAT]), promised that this would be but the start of "a multipronged effort to step up wilderness protection at home." Entrekin-Hoelflich praised the pioneering work of CEMEX, while Sally Collins, director of the new Office of Ecosystems Services and Markets for the US Department of Agriculture, agreed about "the crucial role that intact forests, grasslands and other ecosystems play in sequestering heat-trapping carbon dioxide."[63]

For its part at the Mérida convocation, the NPS announced that, in the words of director Jon Jarvis, it would "bring long-languishing wilderness proposals 'off the shelf.'" In recognition of advances in wildlife science, the NPS director warned that "protected areas have to be larger than they were previously." In addition, said Jarvis, "they have to have connectivity, eventually across country boundaries." Climate change had contributed much to this trans-border phenomenon, and "international agencies will likely need to form corridors that connect protected areas as part of their climate change adaptation plans."[64]

Equally problematic for Jarvis and Sam Hamilton, director of the US Fish and Wildlife Service, was the building of 670 miles of border fencing by the US Department of Homeland Security. "Wilderness forms the essential core of protected areas," added Hamilton, "but wilderness alone will not suffice." It was left to SEMARNAT's director to speak to the new threat to wildlife posed by the barricades. Enkerlin-Hoelflich expressed his concern about what he labeled as "the wall." Yet like other Mexican natural resource officials for a century and more, the director "expressed hope that the wilderness MOU [memorandum of understanding] will focus further attention on the need to create cross-boundary passageways for wildlife." Said Enkerlin-Hoelflich, "We have to make the best of what we've got."[65]

With the endorsement of the Mexican and US leadership, the international park concept accelerated in 2010 as it had two decades earlier. Interior Secretary Kenneth Salazar visited the Big Bend National Park in March, venturing down to the Rio Grande to observe firsthand what he called "the opportunity to share an agenda" to preserve the unique landscape. Hopes ran high that spring, in the estimation of the *Texas Tribune*, that the dream of Franklin Roosevelt "may be closer to reality than ever." The *Tribune* reporter noted that "conversations about uniting Big Bend with the territory in Mexico have been reignited every decade or so since the land deed was signed in 1944," only to be "squashed by politics."[66]

The *Tribune* referred to the "drug violence" that led to "daily death tolls by the dozens in Mexico," as well as "tense international politics"—this a result of fears of terrorist attacks. Yet "the idea now seems to [be] gaining new momentum," said the *Tribune* reporter, with "Big Bend managers and federal representatives . . . seeking approval from the Interior, Homeland Security and State Departments to unite Big Bend with Mexico's designated protected areas." From this would come "the United States' second international park," proclaimed the *Tribune*, a project that would require a binational effort to build visitor facilities and open at least one legal crossing in the park.[67]

True to their word, Presidents Calderón and Obama met at the White House on May 19, 2010, releasing a joint statement that reaffirmed the strategic partnership between the United States and Mexico. The two leaders sought "to improve the lives of all citizens in both our countries, building upon our deep ties, and working with mutual respect and mutual responsibility across a broad arc of issues." Among these were "environmental conservation, clean energy, [and] climate change," all topics that had occupied the minds of Mexican and American park officials for a decade.[68]

When it came to the Big Bend country, the presidents identified the public spaces on both sides of the Rio Grande / Rio Bravo as "one of the largest and most significant ecological complexes in North America." From the national park and Rio Grande Wild and Scenic River on the American side, to the protected areas of Cañon de Santa Elena, Maderas del Carmen, Ocampo, and the newly created Río Bravo del Norte Natural Monument, "increased cooperation . . . would restrict development and enhance security in the region and within this fragile desert ecosystem."[69]

Obama and Calderón tasked Interior Secretary Salazar and SEMARNAT secretary Juan Elvira "to work through appropriate national processes to recognize and designate Big Bend–Río Bravo as a natural area of binational interest." In so doing, the presidents concluded, the landscape would benefit from "wildlife preservation, ecosystem restoration, climate change adaptation, wildland fire management, and invasive species control."[70]

Even as the interior departments of Mexico and the United States moved to actuate the promise of their respective leaders, the issue of border security lurked nearby. The *New York Times* sent Eryn Gable to Big Bend in June 2010 to assess conditions there. Gable applauded what she called "an idea that's been in the making for three-quarters of a century." Yet the *Times* reporter had to admit that "the creation of an international park along the U.S.-Mexico border is still nothing more than a notion." US representative Ciro Rodriguez, he of the 2009 resolution to support the international park, agreed with Gable that "the timing is not appropriate, given what's happening in Mexico." The El Paso congressman preferred to classify the area as "terrain that's not separated by the river but part of the river." His colleague in the US Senate, Kay Bailey Hutchison (R-TX), sought what her spokeswoman called "a clear understanding of how border crossings and other security interests would be protected."[71]

Then a Republican representative from Utah, Rob Bishop, who served as chair of the Congressional Western Caucus, claimed that "border security concerns . . . have been compromised by federal efforts to preserve landscapes and species." To that end, Bishop had introduced in the House a countermeasure to Rodriguez's international park plan. This would "mandate that the Interior and Agriculture Departments not 'impede, prohibit, or restrict activities' by the Homeland Security Department to secure and control the border."[72]

Rhetoric such as that from Hutchison and Bishop joined in the summer of 2010 with other obstacles to international park status. When the massive British Petroleum oil spill occurred in the Gulf of Mexico, Secretary Salazar had to devote all of his time to oversight of cleanup efforts and litigation against the parties responsible for millions of gallons of crude oil washing up on beaches from Louisiana to West Florida. This obscured the real problems that park service officials encountered in drafting the logistics of a binational park or reserve in the Big Bend region.

Rick Frost, an NPS spokesman, told the *New York Times* that "the focus instead is on increased cooperation between the two countries." Such temporizing disheartened champions of the international park like Rick LoBello of El Paso. A longtime advocate of the joining of the two nations along the Rio Grande / Rio Bravo corridor, LoBello marveled at how "up until 10 or 20 years ago, the main problem was Mexico was distrustful of us." That had given way during the first decade of the new century to a sense of respect that had been lacking since the 1930s. "Now that they trust us," LoBello concluded ruefully, "the problem in making it happen is on our side of the border." He noted to the *New York Times* reporter, "I still have some hope but my hope level is not as high as it was."[73]

LoBello's concerns notwithstanding, natural resource agencies on both sides of the river took the Calderón-Obama agreement as a sign that they could proceed with scientific research in the Big Bend region. In October 2010, the Texas Parks and Wildlife Department joined forces with the US Department of the Interior, the US Fish and Wildlife Service, and the US Geological Survey. They signed a memorandum of understanding to expand substantially the zone of interaction in West Texas and northern Mexico. The working group called itself the Big Bend Conservation Cooperative. They agreed to "collaborate on identifying and implementing monitoring, research, and habitat improvement projects with a bi-national group of landowners, managers, and other interested parties" on the river from Fort Quitman to the Amistad Reservoir.[74]

In particular, the cooperative sought "to increase the scientific understanding of the effects of climate change on the natural resources of Big Bend National Park and the Chihuahuan Desert." This would be achieved through the auspices of the Desert Landscape Conservation Cooperative, whereby all parties would "apply Strategic Habitat Conservation planning and cutting-edge mitigation and adaptations strategies that are impacted by climate change." Other outcomes included "engaging our conservation partners in the United States and in Mexico, as well as the public, in the development of sound natural and cultural resource management objectives, programs, and activities."[75]

Coincident with the interior memorandum of understanding planning process was release in December 2010 of a decade-long State of the Parks study of Big Bend, conducted by the nonprofit National Parks Conservation Association

(NPCA). Before the traumatic events of 9/11, the NPCA had identified as critical issues for the Big Bend region its air and water pollution, the diminished stream flows, soil erosion, and the "extirpation of several native species." After ten years of research and policy analysis, the NPCA concluded that the border region suffered from "diminished visitor experiences and widespread effects on all species that rely upon the river for survival." Remedies would be achieved with formation of a "joint US-Mexico International Commission" to design "working agreements and plans to address restoration of the Rio Grande and its tributaries."[76]

After listing the many distinctive features of the border's ecology, from its status as one of the few "Night-Sky" parks in the United States to its "Globally Important Bird Area," the NPCA reiterated statistics about the crises facing the park. Then the NPCA echoed a call from Mexican and American officials from long ago: "The principal goal of the commission should be to develop a plan to establish an international park to better protect natural and cultural resources, encourage environmentally sound and economic development, and institute cooperative border control in the park."[77]

Less than one month after the publication of the NPCA's statement on the critical issues facing the Rio Grande / Rio Bravo corridor in the Big Bend region, events nationwide once again changed the character of public policy toward Mexico in general, and the border in particular. A new Congress took office after the November 2010 elections with a determination to address national security concerns expressed by members of the Republican Party. On April 13, 2011, John McCain and Jon Kyl, Republican senators from the state of Arizona, introduced Senate Bill 803, "to implement a comprehensive border security plan to combat illegal immigration, drug and alien smuggling, and violent activity in the southwest border of the United States." Simultaneously in the House of Representatives, Congressman Rob Bishop and some two dozen other members of his party entered House Resolution 1505, "to prohibit the Secretaries of the Interior and Agriculture from taking action on public lands which impede security on such lands."[78]

Articulating their concerns with language more commonly used in Department of Defense legislation, the bills' sponsors sought to extend Homeland Security authority over all public lands within one hundred miles of America's borders. Gone were the platitudes emanating in the 1990s from the North American Free Trade Agreement, or even the joint communiqué a year earlier from Presidents Obama and Calderón. In their place were demands for the spending of over $4 billion on all manner of military hardware and technology, and the suspension of laws affecting Big Bend National Park like the Antiquities Act (1906), the Wild and Scenic Rivers Act (1968), and even the National Parks Organic Act (1916).

As the border security measures worked their way through the 112th Congress, advocates for partnerships along the Rio Grande / Rio Bravo corridor remained undaunted. In August 2011, the United States announced plans to reopen the border crossing at Boquillas, closed for nine years as a result of fears of illegal activity in the Big Bend region. Park superintendent William Wellman told the Reuters news agency that the closure had "made it much harder" to collaborate with Mexican natural resource officials. Despite the restrictions, Wellman cited as proof of the merits of the partnerships the revival of wildlife, in which "Mexican attempts to restore its half of the ecosystem played an important role." Raymond Skiles, a wildlife biologist for the park, cited the return of the Mexican black bear (first sighted in the late 1980s on park lands). "The future of bears in Big Bend," said Skiles, "depends on there being a healthy population in Mexico."[79]

The endeavors of the CEMEX Project, which by 2011 had restored native grasslands on its five-hundred-thousand-acre property to allow better habitat for desert bighorn sheep (and their predators, like mountain lions), also earned praise from NPS staff and administrators. Peregrine falcons could be seen along the river now, as these birds had "relied more on the extensive mountain ranges in Mexico for food, shelter, and mates." So too did endangered bats migrate across the river. "It's never going to be what it was 100 years ago," Wellman conceded, as "there's just not enough water and too many exotic species." Yet in the spirit of the Calderón-Obama agreement, the park superintendent could say, "We're getting a lot closer to that," words that could have been said seventy years earlier by Lázaro Cárdenas and Franklin Roosevelt.[80]

Wellman's optimism reflected the attitudes of his superiors in the Interior Department, as Secretary Kenneth Salazar announced in October 2011 that he and Juan Elvira, secretary of SEMARNAT, had agreed to "a working plan that identifies the next steps for the continued coordination between the two countries in the protection and preservation of the transnational Big Bend/Río Bravo region." Elvira and Salazar announced establishment of the Cooperative Action for Conservation in the Big Bend/Río Bravo Region. Said Salazar, a descendant of sixteenth-century Spanish-speaking settlers of New Mexico and Colorado, "As neighbors and partners in conservation, the United States and Mexico share more than just a border." Elvira took great pride in stating, "We celebrate putting into actions a model of collaboration for transboundary conservation." Knowing full well how his nation had viewed the region, as well as the journey that the international park idea had traveled, Elvira called it "a dream shared by many past generations; and a legacy for present and future ones."[81]

Highlighting the many distinctive features that the two nations sought to protect—the 268 miles of rivers and three million acres that were home to 448 species of birds, 3,600 species of insects, more than 1,500 plants, and seventy-five species of animals—Elvira, Salazar, and Anthony Wayne, the US ambassador to Mexico, joined in the release of wildlife on the American side of the border, among these 267,000 Rio Grande silvery minnows. Earlier that month, Mexico had released fifteen bird species native to the area, including several types of hawks, American kestrels, and horned owls and burrowing owls. These gestures led Elvira to conclude something that Mexican officials had believed for a long time: "In sum, it is an example of the best our governments and people can pursue through cooperation and joint work." Wayne, echoing the generous spirit of predecessors like Josephus Daniels in the 1930s, told reporters, "For anyone who has visited this spectacular place, one thing is clear: what we share here—the seamless flow of nature across both banks of the river—is far stronger and far more enduring than what divides us."[82]

The dichotomy of friendship and fear could not stop the inevitable, as on April 9, 2013, the US Department of Homeland Security reopened the Boquillas Port of Entry. Travelers on the American side would use their passport and a permit acquired at the Rio Grande Village store to interact remotely with border agents housed in Marfa, Texas. Then the time-honored process of crossing the Rio Grande / Rio Bravo in a rowboat began, followed by the one-mile trip uphill to the old mining town. First by the dozens, then steadily for the next several years, visitors to the gift shops and restaurants drew more residents back to Boquillas. This, in turn, led the state government of Coahuila to build a visitors' center in town. US officials had offered assistance in this endeavor through promotion of the Discover Boquillas campaign. Solimar International, the contractor tasked with developing better relations across the border, worked with local citizens to encourage "biodiversity conservation, partnerships, sales and marketing, and tour-product development."[83]

The reestablishment of cross-border relationships in 2013 also appealed to the World Wildlife Fund. This foundation had formed a consortium of nongovernmental organizations like Catholic Relief Services, Conservation International, World Vision, the Nature Conservancy, the Millennial Water Alliance, and the Coca-Cola Company "to provide integrated approaches to water, sanitation, and hygiene and freshwater conservation" in over twenty countries on four continents. Of the seven river basins included in this initiative, only the Rio Grande / Rio Bravo flowed through North America. Coca-Cola provided the majority of the funding, listing four criteria for its projects: biological diversity, "opportunity for meaningful conservation gains," the potential to enhance resource protection, and the initiative's "importance to the communities in which [the Coca-Cola Company] operates."[84]

Allied with this project in 2013 was the Big Bend–Río Bravo Working Group, consisting of public agencies like the NPS, Texas Parks and Wildlife, the Comisión Nacional de Áreas Naturales Protegidas, and the Mexican National Institute of Ecology and Climate Change (Instituto Nacional de Ecología y Cambio

Climático). This five-year program would address removal of exotic plants and animals from the river corridor. The working group experimented with fire, herbicides, and the plant-eating leaf beetle to effect removal. Then it planted native species along the corridor to keep out invasive strains, with the hope that this would make permanent "the biological diversity of the riparian zone, increase sediment mobility within the river channel, and improve aquatic habitat."[85]

As the NPS advanced toward its centennial in 2016 (a commemoration of the same organic act that House Resolution 1505 sought to suspend along the border in 2013), the partnerships imagined in the heady days of the Calderón-Obama meetings began to lose their momentum. Political differences about border security in faraway places like San Diego and El Paso, and stories of wanton kidnappings and murders, made policy makers in Washington leery of extending the hand of friendship. This harked back to the darker days of the Rio Grande / Rio Bravo, such as Robert T. Hill's 1899 river journey, Pancho Villa's raids, the ideological differences of the late 1930s, or the Cold War tensions of the 1950s and 1960s.

Yet somehow the champions of better relations persisted, albeit in forms and fashions different from those of the first months of the Obama administration. Tom Alex, staff archaeologist at Big Bend, recalled in a November 2013 interview how budget reductions had curtailed funding for cultural resources research dramatically. Instead, Alex and his colleagues would obtain financial support from the Border Resource Preservation project funded by the NPS and the Department of Homeland Security.[86]

Alex examined the impact of illegal immigration traffic on the environment and historical sites north of the Rio Grande. Through the use of overflights and satellite imagery made possible through Department of Homeland Security sources, Alex could outline what he called "thousands of miles of livestock trails," with what looked like "an equal number . . . in similar habitat on the Mexican side of the river." The longtime archaeologist remained hopeful that the reopening of the border "offers new opportunities to collaborate with Mexico's protected areas in the manager of livestock found within Maderas del Carmen, Ocampo, and Santa Elena Canyon protected areas."[87]

Perhaps it was fitting that the divided world of the Rio Grande / Rio Bravo corridor would see in 2015–2016 all that was good and bad with the Mexico-US relationship writ large. In April 2015, Interior Secretary Sally Jewell came to Big Bend National Park to commemorate the second anniversary of the reopening of the Boquillas crossing. Jewell shared the platform with José Guerra Abud, secretary of SEMARNAT. A reporter from the *San Francisco Chronicle* attended the ceremonies and heard the dignitaries say that "the relationship between Big Bend National Park and Boquillas is being viewed as a model that could be applied to other border towns." The population had increased by 30 percent in just two years, and the town boasted a new kindergarten, a health clinic, and a second restaurant alongside the venerable Falcon's, where the NPS and its Mexican counterparts had dined nearly eighty years earlier when first discussing the international partnership.[88]

The World Bank had extended loans to the community for the construction of a solar energy grid, something that the *Chronicle* reporter considered remarkable. "Streetlights, refrigeration, TV, and kitchen appliances," wrote the *Chronicle* staffer, "are now becoming a fact of life in Boquillas." The reporter could not help noticing, however, the archaic charm of the town's earlier life. "The burro rides from the river," said the *Chronicle*, "children skipping around with trinkets to sell and the old buskers serenading restaurant patrons for tips all could be scenes from the old days, frozen in amber."[89]

At year's end, the Sierra Club of El Paso joined with the NPS's Chamizál National Memorial to encourage political leaders in Texas and Mexico to keep the international park dream alive. Rick LoBello of the Greater Big Bend Coalition; Gus Sánchez, superintendent at Chamizál; and representatives of the private research firm Forgotten Frontiers spoke on December 15 on the occasion of the "80th anniversary of the first signed agreement between the United States and Mexico allowing for the creation of International Parks, Forests, and Wild Life Preserves along the United States-Mexican International Boundary."[90]

Jason Abrams and Zach Abrams of Forgotten Frontiers had uncovered long-lost documentation from Albert W. Dorgan of Castolon, Texas, that outlined his one-man campaign in the 1930s and 1940s to bring the two nations together. The Abrams brothers noted that Dorgan had not received enough credit in earlier publications about Big Bend National Park. In the words of Rick LoBello, Jason and Zach Abrams "are planning a gorgeous, professionally designed, but full color hardcover coffee table book revealing this unknown story." Sánchez, a former park ranger at Big Bend, accepted from the Abrams brothers two of Dorgan's maps for the international park, and in the words of LoBello, read an unpublished document from President Harry Truman to Mexican president Manuel Ávila Camacho that called in 1946 for establishment of the park "on behalf of both himself and the 'late President Roosevelt.'"[91]

The spirits of Lázaro Cárdenas and Franklin Roosevelt, and countless other advocates of harmony and friendship on the border between Mexico and the United States, must have smiled wherever they were on that day when the Sierra Club, Forgotten Frontiers, and the NPS gathered once more to state the obvious. The centennial of the NPS's organic act had prompted no end of publications, large and small, about the 401 units of the park system. Most proclaimed the gift of preserving natural beauty that America gave to itself with its publicly funded parks, monuments, seashores, recreation areas, and the like. Some noted those areas where the dream fell short, such as the need for parks to be more inclusive of the next generation of visitors whose demographics will not parallel those of the NPS system's founders.

One writer in particular, Terry Tempest Williams, set herself the task of identifying a dozen sites from Maine to California that would reveal to her the essence of America's century-old love affair with its parks. "Any wind will tell you," wrote the author of many articles and books on nature and the American West, "it is the long view that counts." For Williams, "Big Bend National Park is the long view—stark, lonely, and soul-saving." Once there, Williams marveled: "I have waited all my life to see this kind of vista." Unlike those who lived there, fought and died there, and tried to make a boundary line on a map disappear, Williams had ventured to the border "as a naturalist only, desperate to immerse myself in natural history, not the history of humans." As the author and former NPS ranger Edward Abbey had done in the 1970s when he visited Big Bend, Williams called herself a "misanthrope." All she really wanted, said Williams, was to "simply walk and witness the Chihuahuan Desert, where thousands of species of cactus will ask nothing of me but to be left alone beneath an overarching sky."[92]

Like everyone else who had come and gone through the Rio Grande / Rio Bravo corridor, Williams could not ignore the memories of human interaction and conflict. Standing on the shoreline, she said of Santa Eleña Canyon, "These . . . walls, fourteen hundred feet high, resemble Puebloan pots—black paint on red-fired clay." Looking downstream, as did Walter Prescott Webb in 1937, the nature writer realized that "no map can orient us here." Caught by surprise, even as she sought the mysteries of the national parks, Williams asked herself, "Where does America end and Mexico begin?"

The answer came to her, as it does to all who venture there: "This is its own country, borderless by nature, unowned, unbound, complete." Unaware that forty years earlier the NPS and the Drug Enforcement Agency had fought against Mexican narco-traffickers at Santa Eleña, or that one year later a presidential candidate would demand a wall along the entirety of the Mexico-US border, Williams mused in 2016, "Boundaries are fears made manifest, designed to protect us." Instead, she wrote, "I don't want protection, I want freedom." The ghosts that haunt the river of dreams would understand.[93]

NOTES

PREFACE

1. Arthur R. Gomez, *A Most Singular Country: A History of Occupation in the Big Bend* (Provo, UT: Charles Redd Center for Western Studies, Brigham Young University Press, 1990); John R. Jameson, *The Story of Big Bend National Park* (Austin: University of Texas Press, 1996).

2. Michael Welsh, *Landscape of Ghosts, River of Dreams: An Administrative History of Big Bend National Park* (Santa Fe: National Park Service, 2002), https://www.nps.gov /parkhistory/online_books/bibe/adhi/adhi.htm.

INTRODUCTION

1. W. Dirk Raat, *Mexico and the United States: Ambivalent Vistas*, 4th ed. (Athens: University of Georgia Press, 1992); Dan Flores, *Horizontal Yellow: Nature and History in the Near Southwest* (Albuquerque: University of New Mexico Press, 1999), 147–148.

2. Herbert Eugene Bolton, *Rim of Christendom: A Biography of Eusebio Francisco Kino, Pacific Coast Pioneer* (repr., Tucson: University of Arizona Press, 2015).

3. Jeremy Adelman and Stephen Aron, "From Borderlands to Borders: Empires, Nation-States, and the Peoples in between in North American History," *American Historical Review* 104 (1999): 814–841.

4. Adelman and Aron, 816; Herbert Eugene Bolton, *Rim of Christendom: A Biography of Eusebio Francisco Kino, Pacific Coast Pioneer* (New York: Macmillan, 1936).

5. Adelman and Aron, "From Borderlands to Borders," 816.

6. Pat Kelly, *River of Lost Dreams* (Lincoln: University of Nebraska Press, 1986), 18.

7. David M. Potter, *People of Plenty: Economic Abundance and the American Character* (Chicago: University of Chicago Press, 1958); Howard F. Cline, *Mexico: Revolution to Evolution, 1940–1960* (New York: Oxford University Press, 1962), 231.

8. For a discussion of the construction of the border fence in the early twenty-first century, see Michael Welsh, *A Mission in the Desert: The U.S. Army Corps of Engineers, Albuquerque District, 1985–2010* (Washington, DC: US Government Printing Office, 2015).

CHAPTER 1: ONCE THERE WAS ONLY A RIVER

1. Edward Abbey, *One Life at a Time, Please* (New York: Henry Holt, 1988), 127, 129, 135, 141.

2. "An Act to Establish a National Park Service, and for Other Purposes," approved August 25, 1916 (39 Stat. 535), in *America's National Park System: The Critical Documents*, ed. Lary M. Dilsaver (Lanham, MD: Rowman and Littlefield, 1994), 46.

3. Frank Deckert, *Big Bend: Three Steps to the Sky* (Big Bend National Park, TX: Big Bend Natural History Association, 1981), 4, 7.

4. Gomez, *Most Singular Country*, 1; Deckert, *Big Bend*, 4.

5. Gomez, *Most Singular Country*, 2; Deckert, *Big Bend*, 13. One example of the scholarship of the environment and human interaction is William N. Cronon, *Changes in the Land: Indians, Colonists, and the Ecology of New England* (New York: Hill and Wang, 1983).

6. Tom Alex and Betty Alex, interview by the author, Big Bend National Park, Texas, June 6, 1997; Deckert, *Big Bend*, 14. For analysis of the Jumano presence in the Big Bend country, see Virginia A. Wulfkuhle, "Archeological Manifestations of the Jumano: A Reassessment," University of Texas at Austin, Department of Anthropology, April 1983, Historical Files, Science and Resources Division Library, Big Bend National Park (hereafter BIBE).

7. A good source about the Spanish in the Southwest is David J. Weber, *The Spanish Frontier in North America, 1513–1821* (New Haven, CT: Yale University Press, 1992). For analysis of the complexity and challenge of Indian-Spanish relations, see Ramon A. Gutierrez, *When Jesus Came, the Corn Mothers Went Away: Marriage, Sexuality, and Power in New Mexico, 1500–1846* (Stanford, CA: Stanford University Press, 1991).

8. Gomez, *Most Singular Country*, 10–11; Deckert, *Big Bend*, 33.

9. For a good overview of the Eastern Indé peoples, see Thomas A. Britten, *The Lipan Apaches: People of Wind and Lightning* (Albuquerque: University of New Mexico Press, 2009).

10. Gomez, *Most Singular Country*, 11–12.

11. Gomez, 12–13.

12. Gomez, 16–17; Adelman and Aron, "From Borderlands to Borders," 814.

13. Gomez, *Most Singular Country*, 14, 16–17, 19; Adelman and Aron, "From Borderlands to Borders."

14. For analysis of the Spanish imperial defenses in the desert Southwest, see J. H. Elliott, *Empires of the Atlantic World: Britain and Spain in America, 1492–1830* (New Haven, CT: Yale University Press, 2006).

15. Gomez, *Most Singular Country*, 19–20; Michael Welsh, *U.S. Army Corps of Engineers: Albuquerque District, 1935–1985* (Albuquerque: University of New Mexico Press, 1987), 4–5. For a good discussion of the Royal Corps of Engineers, see Janet R. Fireman, *The Spanish Royal Corps of Engineers in the Western Borderlands, 1764–1815* (Glendale, CA: Arthur H. Clark, 1970).

16. Gomez, *Most Singular Country*, 27–29.

17. Pekka Hamalainen, *The Comanche Empire* (New Haven, CT: Yale University Press, 2008), 64; Miera y Pacheco quoted in Gomez, *Most Singular Country*, 27–29. For a more nuanced view of the impact of Native peoples on the southern plains and northern Mexico, see Andres Reséndez, *The Other Slavery: The Uncovered Story of Indian Enslavement in America* (New York: Houghton Mifflin Harcourt, 2016).

18. David Weber, *Bárbaros: Spaniards and Their Savages in the Age of Enlightenment* (New Haven, CT: Yale University Press, 2005), 91.

19. Weber, 34–36.

20. Weber, 37–40; Max L. Moorhead, *The Apache Frontier: Jacobo Ugarte and Spanish-Indian Relations in Northern New Spain, 1769–1791* (Norman: University of Oklahoma Press, 1968), 200–234.

21. A good introduction to the issues pertaining to the Mexican-American War is Robert W. Johannsen, *To the Halls of the Montezumas: The Mexican War in the American Imagination* (New York: Oxford University Press, 1985).

22. Gomez, *Most Singular Country*, 46, 67. Also see "The Treaty of Guadalupe Hidalgo, 1848," in *Historic Documents of New Mexico*, ed. Richard N. Ellis (Albuquerque: University of New Mexico Press, 1975), 10–20.

23. For an analysis of the Gold Rush and its impact on the West, see Kevin Starr, *Americans and the California Dream, 1850–1910* (New York: Oxford University Press, 1973).

24. Gomez, *Most Singular Country*, 48–51, 53, 55. For a discussion of the early journeys of the US Army into the Davis Mountains, see Michael Welsh, *A Special Place, a Sacred Trust: Preserving the Fort Davis Story* (Santa Fe: National Park Service, 1996), 1–10. Also valuable is Robert M. Utley, *Fort Davis National Historic Site, Texas* (Washington, DC: US Department of the Interior, National Park Service, 1965).

25. Gomez, *Most Singular Country*, 54, 56–58.

26. Gomez, 58–59, 61.

27. Gomez, 63. For an introduction to the army's use of camels in the desert Southwest, see Odie B. Faulk, *The US Camel Corps: An Army Experiment* (New York: Oxford University Press, 1976).

28. Gomez, *Most Singular Country*, 63.

29. Gomez, 68–69, 71; Welsh, *Special Place*, 4–5.

30. Gomez, *Most Singular Country*, 72–75, 77. A good treatment of the Black Seminoles is Kevin Mulroy, *Freedom on the Border: The Seminole Maroons in Florida, the Indian Territory, Coahuila, and Texas* (Lubbock: Texas Tech University Press, 1993).

31. Gomez, *Most Singular Country*, 96–99.

32. Census Office, Department of the Interior, *Eleventh Census of the United States, 1890* (Washington, DC: United States Government Printing Office, 1892). For a discussion of Frederick Jackson Turner and his "frontier thesis," see Turner, *The Frontier in American History* (New York: Holt, 1921).

33. Census Office, Department of the Interior, *Twelfth Census of the United States, 1900* (Washington, DC: US Government Printing Office, 1902).

34. Robert T. Hill, "Running the Cañons of the Rio Grande," *Century Illustrated*, November 1900–April 1901, 371–390. A thorough discussion of the exploration of the nineteenth-century West can be found in William H. Goetzmann, *New Lands, New Men: America and the Second Great Age of Discovery* (New York: Viking, 1986).

35. Quoted in Nancy Alexander, *Father of Texas Geology: Robert T. Hill* (Dallas: Southern Methodist University Press, 1976), 70.

36. Alexander, 18.

37. Hill, "Running the Cañons," 372.

38. Hill, 372.

39. Hill, 372.

40. Hill, 372.

1. Quoted in Robert Shankland, *Steve Mather of the National Parks* (New York: Alfred A. Knopf, 1954), 53. A good treatment of early twentieth-century conservation ideas can be found in Douglas Brinkley, *The Wilderness Warrior: Theodore Roosevelt and the Crusade for America* (New York: HarperCollins, 2009).

2. A good discussion of the link between transportation and park creation can be found in Alfred Runte, *Trains of Discovery: Railroads and the Legacy of Our National Parks* (Lanham, MD: Roberts Rinehart, 2011).

3. Duane F. Guy, ed., *The Story of Palo Duro Canyon* (Lubbock: Texas Tech University Press, 2001), 145–146.

4. Nevin O. Winter, *Texas the Marvellous: The State of the Six Flags* (Boston: Page, 1916), 256. Winter describes the windswept canyon lands as but a smaller version of the more familiar Grand Canyon. Revealing the degree to which Winter was willing to bolster the allure of Palo Duro, he argues, "You may enjoy it [Palo Duro] even more, for the very magnitude of Arizona's wonder sometimes appalls the onlooker. It is so vast that the finite mind has difficulty grasping it." At least in Palo Duro, "the mind can comprehend the details" (262). "Appalling" is probably not the first word that comes to mind when describing the Grand Canyon, and it took a stretch of the imagination to somehow downsize the majestic scale of the Grand Canyon and offer Palo Duro as a suitable replacement, but Winter, in his effort to promote Texas's scenic wonders, felt that such verbal machinations were worth making.

5. Carlysle Graham Raht, *The Romance of Davis Mountains and Big Bend Country* (El Paso: Rahtbooks, 1919), 2.

6. Mark Wasserman, *Everyday Life and Politics in Nineteenth Century Mexico: Men, Women, and War* (Albuquerque: University of New Mexico Press, 2000); Wasserman, *Capitalists, Caciques, and Revolution: The Native Elite and Foreign Enterprise in Chihuahua, Mexico, 1854–1911* (Chapel Hill: University of North Carolina Press, 1984), 5.

7. Manuel Gamio, *Mexican Immigration to the United States: A Study of Human Migration and Adjustment* (New York: Dover, 1971), 160.

8. John Reed, *Insurgent Mexico* (New York: International, 2002), 31.

9. Wasserman, *Capitalists, Caciques, and Revolution*, 133, 135–137, 139.

10. *Fourteenth Census of the United States, 1920* (Washington, DC: US Government Printing Office, 1922).

11. Rupert Norval Richardson, Ernest Wallace, and Adrian N. Anderson, *Texas: The Lone Star State*, 4th ed. (Upper Saddle River, NJ: Prentice-Hall, 1981), 389.

12. Welsh, *Special Place*, 28–29; Elmer J. Edwards, "To the Big Bend Away! Newest National Park Is Widest of the Open Spaces, Offers Most to Vacationists Seeking Nature at Its Rawest," *West Texas Today*, May 1945, 6. *West Texas Today* was published by the West Texas Chamber of Commerce, based in Abilene.

13. Pat M. Neff, *The Battles of Peace* (Fort Worth, TX: Pioneer/Bunker, 1925), 128.

14. James Wright Steely, *Parks for Texas: Enduring Landscapes of the New Deal* (Austin: University of Texas Press, 1999), 231–233.

15. Emma Morrill Shirley, *Administration of Pat M. Neff, Governor of Texas, 1921–1925*, Baylor Bulletin (Waco, TX: Baylor University Press, 1938), 87.

16. Neff, *Battles of Peace*, 131.

17. Walter Prescott Webb, *The Great Plains* (repr., New York: Grosset and Dunlap, 1976); Webb, "The American Revolver and the West," *Scribner's*, February 1927.

18. Quoted in Virginia Madison, *The Big Bend Country of Texas* (Albuquerque: University of New Mexico Press, 1968), 229–230.

19. Quoted in Madison, 229–230.

20. "First Steps in Creating Big Bend National Park Taken by Abilenian," *Abilene (TX) Reporter-News*, June 11, 1944.

21. "First Steps"; "Jameson, *Story of Big Bend*, 19; Michael Welsh, *Dunes and Dreams: A History of White Sands National Monument* (Santa Fe: National Park Service, 1995), 32. J. Frank Dobie had first come to the Big Bend country in 1910 to take a teaching position in the high school of Alpine, Texas. While there only one year, Dobie came to know the Rio Grande, spending much time conducting interviews along the river with its residents. From these experiences would come several of his novels and essays about life in Far West Texas.

22. John Jameson, *Big Bend National Park: The Formative Years* (El Paso: University of Texas at El Paso, 1980), 19–20.

23. Jameson.

24. Paul S. Taylor, *An American Mexican Frontier: Nueces County, Texas* (Chapel Hill: University of North Carolina Press, 1934), 250.

25. Quoted in Douglas Brinkley, *Rightful Heritage: Franklin D. Roosevelt and the Land of America* (New York: HarperCollins, 2016), 316.

26. Jameson, *Story of Big Bend*, 23; Gomez, *Most Singular Country*, 176; House Bill No. 26, "A Bill to Be Entitled an Act Changing the Name of the Texas Canyon State Park to Big Bend State Park," September 1933[?], Box 9, Wallet 24, Folder 4, Everett Ewing Townsend Collection, Archives of the Big Bend, Sul Ross State University, Alpine, TX (hereafter Townsend Collection, ABB).

27. Jameson, *Story of Big Bend*, 23.

28. Jameson, 23; Richard West Sellars, *Preserving Nature in the National Parks: A History* (New Haven, CT: Yale University Press, 1997), 126.

29. Ross A. Maxwell, "Summary of Events That Led to the Establishment of the Big Bend National Park," n.d. [1949?], Record Group (RG) 79, National Park Service (NPS), Southwest Regional Office (SWRO), Santa Fe, Correspondence Relating to National Parks, Monuments, and Recreational Areas, 1927–1953, Box 2, Folder 101: NPS History, Rocky Mountain Region Branch, National Archives and Records Administration, Denver, CO (hereafter DEN NARA); Richard N. Sellars, *Preserving Nature in the National Parks: A History* (New Haven, CT: Yale University Press, 1997), 126, 133; Welsh, *Special Place*, 37.

30. Conrad L. Wirth, assistant director, NPS, State Park Conservation Work, Washington, DC, to Herbert Maier, NPS, Denver, CO, July 24, 1933, RG 79, NPS, SWRO, Santa Fe, Correspondence Relating to CCC, ECW, and ERA Work in National Parks, Forests,

and Monuments and Recreational Areas, 1933–1934, Box 96, Folder 204-01: CCC by Field Officers, DEN NARA.

31. James G. Anderson, "Land Acquisition in the Big Bend National Park of Texas" (MA thesis, Sul Ross State College, 1967), 39; F. A. Dale, district inspector, NPS, Austin, TX, to Major John D. Guthrie, Eight Corps Area (US Army), Fort Sam Houston, TX, September 26, 1933, RG 79, NPS, SWRO, Santa Fe, Correspondence Relating to CCC, ECW, and ERA Work in National Parks, Forests, and Monuments and Recreational Areas, 1933–1934, Box 96, Folder 601-03: (CCC) Camp Sites, DEN NARA.

32. Herbert Maier, district officer, ECW, Austin, TX, to Wirth, October 2, 1933, RG 79, NPS SWRO, Santa Fe, Correspondence Relating to CCC, ECW, and ERA Work in National Parks, Forests, and Monuments and Recreational Areas, 1933–1934, Box 96, Folder 601-03: (CCC) Camp Sites, DEN NARA.

33. Dale to Maier, October 6, 1933, RG 79, NPS, SWRO, Santa Fe, Correspondence Relating to CCC, ECW, and ERA Work in National Parks, Forests, and Monuments and Recreational Areas, 1933–1934, Box 96, Folder 601-03: (CCC) Camp Sites, DEN NARA.

34. Dale to Maier, October 6, 1933.

35. Maier to Townsend, October 12, 1933, RG 79, NPS SWRO, Santa Fe, Correspondence Relating to CCC, ECW, and ERA Work in National Parks, Forests, and Monuments, and Recreational Areas, 1933–1934, Box 96, Folder 601-03: (CCC) Camp Sites, DEN NARA.

36. B. C. Tharp, Department of Botany and Bacteriology, University of Texas, Austin, untitled manuscript, November 16, 1933; C. H. Mueller, "The Vegetation of the Chisos Mountains of West Texas," unpublished manuscript, 1933, all cited in RG 79, NPS, SWRO, Santa Fe, Correspondence Relating to National Parks, Monuments, and Recreational Areas, 1927–1953, Folder NA, Box 94, DEN NARA. Mueller's work came from the introduction to his master's thesis, submitted in 1933.

37. Roger W. Toll, Department of the Interior, Office of National Parks, Buildings, and Reservations, Denver, CO, to Arno B. Cammerer, director, Office of National Parks, Buildings, and Reservations, Washington, DC, March 3, 1934, RG 79, NPS, Central Classified Files (CCF) 1933–1949, Big Bend National Park 207 Files, Box 826, National Archives and Records Administration, Archives II, College Park, MD (hereafter DC NARA II).

38. Jameson, *Story of Big Bend*, 25; Anderson, "Land Acquisition," 40; Toll to Cammerer, March 3, 1934.

39. Maier to Wirth, February 18, 1934, RG 79, NPS, SWRO, Santa Fe, Correspondence Relating to CCC, ECW, and ERA Work in National Forests, Monuments and Recreational Areas, 1933–1934, Big Bend National Park, TX–Bryce Canyon National Monument, UT, Box 97, Folder 601-03.2: (CCC) Abandoned Camps, DEN NARA.

40. Maier to Wirth, February 18, 1934.

41. Maier to Wirth, February 18, 1934.

42. Maier to Wirth, February 18, 1934.

43. Maier to Wirth, February 18, 1934.

44. Maier to Wirth, February 18, 1934.

45. Toll to Maier, February 19, 1934, RG 79, NPS, SWRO, Santa Fe, Correspondence Relating to CCC, ECW, and ERA Work in National Forests, Monuments and Recreational Areas, 1933–1934, Big Bend National Park, TX–Bryce Canyon National Monument, UT, Box 97, Folder 601-03.2: (CCC) Abandoned Camps, DEN NARA.

46. Toll to Maier, February 19, 1934.

47. W. G. Carnes, chief, Western Division, NPS, San Francisco, to Dr. L. I. Hewes, deputy chief Engineer, Bureau of Public Roads, San Francisco, May 4, 1934, RG 79, NPS, SWRO, Santa Fe, Correspondence Relating to National Parks, Monuments and Recreational Areas, 1927–1953, Box 1, Folder 000: General Big Bend, DEN NARA.

48. Gomez, *Most Singular Country*, 179; Anderson, "Land Acquisition," 44; Colp to commanding general, Headquarters, Arizona–New Mexico District, CCC, Fort Bliss, TX, June 1, 1934, RG 79, NPS, SWRO, Santa Fe, Correspondence Relating to National Parks, Monuments and Recreational Areas, 1927–1953, Box 11, Folder 609: (CCC) Leases, DEN NARA.

CHAPTER 3: SCIENCE COMES TO A WILD LAND

1. Sellars, *Preserving Nature*, 86–87, 91–109.

2. Maynard S. Johnson, NPS regional wildlife technician, Bronxville, NY, to Baggley, memorandum, April 24, 1936, RG 79, NPS, CCF 1933–1949, Big Bend 0–32 File, Box 82, DC NARA II. The memorandum includes a report by W. B. McDougall and M. S. Johnson, "Unique Fauna and Flora of the American Side of the Proposed Big Bend International Park."

3. Johnson to Baggley, April 24, 1936.

4. Johnson to Baggley, April 24, 1936.

5. Erik K. Reed, assistant archaeologist, Region III, NPS, Oklahoma City, "Special Report on Archaeological Work in the Big Bend, during the Summer of 1936," September 1936, RG 79, NPS, CCF 1933–1949, Big Bend National Park 207 Files, Box 825, DC NARA II.

6. Reed.

7. Reed.

8. Reed.

9. Reed.

10. Reed.

11. Reed.

12. Reed.

13. Reed.

14. Reed.

15. Ernest G. Marsh Jr., student technician, Department of Botany, University of Texas, Austin, "A Preliminary Report on a Biological Survey of the Santa Rosa and Del Carmen Mountains of Northern Coahuila, Mexico, July 2–September 22, 1936," October 11, 1936, 720-04 Wildlife Survey, Big Bend National Park File, RG 79, NPS, CCF 1933–1949, Big Bend National Park 719–833-05 Files, Box 836, DC NARA II; press release, Region III, NPS, Oklahoma City, October 17, 1936, RG 79, NPS, SWRO, Santa Fe, Correspondence Relating

to CCC, ECW, and ERA Work in National Parks, Forests and Monuments and Recreational Areas, 1933–1934, Box 96, Folder: General Pt. 2, DEN NARA.

16. Marsh, "Preliminary Report"; press release, October 17, 1936.

17. Marsh, "Preliminary Report."

18. Marsh.

19. Marsh.

20. Marsh.

21. Marsh.

22. Marsh.

23. Marsh.

24. Marsh.

25. Marsh.

26. Ernest G. Marsh Jr., "Biological Survey of the Santa Rosa and Del Carmen Mountains of Northern Coahuila, Mexico," July 2–September 22, 1936, RG 79, NPS, CCF 1933–1949, Big Bend National Park 207 Files, Box 825, DC NARA II.

27. Marsh.

28. Marsh.

29. Marsh.

30. Marsh.

31. Marsh.

32. Marsh.

33. Marsh.

34. Marsh.

35. Marsh.

36. Marsh.

37. Marsh.

38. Marsh.

39. Marsh.

40. Marsh.

41. Marsh.

42. Rollin H. Baker, student technician, NPS, to Maier, report, September 13, 1937, report, 207 Big Bend Reports General File, RG 79, NPS, CCF 1933–1949, Big Bend Files, Box 824, DC NARA II.

43. Baker to Maier, September 13, 1937.

44. Baker to Maier, September 13, 1937.

45. James O. Stevenson to Victor Cahalane, memorandum, September 15, 1943, RG 79, NPS, SWRO, Santa Fe, Correspondence Relating to National Parks, Monuments, and Recreational Areas, 1927–1953, Box 20, Folder 720.04: Wild Life Survey, DEN NARA.

46. Stevenson to Cahalane, September 15, 1943. Hermon Bumpus had served as director of the Marine Biological Laboratory at Woods Hole, Massachusetts; president of Tufts College (later Tufts University); and professor of biology at Brown University. Bumpus also would be named the first president of the American Association of Museums.

47. Stevenson to Cahalane, September 15, 1943.

48. Stevenson to Cahalane, September 15, 1943; Hillory A. Tolson, acting NPS director, Chicago, to the acting director, Fish and Wildlife Service, memorandum, March 14, 1944, and Tillotson to the NPS director, memorandum, March 14, 1944, both in 701 Flora Big Bend National Park File, RG 79, NPS, CCF 1933–1949, Big Bend National Park 660-05.8–718 Files, Box 835, DC NARA II.

49. Walter P. Taylor, senior biologist, Fish and Wildlife Service, Walter B. McDougall, park naturalist, NPS, and William B. Davis, acting head, Department of Instruction, Fish and Game, Agricultural and Mechanical College of Texas, "Preliminary Report of an Ecological Survey of Big Bend National Park," March–June 1944, Proposed National Parks Big Bend General Part 8 File, RG 79, NPS, CCF 1933–1949, Big Bend Files, Box 823, DC NARA II.

50. Taylor, McDougall, and Davis.

51. Maxwell to Walter P. Taylor, Wildlife Research Unit, College Station, TX, March 22, 1944, RG 79, NPS, SWRO, Santa Fe, Correspondence Relating to National Parks, Monuments, and Recreational Areas, 1927–1953, Box 20, Folder 720.04: Wild Life Survey, DEN NARA.

52. Taylor, McDougall, and Davis, "Preliminary Report of an Ecological Survey of Big Bend National Park," March–June 1944.

53. Taylor, McDougall, and Davis.

54. Taylor, McDougall, and Davis.

55. Taylor, McDougall, and Davis.

56. Taylor, McDougall, and Davis.

57. Taylor, McDougall, and Davis.

58. Taylor, McDougall, and Davis.

59. Taylor, McDougall, and Davis.

60. Taylor, McDougall, and Davis.

61. Taylor, McDougall, and Davis.

62. Taylor, McDougall, and Davis.

63. Thomas K. Chamberlain, appendix to Taylor, McDougall, and Davis.

64. Chamberlain.

65. Chamberlain.

66. Chamberlain.

67. Chamberlain.

68. Arthur R. Kelley, chief, Archaeological Sites Division, NPS, Chicago, to the NPS director, memorandum, December 10, 1942, RG 79, NPS, SWRO, Santa Fe, Correspondence Relating to National Parks, Monuments, and Recreational Areas, 1927–1953, Folder 800: Protection Services to Public #2, Box 22, DEN NARA.

69. Kelley to NPS director, December 10, 1942.

70. Kelley to NPS director, December 10, 1942.

71. Kelley to NPS director, December 10, 1942.

72. Kelley to NPS director, December 10, 1942.

73. Kelley to NPS director, December 10, 1942.

74. Drury to Morelock, February 10, 1943, 501 Dr. H. W. Morelock Sul Ross File, RG 79, NPS, CCF 1933–1949, Big Bend National Park 208-41-501-02 Files, Box 828, DC NARA II.

75. C. P. Russell, supervisor of interpretation, NPS, Chicago, to Mr. Tripp, memorandum, August 16, 1942, RG 79, NPS, SWRO, Santa Fe, Correspondence Relating to National Parks, Monuments, and Recreational Areas, 1927–1953, Folder 833.06: Museums, Box 22, DEN NARA.

76. Drury to Morelock, February 10, 1943.

77. Drury to Morelock, February 10, 1943.

78. Drury to Morelock, February 10, 1943.

79. Morelock to Drury, February 13, 1943, RG 79, NPS, SWRO, Santa Fe, Correspondence Relating to National Parks, Monuments, and Recreational Areas, 1927–1953, Box 13, Folder 610.01: Purchasing of Land #4 [Folder 2], Big Bend, DEN NARA.

80. Morelock to Drury, February 13, 1943.

CHAPTER 4: DREAMING OF A PARK FOR PEACE

1. Lane Simonian, *Defending the Land of the Jaguar: A History of Conservation in Mexico* (Austin: University of Texas Press, 1995), 68–69, 76–77.

2. Simonian, 76–77.

3. Simonian, 79, 81, 83–84.

4. Simonian, *Defending the Land*, 93–94; Michael C. Meyer and William L. Sherman, *The Course of Mexican History*, 5th ed. (New York: Oxford University Press, 1995), 596, 600.

5. Simonian, *Defending the Land*, 87, 90, 93–94; Meyer and Sherman, *Course of Mexican History*, 596, 600.

6. Simonian, *Defending the Land*, 93–94; Meyer and Sherman, *Course of Mexican History*, 596, 600.

7. Simonian, *Defending the Land*, 94–100. For a discussion of the Mexican park initiative, see Emily Wakild, *Revolutionary Parks: Conservation, Social Justice, and Mexico's National Parks, 1910–1940* (Tucson: University of Arizona Press, 2011). Wakild's thesis is that the early efforts at collaboration between Mexico and the United States in the creation of an international peace park along the Rio Grande / Rio Bravo failed because the Americans did not understand Mexico's goals for national parks to serve its urban populations. Mexico also wanted to preserve small farms and villages, rather than set aside open space for tourism that most benefited the United States.

8. Jameson, *Story of Big Bend*, 104. For additional information about Ickes, see Richard W. Lowitt, *The New Deal and the West* (Bloomington: Indiana University Press, 1984).

9. Josephus Daniels, US ambassador to Mexico, Mexico City, to the secretary of state, Washington, DC, August 16, 1935, RG 79, NPS, SWRO, Santa Fe, Correspondence Relating to National Parks, Monuments and Recreational Areas, 1927–1953, Box 94, Folder: Big Bend Correspondence (Folder 1), DEN NARA.

10. Daniels to the secretary of state, August 16, 1935.

11. Maier to L. R. Fiock, US Bureau of Reclamation, El Paso, TX, October 9, 1935, RG 79, NPS, SWRO, Santa Fe, Correspondence Relating to National Parks, Monuments and Recreational Areas, 1927–1953, Box 94, Folder: Big Bend Correspondence (Folder 1), DEN NARA.

12. Maier to Fiock, October 9, 1935.

13. Maier to Fiock, October 9, 1935.

14. Maier to Fiock, October 9, 1935.

15. Fiock to Maier, October 16, 1935, RG 79, NPS, SWRO, Santa Fe, Correspondence Relating to National Parks, Monuments and Recreational Areas, 1927–1953, Box 94, Folder: Big Bend Correspondence (Folder 1), DEN NARA.

16. Fiock to Maier, October 16, 1935.

17. Fiock to Maier, October 16, 1935.

18. Fiock to Maier, October 16, 1935.

19. Maier to Wirth, October 21, 1935, RG 79, NPS, SWRO, Santa Fe, Correspondence Relating to National Parks, Monuments and Recreational Areas, 1927–1953, Box 94, Folder: Big Bend Correspondence (Folder 1), DEN NARA.

20. L. M. Lawson, American commissioner, International Boundary Commission, El Paso, to Maier, October 23, 1935, RG 79, NPS, SWRO, Santa Fe, Correspondence Relating to National Parks, Monuments and Recreational Areas, 1927–1953, Box 94, Folder: Big Bend Correspondence (Folder 1), DEN NARA.

21. Lawson to Maier, October 23, 1935.

22. Lawson to Maier, October 23, 1935.

23. Maier to Wirth, November 5, 1935, RG 79, NPS, SWRO, Santa Fe, Correspondence Relating to National Parks, Monuments and Recreational Areas, 1927–1953, Box 94, Folder: Big Bend Correspondence (Folder 1), DEN NARA.

24. Maynard Johnson and Walter McDougall to Maier, November 9, 1935, RG 79, NPS, SWRO, Santa Fe, Correspondence Relating to National Parks, Monuments and Recreational Areas, 1927–1953, Box 94, Folder: Big Bend Correspondence (Folder 1), DEN NARA.

25. Johnson and McDougall to Maier, November 9, 1935; Daniel F. Galicia to Maier, November 12, 1935, RG 79, NPS, SWRO, Santa Fe, Correspondence Relating to National Parks, Monuments and Recreational Areas, 1927–1953, Box 94, Folder: Big Bend Correspondence (Folder 1), DEN NARA.

26. A. E. Demaray, acting director, NPS, Washington, DC, to Juan Zinser, chief, Departemento Forestal y Caza y Pesca, care of Mr. George B. Shaw, American consul, Ciudad Juarez, Chihuahua, Mexico, November 19, 1935, RG 79, NPS, SWRO, Santa Fe, Correspondence Relating to National Parks, Monuments and Recreational Areas, 1927–1953, Box 94, Folder: 4th Progress Report on Big Bend—Region III, DEN NARA.

27. Demaray to Zinser, November 19, 1935; Simonian, *Defending the Land*, 101.

28. Herbert Maier, "Report on the Conference with Mexican Representatives Relative to the Proposed Big Bend National Park and Other Border Areas," El Paso, TX, November 24, 1935, RG 79, NPS, SWRO, Santa Fe, Correspondence Relating to National Parks, Monuments and Recreational Areas, 1927–1953, Box 1, Folder 0–30: (NPS) Big

Bend International Park, DEN NARA. Frank Pinkley supervised a group of small NPS sites in Arizona and New Mexico that focused on cultural resources like Indian ruins and Spanish missions; hence the generic term Southwestern National Monuments.

29. Maier.

30. Maier.

31. Maier.

32. Maier.

33. Maier.

34. Maier.

35. Maier.

36. Maier.

37. Maier.

38. Ross A. Maxwell, "Summary of Events That Led to the Establishment of the Big Bend National Park," n.d. [1949?], 6, RG 79, NPS, SWRO, Santa Fe, Correspondence Relating to National Parks, Monuments, and Recreational Areas, 1927–1953, Box 2, Folder 101: NPS History, Rocky Mountain Branch, DEN NARA; Thomason to Townsend, telegram, February 10, 1936, RG 79, NPS, SWRO, Santa Fe, Correspondence Relating to National Parks, Monuments, and Recreational Areas, 1927–1953, Folder: 4th Progress Report on Big Bend—Region III, Box 94, DEN NARA.

39. Maxwell, "Summary of Events," 7.

40. Maxwell, "Summary of Events," 7.

41. Jameson, Story of Big Bend 109.

42. Jameson, Story of Big Bend, 109; Sellars, Preserving Nature, 101.

43. Maier to Juan Thacker, El Paso, TX, March 8, 1936, RG 79, NPS, SWRO, Santa Fe, Correspondence Relating to National Parks, Monuments, and Recreational Areas, 1927–1953, Folder: 4th Progress Report on Big Bend—Region III, Box 94, DEN NARA.

44. Maier to Thacker, March 8, 1936.

45. Maier to Thacker, March 8, 1936.

46. Mrs. Roger Toll, Denver, CO, to McClatchy, April 6, 1936, and McClatchy to Mrs. Toll, April 9, 1936, both in RG 79, NPS, SWRO, Santa Fe, Correspondence Relating to National Parks, Monuments, and Recreational Areas, 1927–1953, Box 9, Folder 503: (NPS) Pictures (General) [Folder 2], DEN NARA.

47. Galicia to McClatchy, March 25, 1936, RG 79, NPS, SWRO, Santa Fe, Correspondence Relating to National Parks, Monuments, and Recreational Areas, 1927–1953, Box 7, Folder 501: Publicity, DEN NARA; Galicia to Wirth, April 3, 1936, RG 79, NPS, SWRO, Santa Fe, Correspondence Relating to National Parks, Monuments, and Recreational Areas, 1927–1953, Box 1, Folder 0–30: (NPS) Big Bend International Park, DEN NARA.

48. Galicia to McClatchy, March 25, 1936; Galicia to Wirth, April 3, 1936.

49. Wirth to regional officer, Region III, NPS, Oklahoma City, June 29, 1936, RG 79, NPS, SWRO, Santa Fe, Correspondence Relating to National Parks, Monuments, and Recreational Areas, 1927–1953, Folder: General April 1, 1936–July 30, 1936, Box 94, DEN NARA.

50. Wirth to regional officer, June 29, 1936.

51. Maier to Wirth, July 3, 1936, RG 79, NPS, SWRO, Santa Fe, Correspondence Relating to National Parks, Monuments, and Recreational Areas, 1927–1953, Folder: General April 1, 1936–July 30, 1936, Box 94, DEN NARA.

52. Maier to Wirth, July 3, 1936.

53. J. T. Roberts, associate landscape architect, NPS, Bureau of Planning and State Cooperation, Austin, TX, "Special Report on Investigation of Proposed Mexican Big Bend National Park," September 9, 1936, RG 79, NPS, SWRO, Santa Fe, Correspondence Relating to CCC, ECW, and ERA Work in National Parks, Forests and Monuments and Recreational Areas, 1933–1934, Box 96, Folder: General Pt. 2, DEN NARA.

54. Roberts. "Tremblores" means "tremblers" in English, similar to "earthquakes" (*temblores*).

55. Roberts.

56. Roberts.

57. Roberts.

58. Roberts.

59. Roberts.

60. Quevedo to Maier, September 14, 1936, RG 79, NPS, SWRO, Santa Fe, Correspondence Relating to National Parks, Monuments and Recreational Areas, 1927–1953, Box 1, Folder 000: General Big Bend, DEN NARA.

61. "Big Bend International Park," *Fort Worth Star-Telegram*, November 4, 1936.

62. "Big Bend International Park."

63. Maier to the NPS director, "Notes on Texas Meetings, November 6th to 9th," memorandum, November 13, 1936, RG 79, NPS, SWRO, Santa Fe, Correspondence Relating to National Parks, Monuments and Recreational Areas, 1927–1953, Folder: Big Bend General, Box 94, DEN NARA.

64. Maier to NPS director, November 13, 1936.

65. Maier to NPS director, November 13, 1936.

66. Maier to NPS director, November 13, 1936.

67. Maier to NPS Director, November 13, 1936.

68. Maier to NPS director, November 13, 1936.

69. Maier to NPS director, November 13, 1936.

70. Maier to NPS director, November 13, 1936.

71. McColm to Arthur Brisbane, King Features Syndicate, New York City, December 1, 1936, RG 79, NPS, SWRO, Santa Fe, Correspondence Relating to National Parks, Monuments and Recreational Areas, 1927–1953, Box 7, Folder 501: Publicity, DEN NARA.

72. McColm to Brisbane, December 1, 1936.

73. H. Conger Jones, "El Parque de la Paz de Mexico," trans. Carmen Reyes Arroyo, *American Forest*, December 1936, Box 9, Wallet 28, Folder 1, Townsend Collection, ABB.

74. Morelock to the Honorable R. A. Bandeen, Stamford, TX, February 8, 1937, RG 79, NPS, SWRO, Santa Fe, Correspondence Relating to National Parks, Monuments and Recreational Areas, 1927–1953, Folder: Big Bend General, Box 94, DEN NARA.

75. Townsend to Morelock, February 11, 1937, RG 79, NPS, SWRO, Santa Fe, Correspondence Relating to National Parks, Monuments and Recreational Areas, 1927–1953, Folder: Big Bend General, Box 94, DEN NARA.

76. Ayers to Maier, telegram, April 16, 1937, RG 79, NPS, SWRO, Santa Fe, Correspondence Relating to National Park, Monuments and Recreational Areas, 1927–1953, Box 1, Folder 0–30: Big Bend International Park Pt. 2, DEN NARA; Maxwell, "Summary of Events," 8.

77. Ayers to Maier.

78. Maier to Departemento Forestal, Caza y Pesca, Mexico City, May 26, 1937; Quevedo to P. L. Boal, chargé d'affaires ad interim, Embassy of the United States of America, Mexico City, June 4, 1937; Boal to the secretary of state, Washington, DC, June 7, 1937, RG 79, NPS, SWRO, Santa Fe, Correspondence Relating to National Parks, Monuments and Recreational Areas, 1927–1953, Box 2, Folder 120-01: House Bills Big Bend, DEN NARA.

79. Maier to Departemento Forestal, Caza y Pesca.

80. Josephus Daniels, US ambassador to Mexico, Raleigh, NC, to Cammerer, June 21, 1937; and secretary of state to the secretary of the interior, memorandum, June 22, 1937, all in RG 79, NPS, SWRO, Santa Fe, Correspondence Relating to National Parks, Monuments and Recreational Areas, 1927–1953, Box 2, Folder 120-01: House Bills Big Bend, DEN NARA.

81. Boal to the secretary of state, June 7, 1937.

82. Boal to the secretary of state, "National Parks Declared Ineffectable for Dotations or Restitutions," memorandum, June 11, 1937, RG 79, NPS, SWRO, Santa Fe, Correspondence Relating to National Parks, Monuments and Recreational Areas, 1927–1953, Box 2, Folder 120: (NPS) Legislation (General), DEN NARA.

83. William P. Bowen, "Mexican National Parks Declared Ineffectable For Ejidial Dotations and Restitutions," n.d., RG 79, NPS, SWRO, Santa Fe, Correspondence Relating to National Parks, Monuments and Recreational Areas, 1927–1953, Box 2, Folder 120: (NPS) Legislation (General), DEN NARA.

84. Bowen.

85. Bowen.

86. Bowen.

87. Bowen.

88. Bowen.

89. Leland D. Case, editor, *Rotarian*, Chicago, to McClatchy, October 19, 1937, RG 79, NPS, SWRO, Santa Fe, Correspondence Relating to National Parks, Monuments and Recreational Areas, 1927–1953, Box 8, Folder 501.02: Magazine Articles, DEN NARA.

90. McClatchy to Case, October 23, 1937, RG 79, NPS, SWRO, Santa Fe, Correspondence Relating to National Parks, Monuments and Recreational Areas, 1927–1953, Box 8, Folder 501.02: Magazine Articles, DEN NARA.

91. McClatchy to Case, October 23, 1937.

92. Friedrich E. Schuler, *Mexico between Hitler and Roosevelt: Mexican Foreign Relations in the Age of Lazaro Cardenas, 1934–1940* (Albuquerque: University of New Mexico Press, 1998), 63, 84.

93. Schuler, 89, 92; Meyer and Sherman, *Course of Mexican History*, 604.

94. Wirth to Cammerer, memorandum, November 21, 1938, RG 79, NPS, SWRO, Santa Fe, Correspondence Relating to National Parks, Monuments and Recreational Areas, 1927–1953, Box 2, Folder 120-07: (NPS) Proposed Legislation Big Bend, DEN NARA.

95. Maier to Galicia, January 11, 1939, RG 79, NPS, SWRO, Santa Fe, Correspondence Relating to National Parks, Monuments and Recreational Areas, 1927–1953, Box 11, Folder 610.01: Purchasing of Lands #1 Big Bend, DEN NARA; Maier to Maxwell, memorandum, April 15, 1939, RG 79, NPS, SWRO, Santa Fe, Correspondence Relating to National Parks, Monuments and Recreational Areas, 1927–1953, Box 1, Folder 0–30: (NPS) Big Bend International Park, DEN NARA; Maxwell to Maier, memorandum, April 17, 1939, RG 79, NPS, SWRO, Santa Fe, Correspondence Relating to National Parks, Monuments and Recreational Areas, 1927–1953, Box 11, Folder 602: (NPS) Boundaries (General), DEN NARA.

96. Wirth to acting regional director, Region III, memorandum, May 3, 1939, RG 79, NPS, SWRO, Santa Fe, Correspondence Relating to National Parks, Monuments and Recreational Areas, 1927–1953, Box 11, Folder 602: (NPS) Boundaries (General), DEN NARA.

97. Maxwell to regional director, Region III, Attn: Mr. Herbert Maier, memorandum, May 22, 1939, RG 79, NPS, SWRO, Santa Fe, Correspondence Relating to National Parks, Monuments and Recreational Areas, 1927–1953, Box 11, Folder 602: (NPS) Boundaries (General), DEN NARA.

98. Maxwell to Maier, memorandum, May 22, 1939, RG 79, NPS, SWRO, Santa Fe, Correspondence Relating to National Parks, Monuments and Recreational Areas, 1927–1953, Box 11, Folder 602: (NPS) Boundaries (General), DEN NARA.

99. Maxwell to Maier, May 22, 1939.

100. Maxwell to Maier, May 22, 1939.

101. Maxwell to Maier, May 22, 1939.

102. Maxwell to Maier, May 22, 1939.

103. Maxwell to Maier, May 22, 1939.

104. Maier to the NPS director, memorandum, May 27, 1939, RG 79, NPS, SWRO, Santa Fe, Correspondence Relating to National Parks, Monuments, and Recreational Areas, 1927–1953, Box 11, Folder 602: (NPS) Boundaries (General), DEN NARA.

105. Demaray to the regional director, Region III, memorandum, July 1, 1939, RG 79, NPS, SWRO, Santa Fe, Correspondence Relating to National Parks, Monuments, and Recreational Areas, 1927–1953, Box 11, Folder 602: (NPS) Boundaries (General), DEN NARA.

106. Maier to the NPS director, memorandum, August 3, 1939, RG 79, NPS, SWRO, Santa Fe, Correspondence Relating to National Parks, Monuments and Recreational Areas, 1927–1953, Box 8, Folder 501.01.1: Roadside Advertising and Road Signs, DEN NARA.

107. Maier to the NPS director, August 3, 1939.

108. Schuler, *Mexico between Hitler and Roosevelt*, 207.

109. Simonian, *Defending the Land*, 107, 109.

110. Simonian, *Defending the Land*, 107, 109; Meyer and Sherman, *Course of Mexican History*, 606; Schuler, *Mexico between Hitler and Roosevelt*, 161–162, 207.

111. George L. Collins, acting chief, Land Planning Division, NPS, Washington, DC, to Wirth, memorandum, January 6, 1940, RG 79, NPS, SWRO, Santa Fe, Correspondence Relating to National Parks, Monuments and Recreational Areas, 1927–1953, Box 11, Folder 602: (NPS) Boundaries (General), DEN NARA; acting secretary of the interior to the secretary of state, Washington, DC, June 1, 1940, RG 79, NPS, SWRO, Santa Fe, Correspondence Relating to National Parks, Monuments and Recreational Areas, 1927–1953, Box 1, Folder 000: General Big Bend, DEN NARA.

112. Horace Morelock, Austin, TX, to Ickes, August 10, 1940, RG 79, NPS, SWRO, Santa Fe, Correspondence Relating to National Parks, Monuments and Recreational Areas, 1927–1953, Box 12, Folder 610.01: Purchasing of Lands #2 [Folder 2] Big Bend, DEN NARA.

113. Morelock to Ickes, August 10, 1940.

114. Morelock to Ickes, August 10, 1940.

115. Morelock to Ickes, August 10, 1940.

116. Alvin J. Wirtz, undersecretary of the interior, Washington, DC, to H. W. Morelock, Austin, TX, August 20, 1940, RG 79, NPS, SWRO, Santa Fe, Correspondence Relating to National Parks, Monuments and Recreational Areas, 1927–1953, Box 12, Folder 610.01: Purchasing of Lands #2 [Folder 2] Big Bend, DEN NARA.

117. McDougall to the regional director, Region III, memorandum, December 18, 1940, Folder 4, Townsend Collection, ABB.

118. McDougall to the regional director, December 18, 1940.

119. J. Pedrero Cordova, commissioner, International Boundary Commission, El Paso, TX, to Townsend, December 21, 1940, Folder 4, Townsend Collection, ABB.

120. Cordova to Townsend, December 21, 1940.

CHAPTER 5: THE RIVER BECOMES A BORDER

1. Conrad L. Wirth, supervisor of recreation and land planning, NPS, Washington, DC, to the regional director, Region III, memorandum, February 23, 1940, Proposed National Parks Big Bend General Par 8 File, RG 79, NPS, CCF 1933–1949, Big Bend Files, Box 823, DC NARA II; Harvey H. Cornell, NPS regional landscape architect, Washington, DC, to Mr. Vint, memorandum, March 12, 1940, Proposed National Parks Big Bend General Part 8 File, RG 79, NPS, CCF 1933–1949, Big Bend Files, Box 833, DC NARA II.

2. John H. Veale, NPS assistant engineer, "Report—Field Trip—March 7–14, 1941, Water Supply and Sewage Disposal, Big Bend State Park," n.d., RG 79, NPS, SWRO, Santa Fe, Correspondence Relating to National Parks, Monuments, and Recreational Areas, 1927–1953, Box 18, Folder 660.03.4: (CCC) Sewage, DEN NARA; Maxwell to the regional director, memorandum, March 17, 1941, and John H. Diehl, regional engineer, NPS, "Reconnaissance and Investigation Report—Big Bend State Park," March 19, 1941, both in RG 79, NPS, SWRO, Santa Fe, Correspondence Relating to CCC, ECW, and ERA Work in National Forests and Monuments and Recreational Areas, 1933–1934, Box 95, Folder: Project 1004, DEN NARA.

3. Maxwell to the regional director, March 17, 1941.

4. J. E. Kell, acting NPS regional chief of planning, to the regional director, memorandum, March 31, 1941, 857 Travel (General) Big Bend File, RG 79, NPS, CCF 1933–1949, Big Bend National Park 847–900.02 Files, Box 837, DC NARA II.

5. Kell to the regional director, March 31, 1941.

6. Kell to the regional director, March 31, 1941.

7. Report of Field Trip of E. F. Preece, February 20–March 15, 1941, inclusive, April 28, 1941, copied, RG 79, NPS, SWRO, Santa Fe, Correspondence Relating to National Parks, Monuments, and Recreational Areas, 1927–1953, Box 15, Folder 620.08: (CCC) Shelter Cabins, DEN NARA.

8. Cornell to the NPS director, Attention: Chief of Planning Vint, memorandum, May 9, 1941, RG 79, NPS, SWRO, Santa Fe, Correspondence Relating to National Parks, Monuments, and Recreational Areas, 1927–1953, Box 15, Folder 620.08: (CCC) Shelter Cabins, DEN NARA.

9. Cornell to the NPS director, May 9, 1941.

10. Milton J. McColm, acting NPS regional director, Santa Fe, NM, to the director, memorandum, March 28, 1942, RG 79, NPS, SWRO, Santa Fe, Correspondence Relating to CCC, ECW, and ERA Work in National Forests, Monuments and Recreational Areas, 1933–1934, Big Bend National Park, TX–Bryce Canyon National Monument, UT, Box 97, Folder 601–03.2: (CCC) Abandoned Camps, DEN NARA; Paul V. Brown, chief, Recreation Land Planning Division, NPS Region III, Santa Fe, NM, to Earl O. Mills, planning counselor, National Resources Planning Board, Dallas, TX, April 15, 1942, RG 79, NPS, SWRO, Santa Fe, Correspondence Relating to National Parks, Monuments, and Recreational Areas, 1927–1953, Box 12, Folder 610.01: Purchasing of Lands #3 [Folder 2] Big Bend, DEN NARA.

11. Tillotson to the NPS director, memorandum, April 28, 1942, 600-03 Big Bend National Park Development Outline File, RG 79, NPS, CCF 1933–1949, Big Bend National Park 600-01–601 Files, Box 832, DC NARA II.

12. Tillotson to the NPS director, April 28, 1942.

13. Tillotson to the NPS director, April 28, 1942.

14. Paul V. Brown, chief, Recreation Planning Division, NPS Region III, "Planning Comments and Use Estimates Big Bend National Park Project," 600-03 Big Bend Development Outline File, RG 79, NPS, CCF 1933–1949, Big Bend National Park 600-01–601 Files, Box 832, DC NARA II.

15. Brown.

16. Brown.

17. Tillotson to Lawrence M. Lawson, international boundary commissioner, El Paso, TX, August 25, 1942, RG 79, NPS, SWRO, Santa Fe, Correspondence Relating to National Parks, Monuments and Recreational Areas, 1927–1953, Box 19, Folder 660-05.4: Reservoirs NPS, DEN NARA.

18. Lawson to Tillotson, August 29, 1942, RG 79, NPS, SWRO, Santa Fe, Correspondence Relating to National Parks, Monuments and Recreational Areas, 1927–1953, Box 19, Folder 660-05.4: Reservoirs NPS, DEN NARA.

19. Lawson to Tillotson, August 29, 1942.

20. Eugene Thompson, administrator, Texas State Parks Board, Big Bend Land Department, to J. V. Ash, chairman, Texas State Parks Board, Bastrop, TX, November 1, 1942, Big Bend National Park Publicity and Statistics Publicity General File, RG 79, NPS, CCF 1933–1949, Big Bend National Park 208-41–501-02 Files, Box 828, DC NARA II.

21. Madison, *Big Bend Country*, 239.

22. Madison, 239.

23. Isabelle F. Story, editor in chief, NPS, Chicago, to William E. Warne, director of information, Department of the Interior, Chicago, memorandum, June 26, 1943, Big Bend National Park Publicity and Statistics Publicity General File, RG 79, NPS, CCF 1933–1949, Big Bend National Park 208-41–501-02 Files, Box 828, DC NARA II.

24. Story to Warne, June 26, 1943.

25. Tillotson to Quinn, July 28, 1943, Big Bend National Park Publicity and Statistics Publicity General File, RG 79, NPS, CCF 1933–1949, Big Bend National Park 208-41–501-02 Files, Box 828, DC NARA II.

26. Tillotson to Quinn, July 28, 1943.

27. Tillotson to Quinn, July 28, 1943.

28. A. M. Mead, San Benito, TX, to Milton West, congressman, Brownsville, TX, September 10, 1943, RG 79, NPS, SWRO, Santa Fe, Correspondence Relating to National Parks, Monuments and Recreational Areas, 1927–1953, Box 19, Folder 660-05.4: Reservoirs (NPS), DEN NARA.

29. C. E. Ainsworth, consulting engineer, International Boundary Commission, El Paso, TX, to Tillotson, November 22, 1943, RG 79, NPS, SWRO, Santa Fe, Correspondence Relating to National Parks, Monuments, and Recreational Areas, 1927–1953, Box 19, Folder 660-05.4 Reservoirs (NPS), DEN NARA.

30. Minor Tillotson, "Suggested Outline of Concessionaire Operations in Big Bend National Park," March 29, 1944, 900-05 Public Utility Operators General File, RG 79, NPS, CCF 1933–1949, Big Bend National Park 900-02–900-05 Files, Box 838, DC NARA II.

31. Tillotson. Tillotson's reference to the sale of "huarachos" at Maria Sada's restaurant was his spelling of the term *huarache* (sandals).

32. Tillotson to the NPS director, April 5, 1944, 900-05 Public Utilities Operators General File, RG 79, NPS, CCF 1933–1949, Big Bend National Park 900-02–900-05 Files, Box 838, DC NARA II.

33. Tillotson to the NPS director, April 5, 1944.

34. Mrs. Josue R. Picon, chair, US section, Committee on the Americas, Women's International League, Detroit, to Drury, December 7, 1943, 101-01 Big Bend National Park History and Legislation Dedications File, RG 79, NPS, CCF 1933–1949, Big Bend National Park Files, Box 824, DC NARA II.

35. Tillotson to the NPS director, memorandum, December 21, 1943, 101-01 Big Bend National Park History and Legislation Dedications File, RG 79, NPS, CCF 1933–1949, Big Bend National Park Files, Box 824, DC NARA II; Zonia Barber, Chicago, to Ickes, May 24, 1944, RG 79, NPS, SWRO, Santa Fe, Correspondence Relating to National Parks, Monuments

and Recreational Areas, 1927–1953, Box 3, Folder 201: Administration (General) Big Bend, DEN NARA.

36. Demaray to the undersecretary, memorandum, April 24, 1944, Historical Files, Science and Resources Division Library, BIBE.

37. Walter P. Taylor, unit leader, US Fish and Wildlife Service, College Station, TX, to Tolson, May 11, 1944, 501-02 Big Bend Magazine Articles File, RG 79, NPS, CCF 1933–1949, Big Bend National Park 208-41-501-02 Files, Box 828, DC NARA II.

38. Taylor to Tolson, May 11, 1944.

39. Taylor to Tolson, May 11, 1944.

40. Roosevelt to President Manuel Ávila Camacho of Mexico, Washington, DC, October 24, 1944, in *Franklin Roosevelt and Conservation, 1911–1945*, ed. Edgar B. Nixon (Washington, DC: US Government Printing Office, 1957), 2:601–602.

41. Roosevelt to Camacho, October 24, 1944, 2:601–602.

42. Remarks given by President Dwight D. Eisenhower at the dedication of Falcón Dam, Texas, October 19, 1953, Texas Archive of the Moving Image, https://texasarchive.org/2013_00972.

43. "Address by Secretary of the Interior Douglas McKay at the Dedication of Big Bend National Park, Texas," November 21, 1955, RG 79, NPS, Box 12, File No. 079 .66.0098 798993, Big Bend National Park Files, Federal Records Center, National Archives and Records Administration, Fort Worth, TX; George Miller, "A Report of the Most Significant Events of the 1956 Fiscal Year at Big Bend National Park, Texas," 1956, Historical Files, Science and Resources Division Library, BIBE.

44. "Address by Secretary of the Interior."

45. "Address by Secretary of the Interior."

46. "Address by Secretary of the Interior."

47. "Address by Secretary of the Interior."

48. "Address by Secretary of the Interior."

49. "Address by Secretary of the Interior."

50. "Address by Secretary of the Interior."

51. "Address by Secretary of the Interior."

52. "Address by Secretary of the Interior."

53. "Address by Secretary of the Interior."

54. "Address by Secretary of the Interior."

55. Madison, *Big Bend Country*, 6.

56. Madison, 6.

57. Madison, 4.

58. Madison, 247–248.

59. Douglas B. Evans, chief naturalist, "Prospectus for the Interpretation of Big Bend National Park," March 7, 1965, Historical Files, Science and Resources Division Library, BIBE.

60. Evans.

61. Evans.

62. Evans.

63. Doug Evans and Doris Evans, interview by the author, Big Bend National Park, TX, October 18, 1996.

64. Garner Hanson, president, National Parks Concessions, interview by the author, Cave City, KY, September 19, 1997.

65. Jerry Rogers, field superintendent, Southwest Support Office, NPS, interview by the author, Santa Fe, August 22, 1997.

66. Rogers, interview by the author.

67. William O. Douglas, *Farewell to Texas: A Vanishing Wilderness* (New York: McGraw-Hill, 1967), 38.

68. Douglas, 40.

69. Douglas, 42.

70. Douglas, 47.

71. Douglas, 56.

72. David J. Jones, resource planner, NPS, "Big Bend Natural Sciences Research Plan," July 1967, Big Bend National Park Files, Southwest Support Office Library, Santa Fe.

73. Jones.

74. Bob Burleson, "An Alternative to the Master Plan and Wilderness Proposal for Big Bend National Park," Americans Backing Better Park Development, Temple, TX, n.d. [January 1972?], Big Bend National Park Files, Southwest Support Office Library, Santa Fe.

75. Burleson.

76. Burleson.

77. Burleson.

78. Burleson.

79. Burleson.

80. Burleson.

81. Burleson.

82. Burleson.

83. "Interpretive Prospectus, Big Bend National Park, Texas," Department of the Interior, NPS, Denver Service Center, October 1974, Big Bend National Park Files, Southwest Support Office Library, Santa Fe.

84. "Interpretive Prospectus."

85. Master plan draft, Big Bend National Park, March 1975, Big Bend National Park Files, Southwest Support Office Library, Santa Fe.

86. Master plan draft.

87. Master plan draft.

88. Master plan draft.

89. Master plan draft.

90. Master plan draft.

CHAPTER 6: GUARDIANS OR WARRIORS?

1. Simonian, *Defending the Land*, 111, 113, 128.

2. Simonian, 128.

3. Julio Carrera, director, Maderas del Carmen Protected Area, Secretaría de Medio Ambiente, Recursos Naturales y Pesca, interview by the author, Big Bend National Park, TX, April 10, 1999.

4. Carlos Marin, chief engineer, International Boundary and Water Commission, interview by the author, El Paso, TX, August 26, 1998.

5. Jameson, *Story of Big Bend*, 121; Etta Koch, interview by the author, Alpine, TX, September 21, 1996; Reece Sholley McNatt, interview by the author, Alamogordo, NM, December 18, 1996.

6. Koch, interview by the author.

7. Curtis Schaafsma, interview by the author, Santa Fe, NM, August 7, 1996.

8. Schaafsma, interview by the author.

9. Schaafsma, interview by the author.

10. Schaafsma, interview by the author.

11. Joe Rumburg, interview by the author, Green Valley, AZ, May 31, 1996. Cosmoline had served as an anticorrosive treatment for metal in the mid-twentieth century.

12. Bob Smith, interview by the author, Three Rivers, CA, September 7, 1996.

13. Smith, interview by the author.

14. Smith, interview by the author.

15. Smith, interview by the author.

16. Smith, interview by the author.

17. Lemuel A. Garrison, *The Making of a Ranger: Forty Years with the National Parks* (Salt Lake City: Howe Books, 1988), 235.

18. Garrison, 233.

19. Monte Fitch, interview by the author, Grand Junction, CO, August 27, 1997.

20. Jameson, *Story of Big Bend*, 123; Russell Dickenson, interview by the author, Seattle, WA, January 28, 1997.

21. Dickenson, interview by the author.

22. Dickenson, interview by the author.

23. Dickenson, interview by the author.

24. Fitch, interview by the author.

25. Fitch, interview by the author.

26. Charles McCurdy, interview by the author, Santa Fe, NM, August 22, 1997; Karen Reyer and Eldon Reyer, interview by the author, Santa Fe, NM, August 6, 1996.

27. McCurdy, interview by the author.

28. McCurdy, interview by the author.

29. McCurdy, interview by the author.

30. McCurdy, interview by the author.

31. McCurdy, interview by the author.

32. Henry Schmidt, interview by the author, Sun City, AZ, December 10, 1996.

33. Schmidt, interview by the author.

34. Schmidt, interview by the author.

35. Bill Wendt, interview by the author, Midpines, CA, September 6, 1996.

36. Wendt, interview by the author.

37. Stanley C. Joseph, interview by the author, Groveland, CA, September 6, 1996.

38. Joseph, interview by the author.

39. Joseph, interview by the author.

40. Jim Milburn, vice president, National Parks Concessions, interview by the author, Cave City, KY, September 19, 1997; Dudley Harrison, county judge, Terrell County, interview by the author, Fort Davis, TX, June 7, 1997.

41. Milburn, interview by the author.

42. Hanson, interview by the author; Robert Arnberger, superintendent, Grand Canyon National Park, AZ, interview by the author, June 3, 1996.

43. Arnberger, interview by the author.

44. Mike Fleming, Science and Resources Management Division, Big Bend National Park, TX, interview by the author, September 23, 1996; Jim Liles, superintendent, Buffalo River National Recreation Area, telephone interview by the author, Harrison, AR, August 21, 1997.

45. Liles, interview by the author.

46. Steve Frye, chief ranger, Glacier National Park, MT, interview by the author, July 25, 1996.

47. Frye, interview by the author.

48. Frye, interview by the author.

49. Frye, interview by the author.

50. Liles, interview by the author; Rick LoBello, director, Carlsbad Caverns Nature Association, interview by the author, Carlsbad Caverns National Park, NM, August 18, 1999.

51. Liles, interview by the author; Frank Deckert, superintendent, Carlsbad Caverns National Park, interview by the author, Carlsbad, NM, September 20, 1996.

52. Deckert, interview by the author; Liles, interview by the author.

53. Deckert, interview by the author; Keith Yarborough, Department of Geography, Sul Ross State University, interview by the author, Alpine, TX, January 17, 1997; Gene Balaz, interview by the author, Green Valley, AZ, May 31, 1996.

54. John Cook, field director, Intermountain Region Field Office, interview by the author, Denver, CO, August 1, 1996.

55. Cook, interview by the author.

56. José Cisneros, superintendent, Big Bend National Park, TX, interview by the author, August 21, 1997; LoBello, interview by the author; Balaz, interview by the author.

57. Balaz, interview by the author.

58. Balaz, interview by the author.

59. Robert Haraden, interview by the author, Seeley Lake, MT, July 24, 1996.

60. Balaz, interview by the author; Liles, interview by the author.

61. Liles, interview by the author.

62. Haraden, interview by the author.

1. Samuel Truett, "Neighbors by Nature: Rethinking Region, Nation, and Environmental History in the U.S.-Mexico Borderlands," *Environmental History* 2, no. 2 (April 1997): 160.

2. Alan Weisman, *La Frontera: The United States Border with Mexico*, photographs by Jay Dusard (New York City: Harcourt Brace Jovanovich, 1986), 63.

3. Weisman, 62–63.

4. Dennis A. Vasquez, chief of interpretation and visitor services, Big Bend National Park, "Working with Mexico: The Development and Status of the Mexican Affairs Program at Big Bend National Park," April 1994, Big Bend National Park Files, Office of Mexican Affairs (MEAF), NPS, Las Cruces, NM. This also was known as the La Paz Agreement, named for the host community in the Mexican state of Baja California del Sur.

5. "Final General Management Plan, Development Concept Plan, Rio Grande Wild and Scenic River, Texas," November 1981, Superintendent's Files, BIBE. Sections of rivers designated as "wild" would have more restrictions on their use than would those labeled "scenic."

6. "Final General Management Plan."

7. "Final General Management Plan." DDT stands for "dichlorodiphenyltrichloroethane," a common agricultural insecticide.

8. "Final General Management Plan."

9. Harrison, interview by the author.

10. Andrew Kurie, Heat Canyon Ranch Inn, TX, "Notes on Rio Grande Wild and Scenic River Designations," July 28, 2000, Superintendent's Files, BIBE; James W. Carrico, interview by the author, Study Butte, TX, January 16, 1997; Harrison, interview by the author. Carrico became the owner of a river-rafting company in Study Butte after retirement from the park service.

11. Marty Ott, Trails Office, NPS, telephone interview by the author, Salt Lake City, UT, August 25, 1997.

12. Ott, interview by the author; Weisman, *La Frontera*, 79–81.

13. Ott, interview by the author; Carrico, interview by the author; Weisman, *La Frontera*, 79–81.

14. Vasquez, "Working with Mexico"; Ramón Olivas, MEAF, NPS, New Mexico State University, interview by the author, Las Cruces, NM, December 18, 1996; Wendt, interview by the author.

15. Vasquez, "Working with Mexico."

16. Olivas, interview by the author; Vasquez, "Working with Mexico."

17. Vasquez, "Working with Mexico."

18. Vasquez.

19. Vasquez.

20. Vasquez.

21. Gloria Uribe, interview by the author, Ciudad Chihuahua, Chihuahua, Mexico, May 21, 1999. For a more in-depth discussion of the centrality of forests in Mexican national

parks and natural resource agency management, see Christopher R. Boyer, ed., *A Land between Waters: Environmental History of Modern Mexico* (Tucson: University of Arizona Press, 2012); and Christopher R. Boyer, *Political Landscapes: Forests, Conservation, and Community in Mexico* (Durham, NC: Duke University Press, 2015). A good summary of the Mexico-US interaction on the river can be found in Steven Mumme, "Water and Environmental Justice at the U.S.-Mexican Border," *Colorado Water* 36, no. 1 (January/February 2019): 8–10.

22. Alfonso LaFon, maestro-investigador, Departemento de Manejo de Recursos Naturales, Facultad de Zootecnica, Universidad Autonoma de Chihuahua, interview by the author, Ciudad Chihuahua, Chihuahua, Mexico, June 1, 1999.

23. LaFon, interview by the author.

24. LaFon, interview by the author; "Big Bend/Boquillas and Maderas del Carmen International Peace Park Proposal," September 11, 1990, Superintendent's Files, BIBE.

25. Daniel Lou Roth, "Mexican and American Policy Alternatives in the Big Bend Region—an Updated Study of the Proposed Mexican National Park in the Sierra del Carmen" (MA thesis, University of Texas, Austin, 1992), 39–42.

26. Vasquez, "Working with Mexico."

27. José A. Cisneros and Valerie J. Naylor, "Uniting *La Frontera*: The Ongoing Efforts to Establish a Transboundary Park," *Environment* 41, no. 3 (April 1999): 13–18.

28. Pablo Dominguez, director, Cañon de Santa Elena Protected Area, interview by the author, Ciudad Chihuahua, Chihuahua, Mexico, May 31, 1999.

29. Cisneros and Naylor, "Uniting *La Frontera*," 14–20.

30. Cisneros and Naylor, 14–20; José Cisneros, interview by the author, Santa Fe, NM, February 4, 2000.

31. Cisneros, interview by the author, February 4, 2000.

32. "'Action Steps' Agreed upon at Protected Area Coordination Meeting," July 26, 2000, July 21, 2001, Superintendent's Files, BIBE.

33. Amy Leinbach Marquis, "Pushing Boundaries," *National Parks Magazine*, Summer 2008; Alejandro Treviño Espinosa, Cementos Mexicanos, interview by the author, Monterrey, Coahuila, Mexico, December 16, 2014. For an example of Robles Gil's photography of the borderlands between Mexico and the United States, see Patricio Robles Gil, *Transboundary Conservation: A New Vision for Protected Areas* (Mexico City: CEMEX, 2005).

34. Leinbach Marquis, "Pushing Boundaries."

35. Leinbach Marquis, "Pushing Boundaries"; Bonnie Reynolds McKinney, *In the Shadow of the Carmens: Afield with a Naturalist in the Northern Mexican Mountains* (Lubbock: Texas Tech University Press, 2012), xix–xx, 6–7, 9–13.

36. Joe Sirotnak, "Binational Cooperation in the Big Bend Region," *George Wright Forum* 28, no. 3 (2011): 292.

37. Sirotnak, 292.

38. "Big Bend International Park Historical Timeline," Greater Big Bend Coalition, accessed May 13, 2016, https://greaterbigbend.wordpress.com/international-park-timeline-2/;

Ralph Blumenthal, "West Texans Sizzle Over a Plan to Sell Their Water," *New York Times*, December 11, 2003.

39. "CIRA: Air Quality in our National Parks," *Colorado State University* 22 (Fall 2004): 3–4.

40. *Big Bend National Park: Final General Management Plan / Environmental Impact Statement* (US Department of the Interior, National Park Service, Big Bend National Park, TX, May 2004), 7–10.

41. *Big Bend National Park*, 12.

42. Lucius Lomax, "Big Bend: 'A Park in Peril,'" *Austin Chronicle*, January 30, 2004; Polly Ross Hughes, "Study Clears Air on Who Causes Big Bend's Haze," *Houston Chronicle*, September 17, 2004.

43. "Joint Declaration of Sister Park Partnerships," March 23, 2006, Superintendent's Files, BIBE; John King, "Seventy Years since the Beginning of Big Bend National Park: Future Vision and Collaboration," keynote speech to El Carmen–Big Bend Conservation Corridor Initiative Workshop, Monterrey, Nuevo Leon, Mexico, April 9, 2006, Superintendent's Files, BIBE.

44. King, "Seventy Years."

45. King, "Seventy Years."

46. "Summary Documents, First Annual Workshop, El Carmen–Big Bend Conservation Corridor Initiative," April 29–30, 2006, Monterrey, Mexico, Superintendent's Files, BIBE.

47. Welsh, *Mission in the Desert*, 208–212; Leinbach Marquis, "Pushing Boundaries."

48. Sharon Wilcox and Brian King, "Peace Parks and Jaguar Trails: Transboundary Conservation in a Globalizing World," *GeoJournal* 71, no. 4 (2008): 221–223.

49. Wilcox and King, 225–226, 228; Emily Levitt, "Park Lands and Politics on the West Texas/Mexico Border," *Journal of Big Bend Studies* 21 (2009): 238.

50. "Big Bend International Park Historical Timeline"; William Wellman, superintendent, to Raymond Skiles, Science and Resources Management Division, Big Bend National Park, memorandum, May 14, 2008, Superintendent's Files, BIBE.

51. Wellman to Skiles, May 14, 2008.

52. "Draft Environmental Assessment, Reestablishment of the Rio Grande Silvery Minnow in the Big Bend Reach of the Rio Grande in Texas," US Fish and Wildlife Service, September 5, 2007, Superintendent's Files, BIBE; "Mexico to Build 'Green Wall' along U.S. Border," Associated Press, June 6, 2006.

53. Sirotnak, "Binational Cooperation," 293.

54. Sirotnak, 293.

55. "Joint Press Conference with President Barack Obama and President Felipe Calderón of Mexico, 4/16/2009," April 16, 2009, White House, Office of the Press Secretary, Mexico City, https://obamawhitehouse.archives.gov/the-press-office/joint-press -conference-with-president-barack-obama-and-president-felipe-calderon-me; House Resolution 695, "Supporting an International Park between Big Bend National Park in the United States and the Protected Areas of the Coahuila and Chihuahua States across

the Border in Mexico," 111th Congress, 1st Session, July 29, 2009, submitted to the Committee on Foreign Affairs, US House of Representatives.

56. "U.S. Secretary of the Interior Ken Salazar and Mexican Minister of Environment and Natural Resources Juan Elvira Decide to Strengthen Conservation Cooperation in Big Bend Area of the U.S.-Mexican Border," news release, US Department of the Interior, August 10, 2009.

57. "U.S. Secretary of the Interior."

58. Cecilia Simon, "The El Carmen-Big Bend Conservation Corridor: A U.S.-Mexico Ecological Project," *Voices of Mexico*, July–September 2006, http://www.revistascisan.unam.mx/Voices/pdfs/7620.pdf.

59. Simon. The Sierra Madre Group operated under the auspices of La Universidad Autónoma de Mexico.

60. Juan Bezaury, "New Natural Monument Connects More Than 3 Million Acres," Nature Conservancy, n.d. [October 2009?], http://www.nature.org/ourinitiatives/regions/northamerica/mexico/explore/new-naturalmonument-connects-more-than-3-million-acres.xml / (source no longer available).

61. Bezaury.

62. April Reese, "U.S., Canada, Mexico Sign Wilderness Agreement," Environment and Energy News, November 9, 2009, https://www.eenews.net/greenwire/2009/11/09/stories/84436; Ben Block, "North American Governments Agree to Protect Wilderness," World Watch Institute, November 11, 2009, https://www.enn.com/articles/40691-north-american-governments-agree-to-protect-wilderness.

63. April Reese, "U.S., Canada, Mexico Sign Wilderness Agreement."

64. April Reese, "U.S., Canada, Mexico Sign Wilderness Agreement."

65. Reese, "U.S., Canada, Mexico"; Block, "North American Governments." The concept of transnational parks designed to preserve larger ecosystems is studied in depth in Adrian Hawkins, Jared Orsi, and Mark Fiege, eds., *National Parks beyond the Nation: Global Perspectives on "America's Best Idea"* (Norman: University of Oklahoma Press, 2016).

66. "Time for a Transboundary Mexico-USA PA at Big Bend NP?," *Texas Tribune*, April 27, 2010.

67. "Mexico/US: Top Officials Support Unified Cross-Border Protection in Visit to Big Bend NP," George Wright Society Administration, March 24, 2010, https://www.georgewrightsociety.org/ (source no longer available); "Time for a Transboundary?"

68. "Mexico/US."

69. "Mexico/US."

70. "Calderón, Obama Support 'Natural Area of Binational Interest' Designation for Río Bravo/Grande PA Complex," George Wright Society Administration, May 20, 2010, https://www.georgewrightsociety.org/ (source no longer available).

71. Eryn Gable, "75 Years On, Effort to Create U.S.-Mexico Park Hampered by Security Concerns," *New York Times*, June 24, 2010.

72. Gable.

73. Gable.

74. Memorandum of Understanding among Texas Parks and Wildlife Department and the United States Department of the Interior, October 4, 2010.

75. Memorandum of Understanding.

76. *State of the Parks, Big Bend National Park: A Resource Assessment* (National Parks Conservation Association, 2010), 7.

77. *State of the Parks*, 7.

78. Senate Bill 803, 112th Congress, 1st Session, April 13, 2011, 11–22; House Resolution 1505, 112th Congress, 2nd Session, April 13, 2011, 1–7.

79. "Park along Texas, Mexico Border Sees Boost from Partnership," Reuters, August 20, 2011.

80. "Park along Texas."

81. "U.S., Mexico Announce Binational Cooperative Conservation Action Plan," press release, US Department of the Interior, October 24, 2011, http://www.nps.gov (source no longer available); "Mexico, United States Pledge to Work Together on Conservation Plan for Big Bend/Río Bravo Region," *National Park Traveler*, October 25, 2011.

82. "U.S., Mexico Announce"; "Mexico, United States Pledge."

83. "Beyond Boquillas: Journey into the Maderas del Carmen," *Big Bend Gazette*, May 5, 2013; *Final Report: Sustainable Tourism Plan for the Communities of Boquillas, Jaboncillos, and Norias, Coahuila, Mexico* (Committee for Environmental Cooperation, July 15, 2013).

84. Karin Krchnak, "Ushering in a Future of Cooperation and Water Security," World Wildlife Fund, March 22, 2013, https://www.worldwildlife.org/stories/ushering-in-a-future-of-cooperation-and-water-security.

85. Krchnak; "Changing a River's Trajectory," World Wildlife Fund, April 15, 2014, https://www.worldwildlife.org/stories/changing-a-river-s-trajectory; "A Passion for Conservation along the Rio Grande," World Wildlife Fund, May 20, 2015, https://www.worldwildlife.org/stories/a-passion-for-conservation-along-the-rio-grande; "Watershed Conservation Fact Sheet," Coca-Cola Company, http://www.cocacolacompany.com (source no longer available); Big Bend-Río Bravo Working Group, *Invasive Species Management in the Big Bend Reach of the Rio Grande-Río Bravo: Five-Year Plan* (November 2013).

86. Tom Alex, interview by the author, Big Bend National Park, November 21, 2013.

87. Alex, interview by the author; "Effects of Undocumented Aliens (UDA's) and Illegal Border Activity on Big Bend Resources—2013 Survey," n.d., Historical Files, Science and Resources Management Division Library, BIBE.

88. "Border Blurs between Big Bend National Park and Mexican Pueblo," *San Francisco Chronicle*, May 15, 2015.

89. "Border Blurs."

90. "El Paso Sierra Club Endorses New Effort to Establish US Mexico International Park," press release, Sierra Club of El Paso, December 6, 2015, https://www.riograndesierraclub.org/el-paso-sierra-club-endorses-new-effort-to-establish-us-mexico-international-park/.

91. "El Paso Sierra Club."

92. Terry Tempest Williams, *The Hour of Land: A Personal Topography of America's National Parks* (New York: Farrar, Straus and Giroux, 2016), ebook. Quotes taken from the introduction, "America's National Parks, by Definition"; and "Big Bend National Park, Texas: Any Wind Will Tell You."

93. Williams, introduction.

BIBLIOGRAPHY

ARCHIVAL COLLECTIONS

Federal

Big Bend National Park
    Historical Files, Science and Resources Division Library
Federal Records Center, National Archives and Records Administration, Fort Worth, TX
    Record Group 79, National Park Service, Big Bend National Park, Southwest
        Regional Office
National Archives and Records Administration, College Park, MD (DC NARA II)
    Record Group 79, National Park Service, Central Classified Files
Rocky Mountain Region Branch, National Archives and Records Administration,
Denver, CO (DEN NARA)
    Record Group 79, National Park Service, Southwest Regional Office
Superintendent's Files, Southwest Support Office, National Park Service, Santa Fe, NM
    Historical Files, Historical Library
    MEAF Files, Office of Mexican Affairs, National Park Service, New Mexico State
        University, Las Cruces, NM

Private

Archives of the Big Bend, Wildenthal Library, Sul Ross State University, Alpine, TX
    Everett Ewing Townsend Collection
    Horace Morelock Collection
National Parks Concessions, Cave City, KY
    NPCI Files

BOOKS

Abbey, Edward. *One Life at a Time, Please.* New York: Henry Holt, 1988.
Alexander, Nancy. *Father of Texas Geology: Robert T. Hill.* Dallas: Southern Methodist
    University Press, 1976.
Arnold, Joseph L. *The Evolution of the 1936 Flood Control Act.* Fort Belvoir, VA: US Army
    Corps of Engineers, Office of History, 1988.
Berger, Dina. *The Development of Mexico's Tourism Industry: Pyramids by Day, Martinis
    by Night.* New York: Palgrave Macmillan, 2006.
Boyer, Christopher R., ed. *A Land between Waters: Environmental History of Modern
    Mexico.* Tucson: University of Arizona Press, 2012.
———. *Political Landscapes: Forests, Conservation, and Community in Mexico.* Durham,
    NC: Duke University Press, 2015.

Brinkley, Douglas. *Rightful Heritage: Franklin D. Roosevelt and the Land of America.* New York: HarperCollins, 2016.

———. *The Wilderness Warrior: Theodore Roosevelt and the Crusade for America.* New York: HarperCollins, 2009.

Britten, Thomas A. *The Lipan Apaches: People of Wind and Lightning.* Albuquerque: University of New Mexico Press, 2009.

Clarke, Jeanne Nineaber. *Roosevelt's Warrior: Harold L. Ickes and the New Deal.* Baltimore: Johns Hopkins University Press, 1996.

Cronon, William N. *Changes in the Land: Indians, Colonists, and the Ecology of New England.* New York: Hill and Wang, 1983.

Deckert, Frank. *Big Bend: Three Steps to the Sky.* Big Bend National Park, TX: Big Bend Natural History Association, 1981.

DeVoto, Bernard. "Let's Close the National Parks." In *DeVoto's West: History, Conservation, and the Public Good,* edited by Edward K. Muller, 203–210. Athens, OH: Swallow / Ohio University Press, 2005.

Dilsaver, Lary M., ed. *America's National Park System: The Critical Documents.* Lanham, MD: Rowman and Littlefield, 1994.

Douglas, William O. *Farewell to Texas: A Vanishing Wilderness.* New York: McGraw-Hill, 1962.

Elliott, J. H. *Empires of the Atlantic World: Britain and Spain in America, 1492–1830.* New Haven, CT: Yale University Press, 2006.

Ellis, Richard N., ed. *Historic Documents of New Mexico.* Albuquerque: University of New Mexico Press, 1975.

Fabry, Judith K. *Guadalupe Mountains National Park: An Administrative History.* Santa Fe: National Park Service, 1988.

Faulk, Odie B. *The US Camel Corps: An Army Experiment.* New York: Oxford University Press, 1976.

Fehrenbach, T. E. *Lone Star: A History of Texas and the Texans.* New York: Macmillan, 1985.

Fireman, Janet R. *The Spanish Royal Corps of Engineers in the Western Borderlands, 1764–1815.* Glendale, CA: Arthur H. Clark, 1970.

Flores, Dan. *Horizontal Yellow: Nature and History in the New Southwest.* Albuquerque: University of New Mexico Press, 1999.

Gamio, Manuel. *Mexican Immigration to the United States: A Study of Human Migration and Adjustment.* New York: Dover, 1971.

Garrison, Lemuel A. *The Making of a Ranger: Forty Years with the National Parks.* Salt Lake City: Howe Books, 1988.

Gates, Paul Wallace. *History of Public Land Law Development.* Washington, DC: US Government Printing Office, 1968.

Goetzmann, William H. *New Lands, New Men: America and the Second Great Age of Discovery.* New York: Viking, 1986.

Gomez, Arthur R. *A Most Singular Country: A History of Occupation in the Big Bend.* Provo, UT: Charles Redd Center for Western Studies, Brigham Young University, 1990.

Gutierrez, Ramon A. *When Jesus Came, the Corn Mothers Went Away: Marriage, Sexuality, and Power in New Mexico, 1500–1846.* Stanford, CA: Stanford University Press, 1991.

Guy, Duane F., ed. *The Story of Palo Duro Canyon.* Lubbock: Texas Tech University Press, 2001.

Hamalainen, Pekka. *The Comanche Empire.* New Haven, CT: Yale University Press, 2008.

Hawkins, Adrian, Jared Orsi, and Mark Fiege, eds. *National Parks beyond the Nation: Global Perspectives on "America's Best Idea."* Norman: University of Oklahoma Press, 2016.

Ise, John. *Our National Park Policy: A Critical History.* Baltimore: Johns Hopkins University Press, 1961.

Jameson, John. *Big Bend National Park: The Formative Years.* El Paso: University of Texas at El Paso, 1980.

———. *The Story of Big Bend National Park.* Austin: University of Texas Press, 1996.

Johannsen, Robert W. *To the Halls of the Montezumas: The Mexican War in the American Imagination.* New York: Oxford University Press, 1985.

Kammen, Michael. *Mystic Chords of Memory: The Transformation of Traditions in American Culture.* New York: Alfred A. Knopf, 1991.

Kelly, Pat. *River of Lost Dreams.* Lincoln: University of Nebraska Press, 1986.

Kirk, Betty. *Covering the Mexican Front: The Battle of Europe versus America.* Norman: University of Oklahoma Press, 1942.

Koch, Etta. *Lizards at the Mantel, Burros at the Door.* Austin: University of Texas Press, 1999.

Lamar, Howard Roberts, ed. *The Reader's Encyclopedia of the American West.* New York: Thomas Y. Crowell, 1977.

Lowitt, Richard W. *The New Deal and the West.* Bloomington: Indiana University Press, 1984.

Madison, Virginia. *The Big Bend Country of Texas.* New York: October House, 1968.

McClelland, Linda Flint. *Building the National Parks: Historic Landscape Design and Construction.* Baltimore: Johns Hopkins University Press, 1998.

McKinney, Bonnie Reynolds. *In the Shadow of the Carmens: Afield with a Naturalist in the Northern Mexican Mountains.* Lubbock: Texas Tech University Press, 2012.

Meyer, Michael C., and William L. Sherman. *The Course of Mexican History.* 5th ed. New York: Oxford University Press, 1995.

Miles, John C. *Guardians of the Parks: A History of the National Parks and Conservation Association.* Washington, DC: Taylor and Francis, 1995.

Moorhead, Max L. *The Apache Frontier: Jacobo Ugarte and Spanish-Indian Relations in Northern New Spain, 1769–1791.* Norman: University of Oklahoma Press, 1968.

Mulroy, Kevin. *Freedom on the Border: The Seminole Maroons in Florida, the Indian Territory, Coahuila, and Texas.* Lubbock: Texas Tech University Press, 1993.

Nash, Gerald D. *The American West in the Twentieth Century: A Short History of an Urban Oasis.* Albuquerque: University of New Mexico Press, 1977.

———. *The American West Transformed: The Impact of the Second World War.* Bloomington: Indiana University Press, 1985.

———. *The West in World War II: Reshaping the Economy.* Lincoln: University of Nebraska Press, 1990.

Neff, Pat M. *The Battles of Peace.* Fort Worth, TX: Pioneer/Bunker, 1925.

Niblo, Stephen R. *Mexico in the 1940s: Modernity, Politics and Corruption.* Wilmington, DE: Scholarly Resources, 1999.

Pike, Fredrick B. *FDR's Good Neighbor Policy: Sixty Years of Generally Gentle Chaos.* Austin: University of Texas Press, 1995.

Ragsdale, Kenneth B. *Quicksilver: Terlingua and the Chisos Mining Company.* College Station: Texas A&M University Press, 1996.

Raht, Carlysle Graham. *The Romance of Davis Mountains and Big Bend Country.* El Paso: Rahtbooks, 1919.

Reed, John. *Insurgent Mexico.* New York: International, 2002.

Reséndez, Andres. *The Other Slavery: The Uncovered Story of Indian Enslavement in America.* New York: Houghton Mifflin Harcourt, 2016.

Richardson, Rupert Norval, Ernest Wallace, and Adrian N. Anderson. *Texas: The Lone Star State.* 4th ed. Upper Saddle River, NJ: Prentice-Hall, 1981.

Robles Gil, Patricio. *Transboundary Conservation: A New Vision for Protected Areas.* Mexico City: CEMEX, 2005.

Rohrbough, Malcolm J. *The Land Office Business: The Settlement and Administration of American Public Lands, 1789–1837.* New York: Oxford University Press, 1968.

Runte, Alfred. *National Parks: The American Experience.* 4th ed. New York: Taylor Trade, 2010.

———. *Trains of Discovery: Railroads and the Legacy of Our National Parks.* Lanham, MD: Roberts Rinehart, 2011.

Schuler, Friedrich E. *Mexico between Hitler and Roosevelt: Mexican Foreign Relations in the Age of Lazaro Cardenas, 1934–1940.* Albuquerque: University of New Mexico Press, 1998.

Sellars, Richard N. *Preserving Nature in the National Parks: A History.* New Haven, CT: Yale University Press, 1997.

Shankland, Robert. *Steve Mather of the National Parks.* New York: Alfred A. Knopf, 1954.

Shirley, Emma Morrill. *Administration of Pat M. Neff, Governor of Texas, 1921–1925.* Baylor Bulletin. Waco, TX: Baylor University Press, 1938.

Simonian, Lane. *Defending the Land of the Jaguar: A History of Conservation in Mexico.* Austin: University of Texas Press, 1995.

Starr, Kevin. *Americans and the California Dream, 1850–1910.* New York: Oxford University Press, 1973.

Steely, James Wright. *Parks for Texas: Enduring Landscapes of the New Deal.* Austin: University of Texas Press, 1999.

Stoddard, T. Lothrop. *Re-forging America: The Story of Our Nationhood.* N.p.: Ostara, 2010.

Swain, Donald C. *Wilderness Defender: Horace M. Albright and Conservation.* Chicago: University of Chicago Press, 1970.

Taylor, Paul S. *An American Mexican Frontier: Nueces County, Texas.* Chapel Hill: University of North Carolina Press, 1934.

Turner, Frederick Jackson. *The Frontier in American History.* New York: Holt, 1921.

Tyler, Ron C. *The Big Bend: A History of the Last Texas Frontier.* College Station: Texas A&M University Press, 1996.

Utley, Robert M. *Fort Davis National Historic Site, Texas.* Washington, DC: US Department of the Interior, National Park Service, 1965.

Wakild, Emily. *Revolutionary Parks: Conservation, Social Justice, and Mexico's National Parks, 1910–1940.* Tucson: University of Arizona Press, 2011.

Wasserman, Mark. *Capitalists, Caciques, and Revolution: The Native Elite and Foreign Enterprise in Chihuahua, Mexico, 1854–1911.* Chapel Hill: University of North Carolina Press, 1984.

———. *Everyday Life and Politics in Nineteenth Century Mexico: Men, Women and War.* Albuquerque: University of New Mexico Press, 2000.

Webb, Walter Prescott. *The Great Plains.* Repr., New York: Grosset and Dunlap, 1976.

Weber, David J. *Bárbaros: Spaniards and Their Savages in the Age of Enlightenment.* New Haven, CT: Yale University Press, 2005.

———. *The Spanish Frontier in North America, 1513–1821.* New Haven, CT: Yale University Press, 1992.

Weisman, Alan, and Jay Dusard. *La Frontera: The United States Border with Mexico.* New York: Harcourt Brace Jovanovich, 1986.

Welsh, Michael. *Dunes and Dreams: A History of White Sands National Monument.* Santa Fe: National Park Service, 1995.

———. *Landscape of Ghosts, River of Dreams: An Administrative History of Big Bend National Park.* Santa Fe: National Park Service, 2002. https://www.nps.gov /parkhistory/online_books/bibe/adhi/adhi.htm.

———. *A Mission in the Desert: The U.S. Army Corps of Engineers, Albuquerque District, 1985–2010.* Washington, DC: US Government Printing Office, 2015.

———. *A Special Place, a Sacred Trust: Preserving the Fort Davis Story.* Santa Fe: National Park Service, 1996.

———. *U.S. Army Corps of Engineers: Albuquerque District, 1935–1985.* Albuquerque: University of New Mexico Press, 1987.

Williams, Terry Tempest. *The Hour of Land: A Personal Topography of America's National Parks.* New York: Farrar, Straus and Giroux, 2016.

Winter, Nevin O. *Texas the Marvellous: The State of the Six Flags.* Boston: Page, 1916.

Wirth, Conrad L. *Parks, Politics, and the People.* Norman: University of Oklahoma Press, 1988.

ARTICLES

Adelman, Jeremy, and Stephen Aron. "From Borderlands to Borders: Empires, Nation-States, and the Peoples in between in North American History." *American Historical Review* 104 (1999): 814–841.

Cisneros, José A., and Valerie J. Naylor. "Uniting *La Frontera*: The Ongoing Efforts to Establish a Transboundary Park." *Environment* 41, no. 3 (April 1999): 12–20.

Edwards, Elmer J. "To the Big Bend Away! Newest National Park Is Widest of the Open Spaces, Offers Most to Vacationists Seeking Nature at Its Rawest." *West Texas Today*, May 1945.

Hill, Robert T. "Running the Cañons of the Rio Grande." *Century Illustrated*, November 1900–April 1901, 371–390.

Leinbach Marquis, Amy. "Pushing Boundaries." *National Parks Magazine*, Summer 2008.

Levitt, Emily. "Park Lands and Politics on the West Texas/Mexico Border." *Journal of Big Bend Studies* 21 (2009): 219–244.

Mumme, Steven. "Water and Environmental Justice at the U.S.-Mexican Border." *Colorado Water* 36, no. 1 (January/February 2019): 8–10.

Sirotnak, Joe. "Binational Cooperation in the Big Bend Region." *George Wright Forum* 28, no. 3 (2011): 291–295.

Timm, Charles A. "Some International Problems Arising from Water Diversion on the United States-Mexico Boundary." *Southwestern Social Science Quarterly* 13, no. 1 (June 1932): 1–15.

Truett, Samuel. "Neighbors by Nature: Rethinking Region, Nation, and Environmental History in the U.S.-Mexico Borderlands." *Environmental History* 2, no. 2 (April 1997): 160–178.

Webb, Walter Prescott. "The American Revolver and the West." *Scribner's*, February 1927.

Welsh, Michael. "A Prophet without Honor: George J. Sanchez and Bilingualism in New Mexico." *New Mexico Historical Review* 69, no. 1 (January 1994): 19–34.

Wilcox, Sharon, and Brian King. "Peace Parks and Jaguar Trails: Transboundary Conservation in a Globalizing World." *GeoJournal* 71, no. 4 (2008): 221–231.

GOVERNMENT PUBLICATIONS

Census Office, Department of the Interior. *Eleventh Census of the United States, 1890.* Washington, DC: US Government Printing Office, 1892.

———. *Fourteenth Census of the United States, 1920.* Washington, DC: US Government Printing Office, 1922.

———. *Thirteenth Census of the United States, 1910.* Washington, DC: US Government Printing Office, 1912.

———. *Twelfth Census of the United States, 1900.* Washington, DC: US Government Printing Office, 1902.

Gomez, Arthur R. *Mariscal Quicksilver Mine and Reduction Works.* Historic American Engineering Record, HAER No. TX. Office of History, Southwest Support Office. Santa Fe: National Park Service, August 1997.

Nixon, Edgar B., ed. *Franklin Roosevelt and Conservation, 1911–1945.* Washington, DC: US Government Printing Office, 1957.

UNPUBLISHED DISSERTATIONS AND THESES

Anderson, James A. "Land Acquisition in the Big Bend National Park of Texas." Master's thesis. Sul Ross State College, 1967.

Roth, Daniel Lou. "Mexican and American Policy Alternatives in the Big Bend Region—An Updated Study of the Proposed Mexican National Park in the Sierra del Carmen." Master's thesis. University of Texas, Austin, 1992.

NEWSPAPERS

Abilene (TX) Reporter-News
Albuquerque Journal
Alpine (TX) Avalanche
Amarillo (TX) Daily News
Austin Dispatch
Austin Statesman
Austin Texan
Corpus Christi Caller-Times
Dallas Morning News
Dallas News
Dallas Times-Herald
El Paso Times
Fort Worth Star-Telegram
Houston Chronicle
Houston Post
Oklahoma City Oklahoman
Pampa (TX) News
San Antonio Express
San Francisco News
Santa Fe New Mexican
Tyler (TX) Telegraph
Wichita Falls (TX) Times

ORAL INTERVIEWS

Alex, Tom. Chief archaeologist, Big Bend National Park, Texas. October 18, 1996; November 21, 2013.
Alex, Tom, and Betty Alex. Big Bend National Park, Texas. June 6, 1997.
Arnberger, Robert. Superintendent, Grand Canyon National Park, Arizona. June 3, 1996.
Babbitt, Bruce. Secretary of the interior, Big Bend National Park, Texas. April 10, 1999.
Balaz, Gene. Green Valley, Arizona. May 31, 1996.
Beard, Val. County magistrate, Brewster County, Alpine, Texas. August 26, 1998.
Carrera, Julio. Director, Maderas del Carmen Protected Area, Secretaría de Medio Ambiente, Recursos Naturales y Pesca, Big Bend National Park, Texas. April 10, 1999.
Carrico, James W. Study Butte, Texas. January 16, 1997.
Cisneros, José. Superintendent, Big Bend National Park, Texas. August 21, 1997; April 23, 1998.

———. Santa Fe, New Mexico. May 6, 1999; February 4, 2000.

Cook, John. Field director, Intermountain Region Field Office, Denver, Colorado. August 1, 1996.

Davila, Vidal. Chief, Sciences and Resource Management Division, Big Bend National Park, Texas. September 5, 1997; August 21, 1998.

Deckert, Frank. Superintendent, Carlsbad Caverns National Park, Carlsbad, New Mexico. September 20, 1996.

Dickenson, Russell. Seattle, Washington. January 28, 1997.

Dominguez, Pablo. Director, Cañon de Santa Eleña Protected Area, Ciudad Chihuahua, Chihuahua, Mexico. May 31, 1999.

Evans, Doug, and Doris Evans. Big Bend National Park, Texas. October 18, 1996.

Fitch, Monte. Grand Junction, Colorado. August 27, 1997.

Fleming, Mike. Science and Resources Management Division, Big Bend National Park, Texas. September 23, 1996.

Frye, Steve. Chief ranger, Glacier National Park, Montana. July 25, 1996.

Grano, Francisco. Marathon, Texas. January 18, 1997.

Hanson, Garner. President, National Parks Concessions, Cave City, Kentucky. September 19, 1997.

Haraden, Robert. Seeley Lake, Montana. July 24, 1996.

Harrison, Dudley. County judge, Terrell County, Fort Davis, Texas. June 7, 1997.

Joseph, Stanley. Groveland, California. September 6, 1999.

Koch, Etta. Alpine, Texas. September 21, 1996.

Krumenaker, Robert. Superintendent, Big Bend National Park, Texas. September 20, 2019.

LaFon, Alfonso. Maestro-investigador, Departemento de Manejo de Recursos Naturales, Facultad de Zootecnia, Universidad Autonoma de Chihuahua, Ciudad Chihuahua, Chihuahua, Mexico. June 1, 1999.

LoBello, Rick. Director, Carlsbad Caverns Nature Association, Carlsbad Caverns National Park, New Mexico. August 18, 1999.

Marin, Carlos. Chief engineer, International Boundary and Water Commission, El Paso, Texas. August 26, 1998.

McCurdy, Charles. Santa Fe, New Mexico. August 22, 1997.

McNatt, Reece Sholley. Alamogordo, New Mexico. December 18, 1996.

Milburn, James. Vice president, National Parks Concessions, Cave City, Kentucky. September 19, 1997.

Olivas, Ramón. Office of Mexican Affairs, National Park Service, New Mexico State University, Las Cruces, New Mexico. December 18, 1996.

Pitcock, Roy, and Louis Pitcock. Graham, Texas. November 28, 1997.

Reyer, Karen, and Eldon Reyer. Santa Fe, New Mexico. August 6, 1996.

Rogers, Jerry. Field superintendent, Southwest Support Office, National Park Service, Santa Fe, New Mexico. August 22, 1997.

Rumburg, Joseph. Green Valley, Arizona. May 31, 1996.

Schaafsma, Curtis. Santa Fe, New Mexico. August 7, 1996.

Schmidt, Henry. Sun City, Arizona. December 10, 1996.

Smith, Bob. Three Rivers, California. September 7, 1996.

Uribe, Gloria. Ciudad Chihuahua, Chihuahua, Mexico. May 31, 1999.

Wendt, Bill. Midpines, California. September 6, 1996.

Yarborough, Keith. Department of Geography, Sul Ross State University, Alpine, Texas. January 17, 1997.

TELEPHONE INTERVIEWS

Liles, Jim. Buffalo National River Recreation Area, Harrison, Arkansas. August 21, 1997.

Ott, Marty. Salt Lake City Trails Office, National Park Service. August 25, 1997.

Treviño Espinosa, Alejandro. Cementos Mexicanos, Monterrey, Coahuila, Mexico. December 16, 2014.

Big Bend National Park (cont.)
and development in the 1970s, 112–16;
Mission 66 initiative and, 107, 123, 125;
National Park scientific surveys (see
scientific surveys); origins of, 30–38;
promotion of the international aspects of,
97–98; species restoration and (see species
restoration); State of the Parks study of
2010, 156–57; James Stevenson's 1943
comments on plans for park development,
51–52; US-Mexico relations and, 31, 32,
102–3, 104–5, 108; US-Mexico treaty
sharing the waters of the Rio Grande and,
103, 119–20; visitation patterns in the
1960s, 109; visitor services and concessions,
101–2, 115; water storage and supply issues,
53, 66–69, 97, 99, 101; Terry Tempest
Williams on, 162
Big Bend region: early interest in Texas for
state and national parks, 24–25; early
Native inhabitants, 6, 7–8, 9, 10 (see also
Apache; Comanche; Native peoples);
Indian raids in the mid- to late-1800s, 14,
15, 17; Virginia Madison's history of, 108;
Mexican interlude, 14; naming of, 15;
National Park scientific surveys (see
scientific surveys); nineteenth-century
American exploration and settlement,
14–22; overview of scholarly and historical
perspectives on, 1–4; physical landscape,
5–7; Carlysle Raht's history of, 25; Spanish
explorers, 8; Spanish settlements and
dominion, 8–12, 13, 14; Treaty of Guadalupe Hidalgo and, 14, 17; United States–
Mexico Boundary Commission, 15–16
Big Bend–Río Bravo Working Group, 159–60
bighorn sheep, 53–54
biological surveys: Rollin Baker's entomological survey, 50–51; Thomas Chamberlain's
marine and fishing survey, 56–58; Maynard
Johnson's study of fauna and flora, 39–40;
Ernest Marsh Jr.'s environmental survey,
43–50; Walter Taylor's 1944 ecological
survey of future interpretive and protection
programs at Big Bend National Park, 53–56
bioregionalism, 150
Bishop, Rob, 155, 156, 157
black bears, 48, 158
Black Seminole, 17, 18

Boal, Pierre de L., 84–85
Bolton, Herbert, 1
Boot Canyon, 51
Boquillas: 1900 census figures, 20; 1920 census
figures, 27; Rollin Baker's entomological
survey and, 51; border reopenings in 2011
and 2013, 158, 159; descriptions of, from the
1940s, 121; descriptions of, from the 1950s,
122–23, 124–25, 127; descriptions of, from
the 1960s, 128; El Carmen–Big Bend
Conservation Corridor Initiative and, 150;
international peace park initiative in the 1990s
and, 142; Ernest Marsh Jr.'s environmental
survey of the Sierra del Carmen and, 46;
Pancho Villa's revolution and, 27; press release
on Big Bend National Park and, 100; state
of border relations in 2015–2016, 160–61
Boquillas Canyon: binational collaborations in
science in the early 2000s and, 147;
Chandler expedition of 1852 and, 16; dam
projects and, 99; Hartz-Echols expedition
of 1859, 17; origins of Big Bend National
Park and, 32, 35; Rio Grande Wild and
Scenic River management plan and, 137; as
signature canyon of the Rio Grande, 7;
water projects plans for the Rio Grande in
the 1930s and, 66–69
Border 21 Mapping Project, 145
border crossings: in the 1950s, 123; in the
1990s, 143; closure in 2001, 146–47;
reopening at Boquillas in 2011 and 2013,
158, 159; revised 1975 park master plan on,
116; security controversies in the 2000s, 149,
154, 155–56, 157
Border Patrol, 123
border relations: Big Bend–Río Bravo Working
Group, 159–60; binational collaborations in
science in the 2000s, 147–49, 151–54, 156,
158–61; border closure in 2001, 146–47;
border reopenings in 2011 and 2013, 158, 159;
border security issues in the 2000s, 149, 154,
155–56, 157; Calderón-Obama agreement of
2010, 154–55, 156; candelilla wax trade and
(see candelilla wax trade); Cooperative
Action for Conservation in the Big Bend/
Rio Bravo Region, 158–59; cotton
smuggling and, 126–27; drug trade and (see
drug trade); El Carmen–Big Bend
Conservation Corridor Initiative, 148–49,

150, 152–53; El Carmen Project, 145–46, 158;
hoof-and-mouth searches, 122, 125, 128;
international peace park initiative and (*see*
international peace park initiative); key
issues and challenges in the 1940s, 119–21;
key issues and challenges in the 1950s,
121–28; key issues and challenges in the
1960s, 128–29; key issues and challenges in
the 1970s, 128–34; key issues and challenges
in the 1980s and 1990s, 135–44; overview of
key issues and challenges, 118–19; state of
relations in 2015–2106, 160–61; trespass
livestock issue (*see* trespass livestock)
Border Resource Preservation project, 160
Border States Conference on Parks, Recreation,
and Wildlife, 136
botanical surveys, 39–40, 45
Bowen, William P., 85–86
Boyd, William C., 27
Boyer, Christopher R., 141
BRAVO. *See* Big Bend Aerosol and Visibility
Observational Study (BRAVO)
Brewster County, 18, 19–20, 27, 33
Brisbane, Arthur, 82
Britten, Thomas A., 9
Brown, Bill, 115
Brown, Paul V., 52, 97, 98, 99
Brown, Perry, 110
Broyles, Phyllis, 126
Broyles, Rod, 126, 127
Bryce, Wendell, 126
buffalo, 75–76
Bumpus, Hermon C., 52, 170n46
Burgess, Glenn, 103–4
Burleson, Bob, 113–15
Burnham, Waddy, 38
Bush, George W., 146
Bustamante, Joaquin C., 80, 93
Butrill, Clyde, 27

Cahalane, Victor, 51, 52
Calderón, Felipe, 152, 153, 154–55
Calderón-Obama agreement, 154–55, 156
California Gold Rush, 14–15
Calles, Plutarco Elías, 64
Camacho, Manuel Ávila, 104, 161
Camel Corps, 16–17
Cammerer, Arno: international peace park
initiative and, 77, 80, 81, 82, 88; land

acquisition for Big Bend National Park
and, 84; Roger Toll's 1934 report on Big
Bend and, 35, 36
Camp Misery, 22
Camp Neville Springs, 18
Camp Peña Colorado, 18
Camp Saint Helena, 27
Canada, 153
candelilla wax: controversy over during World
War II, 99; properties of, 7
candelilla wax trade: challenges in the 1950s,
121–22, 124, 125, 126, 127, 128; challenges
in the 1960s, 128; challenges in the
1970s, 131
Cañon de los Altares, 43
Cañon de Santa Eleña. *See* Santa Eleña
Canyon
Cañon de Santa Eleña Flora and Fauna
Protected Area, 74
Cañon de Sierra Carmel, 16
Carbón plants, 147, 148
Cárdenas, Lázaro: *acuerdo* of 1937, 84; demise
of the international peace park initiative
and, 91; Great Depression and, 63; Mexican
conservation and, 64–65, 73; nationaliza-
tion of oil production in Mexico, 86
Carithers, Joe, 130–32
Carlos III, 11, 13
Carmen Mountain Hunting Club (American
Club), 46, 48, 52, 78–79
Carnes, W. G., 38
Carpenter, Liz, 110
Carrabias, Julia, 142
Carranza, Venustiano, 26, 64
Carrera, Julio, 119, 143
Carrico, Jim, 138, 139
Carson, Johnny, 132
Carter, Amon, 61, 79, 106
"carved rabbit stick," 41
Casa del Nino, 79
Case, Leland D., 86–87
Casner, James, 32, 127, 128
Castolon: Camp Saint Helena, 27; candelilla
wax trade and, 121–22; cotton smuggling
and, 126–27; cultural heritage in Big Bend
National Park and, 109, 115; description of,
from the 1940s, 121; description of, from the
1970s, 129
catfish, 57–58

boundary lines issues, 73, 77–79, 81–82, 83–86, 88–91; last actions in and demise of, 87, 91–94, 95, 128; Mexican land laws and the 1937 *acuerdo* on national parks, 84–86; origins of, 63; promoters of, 79–80, 82–83, 86–87, 92–93, 103–4; revival of interest in the 1990s and 2000s, 92, 141–42, 143–45, 150–51, 154–55, 161; Emily Wakild on, 172n7
Ivey, Rex, 125

Jameson, John, 65, 75, 120
Jane Addams International Peace Park, 65
Jardin Ranch, 46, 48
Jarvis, Jon, 154
Jewell, Sally, 160
Johnson, Elmo, 43, 101
Johnson, Lady Bird, 109–10, 111, 129
Johnson, Lyndon B., 110
Johnson, Maynard, 39–40, 49, 69
Joint Declaration of Sister Park Partnerships, 148
Jones, David J., 112–13
Joseph, Stanley, 127, 128–29
Jumanos, 6, 7–8, 9, 10
Juniper Canyon, 51
Juniperus flaccida (weeping Juniper), 40

Kearny, Stephen Watts, 14
Kell, J. E., 96
Kelley, Arthur, 58–60, 61
Kelly, Pat, 2
Kickapoo, 17
King, Brian, 150
King, John, 147, 148–49
King, Martha, 150
King Features Syndicate, 82
Koch, Etta, 120
Koch, Peter, 120, 125–26
Krueger, Bob, 133, 134
Kyl, Jon, 157

La Bavia Ranch, 45
La Boquilla, 16
La Encantada Ranch, 45
LaFon, Alfonso, 142
Lafora, Nicolás de, 11
La Gacha Ranch, 45
La Gran Apacheria, 10
Lajitas, 12, 74, 125

La Junta de los Ríos, 7, 8, 10, 12, 13
La Linda, 137, 138
La Linda Bridge, 151
La Mariposa Ranch, 45, 47
land laws: Mexican, 84–86
Lane, Franklin, 23
Langberg, Emilio, 15–16
Langford, J. O., 120
Langley, Harry, 38
Langtry, 22
La Rosita Ranch, 45, 48
Lawson, L. M.: international peace park initiative and, 80, 81, 82, 83; US Commission on International Parks and, 74; water projects on the Rio Grande and, 67, 68, 69, 99
lechuguilla, 128
Levitt, Emily, 150
Ligon, J. Stokely, 54
Liles, Jim, 130, 131–32, 133, 134
Limpia Creek, 15
Lipanes (Lipan Apache), 9, 42. *See also* Apache
little canyon bat, 47–48
livestock: hoof-and-mouth searches, 122, 125, 128. *See also* cattle grazing/ranching; trespass livestock
LoBello, Rick: international peace park initiative and, 147, 150, 156, 161; on NPS concerns about terrorist attacks in 1976, 131; on *permisos,* 133
lobo, 49
long-tailed Texas skunks, 48
López, Nicolas, 10
Los Indios Bravos, 8
Los Pueblos, 7–8
Lusk, Gilbert, 135, 136, 137, 140

Maderas del Carmen Flora and Fauna Protected Area, 74, 136, 142, 143, 145–46
Madison, Virginia, 108
maidenhair ferns, 121
Maier, Herbert T.: 1936 field tour of US and Mexican commissioners from Alpine and, 73–74; deaths of Roger Toll and George Meléndez Wright and, 75–76; El Paso conference of 1935 and, 69–70, 71, 72, 73; international peace park initiative and, 77–78, 80, 81, 82, 89, 90–91; land acquisition in Texas for Big Bend National

missions, 8–9, 10
Moran, Thomas, 22
Morelock, Horace W., 92–93, 106
Morelock, Howard, 58, 59, 60, 61, 62, 83
Morgan, Robert D., 38
Morriss, Emery, 60
Moskey, George, 80
mountain lions, 49
Mueller, C. H., 35, 146
Murphy, Daniel O., 18
Murphy, John, 137
Murphysville, 18
Muzquiz, 18, 44, 45, 48
Muzquiz-Boquillas road, 113–16

Nacimiento de los Negros, 18
Nacogdoches, 10
NAFTA. *See* North American Free Trade
  Agreement (NAFTA)
narcotics smuggling, 138–39. *See also* drug
  trade
Nason, George L., 35, 38
National Commission of Natural Protected
  Areas (Mexico), 147
National Environmental Protection Act
  (1969), 113
National Highway Act (1921), 28
National Historic Preservation Act (1966), 110
national monuments, 30–31
National Park Concessions Inc., 110
national parks: Mexico and, 64–65
National Parks Conservation Association,
  156–57
National Park Service (NPS): border relations
  and (*see* border relations); centennial of the
  organic act, 161–62; challenges of
  US-Mexico relationship for promoting Big
  Bend National Park, 102–3; international
  peace park initiative and (*see* international
  peace park initiative); Stephen Mather as
  first director, 23–24; Mission 66 initiative,
  107, 123, 125; National Environmental
  Protection Act and, 113; National Historic
  Preservation Act and, 110; origins of Big
  Bend National Park, 30–38; scientific
  surveys of Big Bend (*see* scientific surveys);
  James Stevenson's comments on plans for
  Big Bend International Park, 51–52; Sul
  Ross State Teachers College and, 58–61, 62;

Wildlife Division and mission of scientific
  research, 39
National Register of Historic Places, 110
National Resources Planning Board, 97, 99
Native peoples: Apache and Comanche, 8, 9,
  10, 12–13, 14, 15 (*see also* Apache; Coman-
  che); Black Seminole, 17, 18; early
  inhabitants of Big Bend, 7–8; Indian
  mercenaries employed by Mexico, 17–18;
  Jumanos, 6, 7–8, 9, 10; raids along the
  US-Mexico border in the mid- to
  late-1800s, 14, 15, 17; Erik Reed's archaeo-
  logical survey of Big Bend, 40–43
natural resources: review of 1964, 116–17;
  Walter Taylor's 1944 ecological survey of, 55
Nature Conservancy, 153
Naylor, Valerie J., 144
Neff, Pat Morris, 28–29
Neighbors, Robert S., 15
Ness, Howard, 140
New Mexico State University, 140
New York Times, 155, 156
Ninth World Wilderness Congress, 153–54
North American Free Trade Agreement
  (NAFTA), 118, 141, 142
NPS. *See* National Park Service (NPS)
Nueva Vizcaya, 8–9
Nuuche, 12

Obama, Barack, 151, 152, 154–55
Ocampo Protected Area, 151, 152
Oconor, Hugo, 12, 13
Office of Ecosystems Services and Markets,
  153–54
Ojinaga, 7
Olivas, Ramón, 139, 140
One Life at a Time, Please (Abbey), 5
opossums, 47
Organ Pipe Cactus National Monument, 69, 72
Ott, Marty, 138, 139
overgrazing, 1, 50
Ozark bluff-dwellers, 41

Palo Duro Canyon, 24–25, 166n4
Panther Junction, 124
"Park Lands and Politics on the West Texas/
  Mexico Border" (Levitt), 150
Partearroy, W. C. de, 93
Patarabueyes, 41, 42–43

Roberts, J. T., 78–79
Robinson, Forest, 33
rock bowls, 53
Rockefeller, Nelson, 60, 61
Rodriguez, Ciro, 150, 152, 155
Rodriguez-Chamuscado expedition, 9
Rogers, Jerry, 110–11
Romance of Davis Mountains and Big Bend Country, The (Raht), 25
Rooney, Francis, 18
Roosevelt, Franklin Delano: Big Bend National Park and the desire for good US-Mexico relations, 3, 32, 63, 104–5, 161; Good Neighbor Policy, 65; International Boundary Commission and, 68–69; planned dedication ceremony for Big Bend National Park and, 101; presidential election of 1936, 80; support for Big Bend National Park, 31–32
Roosevelt, Theodore, 23, 63–64
Rotarian, 86–87
Rotary International, 86–87, 144, 147
Roth, Daniel L., 142–43
Royal Corps of Engineers, 11
Rubí, Marqués de, 11
Rumburg, Joe, 121–22, 126
Russell, Carl, 60, 61

Sabeata, Juan, 10
Sada, Maria, 102
Sagebrush Rebellion, 134, 138
Sager, Merel, 80, 81
Salazar, Kenneth, 152, 154, 155, 156, 158–59
Salineño, 68
Saltillo, 136
San Antonio, 10
San Carlos, 12, 13, 14, 16, 17, 74
Sánchez, Gus, 161
sandals, 41
Sanderson, 99
San Francisco Canyon, 137
San Francisco Chronicle, 160–61
San Juan Bautista, 11
Santa Anna, Antonio López de, 14
Santa Anna Canyon, 45
Santacruz, Armando, Jr., 66, 71
Santa Eleña (town), 128–29, 131, 139
Santa Eleña Canyon: Rollin Baker's entomo-logical survey of, 51; candelilla wax trade

and, 125; Cañon de Santa Eleña Flora and Fauna Protected Area, 74; Chandler expedition of 1852 and, 16; cotton smuggling and, 126–27; Hartz-Echols expedition of 1859, 17; international peace park initiative in the 1990s and, 143; origins of Big Bend National Park and, 32, 35, 36–37; plans for water projects in the 1930s, 66–69; Río Bravo del Norte Natural Monument and, 151; river rafting and, 120–21, 126; a signature canyon of the Rio Grande, 7; Terry Tempest Williams on, 162
Santa Rosa Mountains, 45, 46, 48
Santo Domingo, 45, 49
San Vicente: demolition of, 110; descriptions of, in the 1940s, 121; Langberg expedition and, 16; Mexican *colonia,* 17; Maggie Smith and, 124; Spanish presidio at, 12, 13, 16, 17
San Vicente Crossing, 132
Saturday Evening Post, 92
Schaafsma, Curtis, 120–21
Schaafsma, Harold, 120
Schaafsma, Polly, 120
Schmidt, Hank, 127
school lands, 32
Schuler, Friedrich, 87, 91–92
scientific surveys: Rollin Baker's entomological survey, 50–51; Thomas Chamberlain's marine and fishing survey, 56–58; importance of the National Park surveys for Big Bend, 61–62; Maynard Johnson's survey of fauna and flora, 39–40; Ernest Marsh Jr.'s environmental survey, 43–50; natural resources review of 1964, 116–17; Erik Reed's archaeological survey, 40–43; Walter Taylor's ecological survey, 53–56
Scribner's magazine, 20, 29
search-and-destroy tactics, 124
Secretariat of the Environment, Natural Resources, and Fisheries (SEMARNAP; Mexico), 141, 142, 143, 144, 154
Secure Fence Act (2006), 149
SEDUE. *See* Ministry of Urban Development and Ecology (SEDUE; Mexico)
Sellars, Richard, 32, 39
SEMARNAP. *See* Secretariat of the Environment, Natural Resources, and Fisheries (SEMARNAP; Mexico)
Seminole, 17, 18

Seminole Negro Scouts, 18
September 11 terrorist attacks, 135, 146
Serrano, Jose H., 71
Seven Years' War, 11
Sheppard, Morris, 31
Sherman, William L., 64, 88, 91
Sholley, George, 122, 123, 124
Sierra Club, 142, 161
Sierra del Carmen: Carmen Mountain
    Hunting Club, 46, 48, 52, 78–79; William
    Douglas on, 112; Ernest Marsh Jr.'s
    environmental survey of, 44–50; mining in
    the 1940s, 121; Río Bravo del Norte Natural
    Monument and, 151
Sierra del Carmen National Park, 84
Sierra Diablo Mountains, 54
Sierra Fronterisa. See Fronteriza Mountains
Sierra Madre Group, 152, 153
Simonian, Lane, 63, 64–65, 71, 91
Sirotnak, Joe, 146, 147
Skiles, Raymond, 151, 158
skunks, 48
slaves and slave trade, 9, 13
Smith, Bob, 122–23, 124
Smith, Maggie, 120, 122, 123, 124
Smith, William F., 15
smuggling, 126–27, 129. See also drug trade
Society of American Foresters, 73
Society of Mammologists, 39
solar energy, 161
Solimar International, 159
souvenir shops, 102
Spain: explorers of the Big Bend region, 8;
    settlements and dominion in the
    Southwest, 8–12, 13, 14
species restoration: El Carmen–Big Bend
    Conservation Corridor Initiative and, 149,
    158; importance of Mexico in, 54–55, 61–62;
    Walter Taylor's 1944 ecological survey on,
    53–55
sport fishing, 56–58
spotted skunks, 48
Sprecher, Stan, 120–21
springs, 53
Stevenson, Coke, 99–100
Stevenson, James O., 49, 51–52
Stillwell Creek, 88
Stillwell Crossing, 89
Stillwell ranches, 88–89

Story, Isabelle, 100
Study Butte, 124
Sue Peaks, 90
sulfuric acid, 124, 128
Sul Ross State Teachers College, 58–61, 62, 99,
    108, 131–32

Taft, William Howard, 23
"tanks," 53
Taylor, Paul S., 31
Taylor, Walter P., 53–56, 103, 146
Taylor, Zachary, 14
Terlingua Creek, 6, 137
Terlingua precinct, 20
Texans for the Preservation of the Rio
    Grande, 138
Texas: deed-transfer ceremony for Big Bend
    National Park and, 99–100; early interest in
    creating state and national parks, 24–25,
    27–29; Governor Pat Neff, 28–29; land
    acquisition for Big Bend National Park
    and, 84, 90, 101; origins of Big Bend
    National Park, 30–38; promoters of the
    international peace park initiative, 79–80,
    82–83; Everett Townsend and, 29–30;
    Walter Webb and, 29
Texas Canyons State Park, 30
Texas Explorers Club, 133
Texas Fish, Game, and Oyster
    Commission, 27
Texas Highway Association, 28
Texas jackrabbits, 40
Texas Panhandle, 24–25
Texas Parks and Wildlife Department, 156
Texas Rangers, 29
Texas State Parks Board, 28, 36, 38, 120
Texas the Marvellous (Winter), 24
Texas Tribune, 154
Thacker, Juan, 71, 75, 80
Tharp, B. C., 35
Thomason, Ewing, 74, 101
Thompson, Ben, 76
Tillotson, Minor, 52, 93–94, 97–98, 99,
    100–102
timber cutting, 54–55
tinajas, 53
Toll, Roger, 33, 35–36, 37, 74, 75–76
Tolson, Hillory, 103
Tonight Show, 132

Michael Welsh received his PhD in the history of the American West in 1983 from the University of New Mexico. He has taught regional history courses at the University of New Mexico, Oregon State University, Cameron University (Oklahoma), and for the past thirty years at the University of Northern Colorado. His publications include five studies for the US Army Corps of Engineers in the American West. Among these are *U.S. Army Corps of Engineers: Albuquerque District, 1935–1985* (1987) and *A Mission in the Desert: U.S. Army Corps of Engineers, Albuquerque District, 1985–2010* (2015). He also has written five studies of national parks in the American West, including *Landscape of Ghosts, River of Dreams: An Administrative History of Big Bend National Park* (2002). His most recent monograph is coauthored with Gregory J. Hobbs, *Confluence: The Story of Greeley Water* (2020).